UNWRAPPING INCREASE, DESTINY, RELATIONSHIPS, GOD, AND THE GIFTS OF THE SPIRIT

THE GIFTS OF FREEDOM SERIES

UNWRAPPING INCREASE, DESTINY, RELATIONSHIPS, GOD, AND THE GIFTS OF THE SPIRIT

BOOK THREE

THE GIFTS OF FREEDOM SERIES

GREG RICE

DESTINY IMAGE® PUBLISHERS, INC.
P.O. Box 310, Shippensburg, PA 17257-0310

"Speaking to the Purposes of God for this Generation and for the Generations to Come."

This book and all other Destiny Image, Revival Press, Mercy Place, Fresh Bread, Destiny Image Fiction, and Treasure House books are available at Christian bookstores and distributors worldwide.

For a U.S. bookstore nearest you, call **1-800-722-6774.**

For more information on foreign distributors, call **717-532-3040.**

Reach us on the Internet: **www.destinyimage.com.**

ISBN 10: 0-7684-2746-0

ISBN 13: 978-0-7684-2746-2

For Worldwide Distribution, Printed in the U.S.A.

1 2 3 4 5 6 7 8 9 10 11 / 12 11 10 09

DEDICATED TO

MY SON, ROBERT RICE,

and men and women who are spiritual paupers,
men and women behind bars, men and women in rehab,

and

You.

I pray that through this book you will gain greater freedom,
a deeper understanding of God, and a closer relationship with Him.

CONTENTS

PREFACE

W hat does God want you to do with your life? The answers you get from Christians would vary; some would say "good church attendance," another would say "giving the church your financial support," or maybe you've heard "being active in church programs!" But none of these alone will truly satisfy your heart.

You were created for relationships, which is what the five gifts in this book are all about. First is our relationship with God. In fact, we the Church are described as the Bride of Christ preparing for the wedding. After that comes the Bible's definition of how our relationships with other people should look. Using the gifts God offers will allow your relationships to truly satisfy your heart and give purpose to your life.

This book will answer the question, *What does God desire for your life?* It is not just being active in His Church, but truly becoming His living Church.

As you come to Him, the living Stone—rejected by men but chosen by God and precious to Him—you also, like living stones, are being built into a spiritual house to be a holy priesthood, offering spiritual sacrifices acceptable to God through Jesus Christ (1 Peter 2:4-5).

INTRODUCTION

BOOK ONE: IN THE BEGINNING

In Book One, we looked at how we were created by God to be in relationship with Him—a relationship of mutual love. Originally, this was easy because Adam and Eve were created in His image and likeness and enjoyed a spirit-to-Spirit connection with Him, which allowed them to keep His essence of love alive in them. They radiated with God's love, in a pure and intimate relationship with their Creator. God gave them freedom of choice, the free will which allowed them to love and choose perfect love or to reject His will for their lives and sin. They rebelled and chose to reject God (see Genesis 3).

Today many people still reject Him, like Adam and Eve, because they believe they are wiser, they can work life out on their own, and they have a better plan than their Creator. However, God's desire is for His creation to *thrive* in life by walking with His Spirit's guidance and according to instruction from His Word.

When Adam and Eve disobeyed God, they brought sin into the world—that is, things outside of God's perfect plan. They opened a Pandora's Box. With sin came death and humanity's bondage in and to this world. Then humanity had to toil, work, and sweat to survive, having lost a functioning spirit-to-Spirit connection with God. As humanity, we brought this curse on ourselves, and our daily experience of it brings us back to the truth—we need God.

The trouble is, we can't find God on our own! Our only hope of getting back on course is in salvation through Jesus Christ. His death on the cross gives us the opportunity for new life and complete forgiveness of our sin, if we accept it.

When we receive this first Gift of Life, we accept the second with it—the Gift of the Holy Spirit. Indeed this spirit-to-Spirit reconnection is the vehicle for achieving real intimacy with Him. His image and likeness can once again exude from our lives with a real time connection. It is through the Holy Spirit that we receive the other gifts, except for the Gift of Faith.

The Gift of Faith was already given to us at birth, but it must be received, unwrapped, and used in our relationship with God for it to bring life. Faith is a verb, an action; that's the only way to use it! An action of faith pleases God; it's the key to His heart (see Heb. 11:6). This means living out and acting upon His promises as if your life depended on it. Our actions please God because the Gift of Faith is the foundation on which we live, allowing us to unwrap and unleash all the other gifts available to us while we're here on earth.

The first gift we can unwrap with our faith is the Gift of Adversity. In all adversity, no matter what the cause, God has imbedded some form of potential redemption that we can unwrap with our faith.

BOOK TWO: BUILDING YOUR SPIRITUAL HOME

The gift of new life in Jesus is just that, a new and unfamiliar way of living—Jesus called it being "born again" (see John 3:3). If you truly are spiritually born again, just like a newborn, you need to learn how to crawl, walk, and eat. How do children learn these essential components of life? By being willing to accept guidance, teaching, and help until they are mature and can stand and eat on their own.

If *Book One* is about building a spiritual foundation, *Book Two* involves assessing and using those materials to build a solid spiritual home using three additional gifts that God offers each of us.

At Jesus' birth, the wise men brought Him gifts of gold, frankincense, and myrrh. These gifts were symbolic, and they also served a practical function for Jesus and His family—they were vital gifts. Today, they are still just as essential to His family; that's you and me!

The Gift of Gold represents God's promise of provision in our lives. When the gift is fully unwrapped with our faith, then we also find the peace of God. Receiving this peace allows us to better resist temptations in the world and to follow the path that God has laid out for us.

The Gift of Frankincense represents praise, worship, and prayer, through which we develop our intimacy with God. Praise and worship are designed to clarify and confirm the relationship between God and us. Prayer is a communication link that establishes expectation; in it, we hold a two-way dialog with the Creator of Heaven and earth.

The Gift of Myrrh represents death. Like Jesus, our first death should be our death to ourselves or our decision to give up our will and allow God's will to replace it in our lives on earth. This is the primary way to clear the path for God's will and destiny to flow into our lives. This is our first death. Jesus' first death was also successfully used to establish His spiritual Kingdom on earth. Jesus' second death on the Cross, His physical death, was the vehicle used to bring us back into relationship with God and to give us eternal life.

Book Three: BRINGING LIFE TO YOUR SPIRITUAL HOME

Now that you've established your spiritual home, you may be asking, "How do I turn this house into a home? How do I make it vibrant? How do I live an abundant life with everything that God has to offer me?"

The answer is found in the last five gifts, which are all about relationship. These gifts, covered in this book, are the Gift of Increase, the Gifts of the Spirit, the Gift of Relationship, the Gift of Destiny, and the Gift of God Himself, the Head of the Trinity. They address how we relate to God, living an abundant life and exuding His image and likeness. And they address how we relate to others in a way that exudes His image and likeness. The Gifts of Destiny and of God Himself speak primarily to our ideal relationship with God. The Gifts of the Spirit and of Relationship revolve around our connection with others—the quality of which affects our relationship with God. And within the Gift of Increase both our earthly and heavenly relationships are intertwined.

A big difference exists between knowing information and becoming a teacher, between reading a baby book and becoming a mom or dad. The difference involves establishing relationships in order to bring knowledge alive. This book is about bringing your house alive.

The Gifts of Freedom series was written to turn a spiritual infant into a warrior for God—for this is your true calling. Remember, you do not need to speed through this book. Take the time you need, and allow God to interact with you as you consider the biblical truths He presents to you. Also consider how each of the **Action & Visualization** instructions I offer can bring a long-term change in your life. These spots are meant to be a time to pause and apply what you have read. Perhaps they may provide a good time to lay the book down and to live out what you just read.

Let's unwrap these next five gifts.

Chapter 1

GIFT #8—INCREASE (PART 1)

WHERE, HOW, AND WHY IS THERE INCREASE?

Before you begin to read, pray that the Holy Spirit will give you
and all readers of this book understanding and application.

*I planted, Apollos watered, but God **gave** the **increase**. So then neither he who plants is anything, nor he who waters, but God who **gives** the **increase*** (1 Corinthians 3:6-7 NKJV).

Who doesn't want to put their time and energy into something that is going to be successful—something that will show an increase? Financially, we all want to see our investments double or multiply over time. Whether we have a home, a business venture, an IRA, or a stock portfolio, we are in many ways gambling when we invest. We *hope* for an increase, but in most cases, we have no certainty of one. The investments we make in the physical world (our fallen world) are always risky because the markets are unstable, they fluctuate, and sometimes they even crash. Open the business section of any newspaper, any day of the week, and you'll nearly always read something about economic instability.

An investment in God's market, however, is an investment in a Kingdom where the principles never change and where we are indeed assured of eternal truths and rewards. With that in mind, consider why we put our trust and hope in the business market for financial gain. Do we do it for happiness, for security? Isn't God the Giver of every good and perfect gift; isn't He the true Source and Giver of increase?

☩ *Every good and perfect gift is from above, coming down from the Father of he heavenly lights, who does not change like shifting shadows* (James 1:17).

Yes, God is the Giver of all increase, advancement, and victory, whether in the spiritual, physical, or financial realms. The Gift of Increase has the power to free you in many ways. It has a ripple effect, like a rock landing in a pond.

In this chapter, we'll explore how increase within God's Kingdom is rooted in the investment of our time, attention, heart, and yes, even our money, in the Kingdom of God—which is the *only* truly sound investment. You'll discover that, while you do have a role to play in the process (the opening verse of the chapter indicates both planting and watering), the actual increase comes by God's hand. It is His sovereign, reserved right to determine when and how it happens and to actually release the increase. However, it's important to remember your part does require an action of faith, which is what pleases God and is the key to His heart (see Hebrews 11:6). Yes, increase can come to you by the process of enhancing your relationship with God.

Increase From the Beginning

God's plan is to give increase and multiplication. From nature we see that all life has a growth pattern and that it multiplies itself. This is evident from the very beginning of Creation:

✟ *God blessed them and said to them, "Be fruitful and increase in number; fill the earth and subdue it..."* (Genesis 1:28).

God gave Noah a similar command regarding the animals:

✟ *Bring out every kind of living creature that is with you—the birds, the animals, and all the creatures that move along the ground—so they can multiply on the earth and be fruitful and increase in number upon it* (Genesis 8:17).

And an angel told Abram's (Abraham's) wife, Sarah, that God would bless them with the Gift of Increase as well:

✟ *The angel added, "I will so increase your descendants that they will be too numerous to count"* (Genesis 16:10).

INCREASE IN GENERATIONS

Abram, whose faith God counted as righteousness, was also blessed by God with wealth:

✟ *Abram had become very wealthy in livestock and in silver and gold* (Genesis 13:2).

And his son, Isaac, was also blessed with wealth:

✠ *The man became rich, and his wealth continued to grow until he became very wealthy* (Genesis 26:13).

And so, too, his grandson, Jacob, was blessed with wealth:

✠ *In this way the man grew exceedingly prosperous and came to own large flocks, and maidservants and menservants, and camels and donkeys* (Genesis 30:43).

In fact, in the Old Testament, increase is often portrayed as a blessing that is carried down from generation to generation. Consider the following verses:

✠ *May the Lord, the God of your fathers, increase you a thousand times and bless you as He has promised* (Deuteronomy 1:11).

✠ *May the Lord make you increase, both you and your children* (Psalm 115:14).

Increase as Blessing

When you start receiving God's Gift of Increase (including wealth) as a *blessing*, you will discover that it is a trouble-free gift to those who have faith and know it is from God.

✠ *The blessing of the Lord brings wealth, and He adds no trouble to it* (Proverbs 10:22).

Of course, wealth in itself is not always good unless it is a blessing from God.

✝ *...the abundance of a man permits him no sleep* (Ecclesiastes 5:12).

Increase comes to the righteous and wicked *alike*. However, it is our faith in God that makes the gift a true blessing in which we can joyously *rest*. Increase without *faith* will only cause constant anxiety—the struggle to maintain and protect the gift. Without faith, the rich man will worry about how to keep his wealth. But the righteous know that prosperity is one of many gifts from God and understand that God has good intentions to freely give us His good gifts.

✝ *He [God] who did not spare His own Son, but delivered Him up for us all, how shall He not with Him also freely give us all things* (Romans 8:32 NKJV).

✝ *We have not received the spirit of the world but the Spirit who is from God, that we may understand what God has freely given us* (1 Corinthians 2:12).

The Bible even gives insight on our ability to enjoy what we receive, whether *little* or *great*—even our enjoyment is a gift from God.

✝ *Moreover, when God gives any man wealth and possessions, and enables him to enjoy them, to accept his lot and be happy in his work—this is a gift of God* (Ecclesiastes 5:19).

FAITH IN GOD RELEASES INCREASE

Symbolically speaking, you will have winter and summer seasons in life. However, as you grow closer to God and gain wisdom, you will come to understand that He has a special gift of riches and honor designed just for you and that the gift is within your reach.

✟ *With [God] are riches and honor, enduring wealth and prosperity* (Proverbs 8:18).

✟ *But remember the Lord your God, for it is He who gives you the ability to produce wealth, and so confirms His covenant, which He swore to your forefathers, as it is today* (Deuteronomy 8:18).

Remember, it is by *faith* that we unwrap the gifts of God. In this case, we must have faith that God's gifts are perfect for us, though they are not always readily apparent, and that they are going to be beneficial and complete.

We need faith to accept that God's provision is sufficient to cover all of our needs. Only then will we possess all the benefits of the gift and *all* that God has to offer. For example, the Israelites were offered access to their Promised Land, but since they did not spiritually receive and unwrap this gift from God, they could not enjoy and maintain possession of the gift and all that God had promised them.

✟ *So we see that they were not able to enter, because of their unbelief* (Hebrews 3:19).

Though many times we are allowed to maintain a gift physically, if we do not receive it with faith, we do not get *full* possession of all its benefits (rest, joy, and fulfillment). It's only through an intimate relationship with God that we can understand and, therefore, obtain all the benefits from the gifts that He offers us while on earth. This is one reason you should not be envious when you see the unrighteous gain great wealth, fame, power, etc.; it will not be joyful and fulfilling to them, and indeed, it is sometimes a curse. However, those who have exercised their faith through intimacy with God will find rest, joy, and fulfillment in the spoils that come from God (even when the spoils don't seem like much).

✠ *Now we who have **believed** enter that rest...* (Hebrews 4:3).

Action & Visualization

Regardless of the gifts you receive, use your faith and relationship with God to get the fullest benefit from them.

Faith Helps Bring Increase

God also works with His followers, combining their faith with His power to bring multiplication. We see this in the story of Elisha and the widow:

✠ *The wife of a man from the company of the prophets cried out to Elisha, "Your servant my husband is dead, and you know that he revered the Lord. But now his creditor is coming to take my two boys as his slaves." Elisha replied to her, "How can I help you? Tell me, what do you have in your house?" "Your servant has nothing there at all,"* she said, "except a little oil." Elisha said, "Go around and ask all your neighbors for empty jars. **Don't ask for just a few**. Then go inside and shut the door behind you and your sons. Pour oil into all the jars, and as each is filled, put it to one side." She left him and afterward shut the door behind her and her sons. They brought the jars to her and she kept pouring. When all the jars were full, she said to her son, "Bring me another one." But he replied, **"There is not a jar left."** **Then the oil stopped flowing.** She went and told the man of God, and he said, "Go, sell the oil and pay your debts. You and your sons can live on what is left" (2 Kings 4:1-7).

The widow said she had nothing but a small amount of oil. We too often start with a small amount of resources—money, energy, talents, education (our seeds may be many or few). God wants us to step out and plant these seeds, having faith in His power to give the increase to our planted seeds.

In this story, the prophet Elisha asked the widow to collect as many jars as she could—as many as her faith would allow. The number of jars she collected, you could say, represented her level of faith. The oil was multiplied by God, filling all of the jars—according to the measure of her faith. Indeed, in this case, when her faith ended, *the oil stopped flowing.* Likewise, when we do something in faith, God can multiply our resources, sometimes beyond our understanding, allowing us to accomplish His will.

In the Gospel of John, Chapter 6, we find a similar story. A boy gives Jesus five loaves of bread and two small fish, which Jesus multiplies to feed 5,000 people (see John 6:1-13). Not only did Jesus provide increase in order to feed the crowd, but there were 12 baskets of leftovers. That's far more than the boy brought to Jesus in the first place.

The boy's generosity and willingness to surrender his meal to Jesus in faith allowed him to combine what he had with Jesus' power in order to accomplish God's will. For the part he played, the boy received a return or increase. This is a vivid picture of how God can turn what seems like a little into a lot—this is supernatural multiplication. God can do the same for you when you act in faith by trusting Him with what little you have. *Whatever you give God in faith, He will return it to you in abundance.*

Jesus' disciples acted in faith when they went out with no money and only the clothes they were wearing—and God worked with them and through them.

✞ *Then the disciples went out and preached everywhere, and the Lord worked with them and confirmed His word by the signs that accompanied it* (Mark 16:20).

You can rely on Him and His power when you are acting in His will.

✞ *Not that we are competent in ourselves to claim anything for ourselves, but our competence comes from God* (2 Corinthians 3:5).

Action & Visualization

Give God what you have so that He can return you an increase.

Only God Gives Increase

God is the only source of increase in wealth, in honor, and in strength:

✞ *Wealth and honor come from You; You are the ruler of all things. In Your hands are strength and power to exalt and give strength to all* (1 Chronicles 29:12).

✠ *To this John replied, "A man can receive only what is given him from heaven" (John 3:27).*

Another type of increase comes in the form of personal victories over the difficulties in your life. Just as with material increase, we must trust God for increase in victory.

✠ *With God we will gain the victory... (Psalm 60:12).*

✠ *[God] holds victory in store for the upright... (Proverbs 2:7).*

Not only does God give it, He also sustains it. All growth (increase) in our lives has to be built up and maintained by God; otherwise it is meaningless.

✠ *Unless the Lord builds the house, its builders labor in vain. Unless the Lord watches over the city, the watchmen stand guard in vain. In vain you rise early and stay up late, toiling for food to eat—for He grants sleep to those He loves (Psalm 127:1-2).*

This passage shows that confidence in Him (our Provider) will allow us to rest and to be comfortable with our gifts when they are delivered. When we see ourselves as our ultimate provider, we're acting out our disbelief in the Provider. In so doing, we miss the path He intends for us. But when we do place our faith in God, and obtain His power of increase, growth, and victory, then we effectively allow Him to show Himself in our lives.

✠ *But we have this treasure in jars of clay to show that this all-surpassing power is from God and not from us (2 Corinthians 4:7).*

WHY ONLY GOD?

So why has God reserved the right to determine increase, growth, and victory? Why is He the sole author? Why can't we just go out and get it ourselves?

To answer this question we need to remember that God gave us freedom of choice—*independence*—so that we would have the ability to have a loving relationship with Him. God cannot force or demand love—if He did, it wouldn't be love. So we can only exhibit love through our freedom of choice and independence. Without independence love can not exist; however, with this independence we have chosen to bring evil into the world. So how can God counteract this evil while at the same time allowing our independence? If we have complete independence, how can God have complete control as well?

First, this divine right enables God to remain in ultimate control of the world while at the same time offering us our freedom of choice. If He controls the increase, then ultimately, He controls the end result. Of course God allows consequences to happen according to our choices, but by controlling the increase, God can imbed an opportunity for redemption, an opportunity for us to get back on track, even when we make the wrong choice. It also gives God room to work in our lives, to be a rewarder, to exercise His grace, to show His love, and to accomplish His will. By controlling the increase, God determines where the power, the money, and the blessings go; thus He can accomplish His will for us in the end. Consider this example of God using His power of increase as a means to accomplishing His will:

I will increase the fruit of the trees and the crops of the field, so that you will no longer suffer disgrace among the nations because of famine (Ezekiel 36:30).

Second, it pulls us closer to Him. If increase were solely up to our own efforts, would we perceive our need for God? Would as many of us really seek Him or as earnestly? However, because we have to trust God for increase, for our very physical sustenance, we are led to realize our dependence on Him. Since we are also spiritually needy, our realization of our physical dependence leads us to a realization of our spiritual dependence on God and His grace. This dependence compels us to seek a closer and more intimate relationship with God and therefore we find fulfillment.

Third, dependence on God keeps us from becoming prideful. Keep in mind that pride was the cause of satan's fall from Heaven:

You said in your heart, "I will ascend to heaven; I will raise my throne above the stars of God" ...But you are brought down to the grave, to the depths of the pit (Isaiah 14:13,15).

Ezekiel describes satan's pride:

*...You [satan] were the model of perfection, full of wisdom and perfect in beauty. You were in Eden, the garden of God; every precious stone adorned you: ruby, topaz and emerald, chrysolite, onyx and jasper, sapphire, turquoise, and beryl. Your settings and mountings were made of gold; on the day you were created they were prepared. You were anointed as a guardian cherub, for so I ordained you. You were on the holy mount of God; you walked among the fiery stones. You were blameless in your ways from the day you were created till wickedness was found in you...Your heart became **proud** on account of your beauty, and you corrupted your wisdom because of your splendor. So I threw you to the earth; I made a spectacle of you before kings* (Ezekiel 28:12-15,17).

The lesson here is pretty clear: *pride cometh before a fall* (see Prov. 16:18). Remember the invisible law of gravity? Well this is the invisible *law of pride*. Just as, in the natural, slipping off a high ledge will cause your body to fall, so in the spiritual realm, pride will cause your demise.

✝ *Pride goes before destruction; a haughty spirit before a fall* (Proverbs 16:18).

✝ *When pride comes, then comes disgrace, but with humility comes wisdom* (Proverbs 11:2).

✝ *A man's pride brings him low, but a man of lowly spirit gains honor* (Proverbs 29:23).

Pride is not the will of God, but came as a result of living in a fallen world and being swept up in it.

✝ *For everything in the world—the cravings of sinful man, the lust of his eyes and the boasting of what he has and does—comes not from the Father but from the world* (1 John 2:16).

When we understand that we don't control our increase, human pride takes a back seat and humility kicks in. Only when we are in this state of humility can we see and accept God's plan and purpose for our lives. This applies to all kinds of increase, including our salvation (which is the greatest increase we receive since it grants us the promise of Heaven and an eternity with God):

✠ *For it is by grace you have been saved, through faith—and this not from yourselves, it is the gift of God—**not** by works, so that no one can boast* (Ephesians 2:8-9).

God knows that, if we could earn our salvation through works, we would be boastful and proud. Our eyes would be on ourselves and not on Him. This is one reason our salvation is a *gift*—to help us keep our eyes on Him and on His plan. It is for this same reason that *all* increase (physical, financial, and spiritual) is a gift.

✠ *Every good and perfect gift is from above...* (James 1:17).

The danger of pride is also part of the reason God requires faith in order to receive His gifts. Just as we had to humble ourselves and have faith in God in order to receive the Gift of Life, so too our actions of faith can unwrap the Gift of Increase. Further, we can't fully use the gift until we unwrap all of it. In other words, our levels of action in faith simply represent our levels of intimacy with God. Each step that we walk in faith brings us *closer* to Him. It's what pleases Him, and it is the very key to His heart.

✠ *And without faith it is impossible to please God...* (Hebrews 11:6).

God arranged things this way because He knew humanity had a prideful spirit. He seeks ways to protect us from ourselves, from our actions against ourselves and His creation. Look at what happened when people thought they could build a tower or way to get to Heaven without God:

✠ *Then they said, "Come, let us build ourselves a city, with a tower that reaches to the heavens, so that we may make a name for ourselves and not be scattered over the face of the whole earth"* (Genesis 11:4).

They wanted to touch Heaven in a physical, external way without God. But God wants us to reach for Heaven through our relationship with Him, through our internal, spirit-to-Spirit connection. Because the people at the Tower of Babel sought to reach Him through the wrong means, God scattered them so that they would have to seek Him in the right way.

✠ *So the Lord scattered them from there over all the earth, and they stopped building the city* (Genesis 11:8).

The Babylonians, approximately 700 years later, provide another example. Look at what happened to them when they allowed their pride to take over:

✠ *You have trusted in your wickedness* [operating outside of God's will] *and have said, "No one sees me." Your wisdom and knowledge mislead you when you say to yourself, "I am, and there is none* [no God] *besides me." Disaster will come upon you, and you will not know how to conjure it away. A calamity will fall upon you that you cannot ward off with a ransom; a catastrophe you cannot foresee will suddenly come upon you* (Isaiah 47:10-11).

Simply put, pride in your efforts is not a vehicle toward intimacy with God. On the other hand, God has designed in the Gift of Increase a way for us to gain greater intimacy with Himself if we so choose.

IMPORTANCE OF CREDITING GOD

Why does calamity happen when we develop pride? Sadly, it's because we start seeing ourselves as masters of our own universe; essentially, we are in certain areas of our life trying to dethrone God. In those areas, we put ourselves in His position. When we develop pride, we are saying, at best, "He doesn't matter," or at worst, "He doesn't exist." How can we ever fulfill our purpose of developing a loving relationship with Him and exuding His image and likeness into the creation if we think this way?

Consider God for a moment. How would you feel if you prepared and cooked all day for a dinner party and your spouse took credit for all of your hard work? Relationship means acknowledging and giving credit where credit is due. The same is true in our relationship with God. We must not try to take credit for God's work.

☩ *Like clouds and wind without rain is a man who boasts of gifts he does not give* (Proverbs 25:14).

When good things happen to you, it is always important to remember God and to give Him the glory:

☩ *Let them give glory to the Lord...* (Isaiah 42:12).

☩ *Fear God and give Him glory...* (Revelation 14:7).

God does not just demand credit for His gifts for credit sake alone. He knows this is the first step for you to understand how to find true fulfillment in life. He actually rewards those who give Him the credit He rightfully deserves:

✛ *Humility and the fear of the Lord bring wealth and honor and life* (Proverbs 22:4).

Conversely, you have read that a boastful and thankless attitude takes the credit away from God and will not be rewarded. Moreover, our boasting about what we have today is in vain because we never know what tomorrow will bring.

✛ *Do not boast about tomorrow, for you do not know what a day may bring forth* (Proverbs 27:1).

A story in the Gospel of Luke illustrates the need for a humble and thankful attitude in order for you to find and receive the ultimate desire that God has for your life. On the road, Jesus meets ten lepers and gives them instruction on how to be healed:

✛ *When [Jesus] saw them, He said "Go show yourselves to the priests." And as they went, they were cleansed* (Luke 17:14).

They all followed His instructions and were cleansed. This is an example of the first step; acting on faith is the road to your miracle. But read what happens next:

✛ *One of them, when he saw he was healed, came back, **praising** God in a loud voice. He threw himself at Jesus' feet and thanked Him— and he was a Samaritan. Jesus asked, "Were not all ten cleansed? Where are the other nine? Was no one found to return and give **praise** to God except this foreigner?" Then He said to him, "Rise and go; your faith has made you **well**"* (Luke 17:15-19).

Not only was this Samaritan leper cleansed, but he was also *made well* as a result of giving God the glory. Jesus healed the ten lepers' physical disease, which was a result or physical manifestation of their spiritual sickness. One leper came back to praise God for the physical healing and therefore received spiritual healing as well. By so doing, he got to the root of what was creating problems in his physical life. When you are praising God and giving Him credit for all the things He gives you, you are developing greater intimacy with God through which His presence will free you.

Our best life revolves around an interconnected relationship with God. This creates intimacy and aligns us with our Creator. The better we understand our responsibility and God's nature, the better we are able to align ourselves with God. You see, God does not want to get the credit just to get the credit. He knows that giving Him the credit is good for us because it forces us to align ourselves with Him and the purpose for which He created each one of us. When we are aligning ourselves with God and His plan, we are creating intimacy with which comes manifestations of God. Aligning ourselves with God, of course, also puts us in a better position to receive, unwrap, and use all the increase that He offers. We begin to realize that it is *not* our company, our boss, or our clients who are the providers; it is God *alone*. Therefore, He should be our *only* God and our *main* focus.

Action & Visualization

Be humble in all things and always give God credit so that your vision will be clear enough to see His will in your life.

Sowing and Reaping

One of the key aspects to finding increase is the principle of *sowing and reaping*. This principle applies spiritually, intellectually, physically, and financially. We have two parts to play in this process: we sow in *faith*, and we reap in *thanks*. God has two parts to play as well: He supplies the seed, and once we sow, God then gives the increase.

For us, faith is an essential component—that's why the two chapters on faith in *Book One* are important to understand before you can fully understand and appreciate the principle of sowing and reaping. Like the preceding gifts, faith is the *catalyst* for this gift too. How do you put faith into this principle of sowing and reaping? Your level of faith will likely determine *what* and *how much* of your resources you're actually willing to plant. Obviously, if you have no faith in the principle of growth, you will plant nothing that has any value to you. And conversely, the higher the level of faith you have, the more willing you'll be to plant the things of greater value in your life.

I have discovered nine spiritual truths that relate to this principle of sowing and reaping. These nine truths will affect you every day of your life, whether you are intentionally acting according to them or not. Therefore, it is important to fully understand their powerful effects and consequences in the same way that you have learned to adjust your life to gravity—allowing it to help you and not harm you.

Truth #1: You Reap What You Sow

How do we understand the spiritual truths of sowing and reaping? One way that spiritual truths are revealed is through nature:

For since the creation of the world His invisible attributes are clearly seen, being understood by the things that are made, even His eternal power and Godhead, so that they are without excuse... (Romans 1:20 NKJV).

In nature we see the principle of sowing and reaping played out. This first truth on sowing and reaping, along with the second and third, are found in Galatians 6:

✠ *Do not be deceived, God is not mocked; for whatever a man sows, that he will also reap* (Galatians 6:7 NKJV).

Simply put, in nature, when you plant an apple seed, you get an apple tree; when you plant an orange seed, you get an orange tree; when you sow something, you reap more of the same.

Sowing Not Just Seeds

This concept applies to all areas of life. You can even sow and reap the harvest of many things, even *time*. Yes, time. I learned this after I'd begun planting my time—a tithe, so to speak—by doing work for the Church. Sowing our time can allow us to reap what the Christian author, Mario Murillo, calls "God speed."[1] This kind of harvest was demonstrated to me the day I read the chapter on "God speed" in his book *I Am the Christian the Devil Warned You About*. That day, when I left the 38-story building in which I lived, I was pressed for time en route to church to help my pastor. Getting an elevator in my building usually took a long time; however, that day as I came down the 19th floor hallway, before I could even press the button, the elevator door opened. I went straight in, and it went straight down. Then when I got to the street, there was only one cab in sight—but it had a customer in it. That cab pulled right up, the passenger jumped out, I got in and the cab sped off.

As I got in, the cab driver radioed the dispatcher that he was not going to the Ala Moana Mall *anymore*. The previous customer he had—*without explanation*—aborted the trip midway through. He was now headed to the

Word of Life Christian Center. It was as if God had ripped that other customer right out of the cab so that I could get to church quickly. When I got back to my building that afternoon, the elevators continued to open on my floor as I approached them, allowing me to do things in less time. I found out later that the building managers had reprogrammed the elevators to go to the 19th floor (midpoint of the building) and wait there when not in use.

The elevator's timing was not a miracle intervention by God like the parting of the Red Sea, but it made an impression on me. Every day since then, I have been vividly reminded of the chapter that I had read about God speed. I think the reprogramming was a God-inspired occurrence that helped make the elevators more efficient, and that illustrated to me (and now you) that even *time* can be increased when we learn to trust God with it.

Several times it is recorded in the New Testament that Jesus and His disciples experienced supernatural transportation, freak weather occurrences, or other supernatural interventions by God to get from one place to another.

✟ *And he* [the eunuch] *gave orders to stop the chariot. Then both Philip and the eunuch went down to the water and Philip baptized him. When they came up out of the water, **the Spirit of the Lord suddenly took Philip away**, and the eunuch did not see him again, but went on his way rejoicing. Philip, however, appeared at Azotus and traveled about, preaching the gospel in all the towns until he reached Caesarea (Acts 8:38-40).*

✟ *After Paul had seen the vision, we got ready at once to leave for Macedonia, concluding that God had called us to preach the gospel to them. From Troas we put out to sea and sailed straight for Samothrace and the **next** day on to Neopolis (Acts 16:10-12). (This*

125-mile trip under natural circumstance would take two days; however, with freak winds known to the region, God allowed them to make it in one day.)

✠ *All the people in the synagogue were furious when they heard this* [what Jesus said]. *They got up, drove Him out of the town, and took Him to the brow of the hill on which the town was built, in order to throw Him down the cliff. But He walked right through the crowd and went on His way* [to Capernaum to give His time to teaching] (Luke 4:28-30).

As we continue, I will reveal other kinds of things you can sow that will reap a harvest, and if you are in God's will, a harvest of life-long blessings.

How Much Increase?

You probably are wondering if there's a relationship between the amount of sowing and the increase. According to the Bible, the answer is *yes*. Read what the apostle Paul writes to the Corinthian Christians:

✠ *...He who sows sparingly will also reap sparingly, and he who sows bountifully will also reap bountifully* (2 Corinthians 9:6 NKJV).

And of course, what can ultimately happen if we don't sow at all?

✠ *A sluggard does not plow in season; so at harvest time he looks but finds nothing* (Proverbs 20:4).

Does this mean that if you sow a seed you will be guaranteed a harvest? If we look deeper at the analogy in nature, we find that the answer is *no*. Crops sometimes fail! Crop failure can be good when we have planted the wrong seed. I have prayed for crop failure at times, for divine mercy. This is why we always need to keep in mind *who* is in charge of the harvest:

✟ *I planted, Apollos watered, but God* **gave** *the* **increase** (1 Corinthians 3:6 NKJV).

Though Apollos and Paul had a role to play in the sowing, God was still in charge of the result. How hard we work doesn't immediately or exactly translate proportionately into the harvest. But that shouldn't dissuade us from planting and doing so bountifully; for when God chooses to provide increase (as you see from the previous verse), He will do so according to our sowing.

Truth #2: Sow Spiritually to Reap an Eternal Harvest

The next verse in Galatians clarifies this second truth that sowing and reaping do not just apply to things in the physical realm, but also in the spiritual realm:

✟ *For he who sows to his flesh will of the flesh reap corruption, but he who sows to the Spirit will of the Spirit reap everlasting life* (Galatians 6:8 NKJV).

If you only sow things of the flesh—earthly desires, for example—you will only reap things of the flesh, things that are not godly. However, if you follow the leading of the Spirit with your sowing, then you will reap a harvest of everlasting value.

TRUTH #3: SEED + TIME = HARVEST

In the next verse in the Galatians passage, God highlights the third truth:

And let us not grow weary while doing good, for in due season we shall reap if we do not lose heart (Galatians 6:9 NKJV).

When the apostle Paul writes "doing good," he's talking about the sowing process—the planting of *spiritual* seed. "In due season" refers to God's timing—not ours. "We shall reap" refers to the harvest or increase that will come. This is not just a material harvest. It also includes a harvest of spiritual fruit, like love, joy, and peace (see Galatians 5:22-23); spiritual gifts, like prophecy and healing; and gifts of salvation for people you know.

Yes, God can also return your physical sowing with a spiritual harvest:

Now He who supplies seed to the sower and bread for food will also supply and increase your store of seed and will enlarge the harvest of your righteousness [right-standing with God] (2 Corinthians 9:10).

Do not store up for yourselves treasures on earth, where moth and rust destroy, and where thieves break in and steal. But store up for yourselves treasures in heaven, where moth and rust do not destroy, and where thieves do not break in and steal. For where your treasure is, there your heart will be also (Matthew 6:19-21).

Galatians 6:9 concludes with the phrase, *"if we do not lose heart,"* which leads us to a critical part of the third truth that we must understand about the principle of sowing and reaping in order to be successful at living life in God.

It's important to not miss the implications of the phrases "in due season" and "if we do not lose heart." I believe they are God's way of reminding us to hang in there—to use our faith. God makes it clear that our role is keeping our faith steadfast—trusting in what we hope for (His promises) and not necessarily in what we see. This is God's way of doing things—*if we don't lose heart.*

Let's consider some of the ramifications of the truth of Seed + Time = Harvest. When you plant an apple seed, you are *not* going to grow an orange tree. Nor will you have apples to eat the next day, because it *takes time* for the tree to bear fruit. Time allows God to work in and through us, growing our faith.

Be patient, then, brothers, until the Lord's coming [in your life]. *See how the farmer waits for the land to yield its valuable crop and how patient he is for the autumn and spring rains. You too, be patient and stand firm, because the Lord's coming is near* (James 5:7-8).

When the Lord comes, He will bring an increase because His essence is increase. God is the God of increase and multiplication. God has set this spiritual truth of Seed + Time = Harvest to work in everything. For example, if you plant seeds of kindness, in time you will receive a harvest in kindness. If you plant smiles, you'll receive more smiles. The truth also applies to bad seeds:

As I have observed, those who plow evil and those who sow trouble reap it (Job 4:8).

In the case of the bad seeds we plant the delayed time gives us the opportunity for redemption and hopefully mercy—a crop failure.

It Requires Work

When these first three truths were initially revealed to me, after I was saved, I felt like I was hearing *bad news*. Honestly, most of the seeds I had sown weren't good. On the other hand, learning these truths gave me a blueprint for how to turn things around. They helped me to see what I had to do to work my way out of the hole that I had dug for myself. Don't be afraid of that word *work*; for it is with toil that we will reap our harvest. Because of The Fall, much effort and toil are required in sowing and reaping (even in spiritual things).

☦ *...Cursed is the ground because of you; through painful toil you will eat of it all the days of your life. It will produce thorns and thistles for you.... By the sweat of our brow you will eat your food...* (Genesis 3:17-19).

You will learn through your trials that even the act of sowing and reaping is a simple and powerful way to please God. It will draw you toward intimate relationship with Him because it requires you to use your faith; plus, the great effort that it requires will lead you to seek His rest.

Truly work is important to our faith. While the Gift of Salvation is free—you can't earn it—God does ask us to work on our spiritual lives. As the apostle Paul said, we must each *work* out our own salvation (see Phil. 2:12). A key focus for our work of faith is the principle of sowing and reaping.

Truth #4: God Determines the Increase

God has reserved the right to determine the increase that we receive so that He can dispense it only for our good. He will not release it at a time that would be bad for us, causing us to stumble. Only He knows the *best* time for release.

Despite the way that I've written out Truth #3, Seed + Time = Harvest, it is not a mathematical formula. It does not say that if we plant *x* dollars we will reap *y* dollars in return. We only have to look at nature to see evidence of this. We can't know all of the reasons for the size or the timing of a harvest. But remember, God is working in all things to accomplish His goals, which are often beyond our understanding. What God wants us to remember is this:

✠ *And we know that all things work together for good to those who love God, to those who are the called according to His purpose* (Romans 8:28 NKJV).

What does all this mean? It means, have faith! Have faith that God is working all things together for our good. OK, how do we have this faith? Remember that faith is an action. Our first action is to plant the seed. Sometimes we live our faith out through being joyful in difficult circumstances (like when a crop fails or when the wait for a promised harvest seems interminably long). And then we plant again. And again. Most of all, faith in action does not lose heart; it remains steadfast and brave.

Look at the farmer. He has complete trust and confidence in Seed + Time = Harvest. When he experiences a crop failure, he doesn't stop planting. He starts all over again. He trusts that eventually a harvest will rise, and he refuses to give up. While he may have to endure tough times, it is his ability to "not lose heart" that keeps the hope of a harvest alive. It's that steadfast hope and faith in the harvest that allows him to toil on in the face of seeming setbacks. Remember, faith means *persistence*. And let's not forget, the bigger the setback or the longer the wait, the more we must exercise our faith—and this is a God-honoring position, one that will not go unnoticed by the Giver of all increase.

Action & Visualization

Plant seeds that you believe God wants you to sow, and don't lose heart if the harvest doesn't come according to your expectations. Keep on planting.

Truth #5: The Seed Is Within

God puts the seed required for multiplication in each of His creations. This truth is found in this verse:

*Then God said, "Let the earth bring forth grass, the herb that yields seed, and the fruit tree that yields fruit according to its kind, **whose seed is in itself...**" (Genesis 1:11 NKJV).*

"Whose seed is in itself"? God is saying that fruit has within itself the ability to multiply. Study an apple or an orange, and you will see this truth in vivid display. Here's what it means to us spiritually: when God gives the Gift of Increase, He is simultaneously giving the gift of seed. Our increase is always for the purpose of more sowing according to His plan. This concept applies to many things, including all things that grow (including you and me), money, actions, and much more. Just like a farmer, we maintain a *cycle* of sowing and reaping as God gives us increase.

TRUTH #6: BOTH SUSTENANCE AND SEED

As I said earlier, God gives the seeds, and when we plant them, He is responsible for the *increase*. We are responsible for the *sowing*. Let's take it a step farther. Look at this verse in Isaiah:

For as the rain comes down...And make[s] *it* [the soil] *bring forth and bud, that it may give seed to the **sower** and **bread to the eater**...* (Isaiah 55:10 NKJV).

As I understand it, this verse means that God gives us the seeds, and we divvy them up. Which should be planted? Which should be used for sustenance? The decision is ours.

Look at an apple; it is both food and seed. Farmers know that if they consume all of their crops and leave nothing for planting, they will not have any income the next year. Money can also be both food and seed. You can consume it, or you can plant it. It is up to you to determine what portion will be *seed* and what will be your *food*. Sometimes we withhold "planting seed" out of fear that our God-given resources will dry up, meaning we store it up or horde it. But planting wisely now is important to both our immediate and our distant future.

ACTION & VISUALIZATION

Wisely consider the dispensing of your harvest.
What will you use for seed, and what will you use for food?

Truth #7: Live by Faith

As discussed in detail at the beginning of this chapter, growth, increase, and multiplication are part of God's nature. And we position ourselves to receive them when we live by faith. But how do we do this practically?

Since God gives the seed, we do not determine how much we start with. Some begin with abundance while others begin with less. The woman described in Luke 21:2 had only two small coins to give to an offering, and when she gave those coins, Jesus praised her over all the others who gave much more. Jesus said that by giving the two coins—all that she had—this woman did more than all the rest.

The message of this is clear—it wasn't the dollar amount of her gift, but what it represented at the heart and faith level. It was all she had! This was a powerful action of faith, and it pleased God so much that He recognized her for all of eternity in Scripture. Remember, God looks at the heart not the outward appearance as the world does.

But the Lord said to Samuel, "Do not consider his appearance or his height, for I have rejected him. The Lord does not look at the things man looks at. Man looks at the outward appearance, but the Lord looks at the heart (1 Samuel 16:7).

Likewise it isn't the appearance or size of the gift you give that impresses Him; it's the intentions (motives) of the giver's heart that finds favor with Him. Neither is it about the amount of money that you have; instead, it's about what you do with the money that He gives you.

This is also illustrated in Matthew 25 through the parable of the talents. In this story, three men are given varying amounts of money (*talents* in the Bible passage). One is given five talents, one is given two, and the third is given one. What was most important in this story was not the number of talents each man was given, but how he invested them (see Matthew 25:14-30). We all have something to give—something to improve the Body of Christ, whether it is our money, time, talents, etc. This is one of our callings as Christians, and God desires that we use these gifts (money, time, resources, ability, information, emotions, etc.) in ways that build up the Body of Christ and, in that process, ourselves. This is done in faith by planting or using what we have been given.

Faith vs. Flesh

Unfortunately, living by faith is not easy. When we seek to embrace God's spiritual things, we must fight against our flesh and temporal desires. Our fleshly desires—our sinful nature—usually point us toward comfort and pleasing ourselves. This is in sharp contrast to what God desires: He wants us to follow Him and please Him with all of our actions. Our flesh and spirit are at war with each other:

⊕ *For the flesh lusts against the Spirit, and the Spirit against the flesh; and these are contrary to one another, so that you do not do the things that you wish* (Galatians 5:17 NKJV).

We need to be aware of this so that we can make every effort to win the battle over the flesh because:

⊕ *...flesh and blood cannot inherit the Kingdom of God* [in our daily lives]*...* (1 Corinthians 15:50 NKJV).

It is not only our fleshly desires that challenge our faith, but also our fleshly minds. The Bible says a mind without the Spirit of God cannot understand spiritual things.

✠ *But the natural man does not receive the things of the Spirit of God, for they are foolishness to him; nor can he know them, because they are spiritually discerned* (1 Corinthians 2:14 NKJV).

Thus, in order to live a life of faith, we must overcome our desires in life. The famous philosopher Aristotle said, "I count him braver who overcomes his desires than him who overcomes his enemies;" for the hardest victory is over self.[2] Only when we allow ourselves to be led by the Spirit are we able to act in faith and please God, thus placing ourselves in a better position to receive whatever increase He has planned for us. For example, take note of this:

✠ *...for God loves a cheerful giver* (2 Corinthians 9:7).

It is not only important to be an obedient planter and giver, but also to be a *willing* and cheerful one. And the ability to be a *cheerful* giver comes only through subduing the flesh and living in faith.

Note also in the verse that follows that God requires two things of us to allow us to eat the best of the land:

✠ *If you are **willing** and **obedient**, you will eat the best from the land* (Isaiah 1:19).

It's not just your obedience that God desires, but also your willingness. This, again, is an act of faith—a decision to go one step beyond obedience (which you could perform grudgingly) to willingness (which is a position of trusting in God's goodness). You will then have all that God purposed for you—abundant life.

Truth #8: You Must Die to Self

Proper planting requires that you let go of what you plant in order to let God use both you and your seed for His purposes. This truth was most clearly revealed to me in this verse:

✝ *Foolish one, what you sow is **not** made alive unless it **dies*** (1 Corinthians 15:36 NKJV).

Think about this: "What you sow is not made alive unless it dies." The apple seed must cease to exist as a seed before it can become an apple tree. In other words, you likewise have to die to yourself to bear fruit. God's will must come before your own—leaving fleshly desires behind. Think about this in relation to other areas of your life. Perhaps your hold on your money or finances has to die before you can receive the increase that God desires for you. When you give, are you giving so that you can have some additional control over a person or entity? When you give, is it to be known and to receive praises? Or are you giving simply and quietly, without fanfare, solely to follow God's will in your life and to exude His love?

Action & Visualization

Give for God's purposes and not your own.

Truth #9: The Timeline Is Shortening

The spiritual growth timeline, from seed to harvest, is becoming shorter and shorter as we approach the return of Jesus. This truth should inspire us to sow generously and often. The Bible says that in the last days cycles will grow shorter and shorter.

✠ *"Behold, the days are coming", says the Lord, "When the plowman shall overtake the reaper, and the treader of grapes him who sows seed...* (Amos 9:13 NKJV).

We see another vivid example of this in the cycling rate at which human knowledge has increased over time. According to a study by French economist George Anderlo, if all scientific knowledge accumulated prior to A.D. 1 equaled one Unit of Information then it took 1,500 years to double the first time to two Units of information. The next doubling of information, from two to four Units took only 250 years or up until 1750. By 1900, only 150 years later, it had doubled yet again up to eight Units. The speed of doubling continues to get faster and faster. Sixteen Units of information was reached in 1950 with the passage of only fifty years, and this doubled again in just ten years to a total of 32 Units. Another seven years to 64 Units, and then in just six years to 128 Units of information. This was in 1973, the year of Anderlos study. The doubling speed of information has continued to accelerate and is now estimated to occur about every 18 months. With the coming of the Internet, information in certain specialized areas may double every year.[3] Think about it: between the first day of college classes and graduation day, the knowledge in our world will have doubled *four* times.

Ninety percent of all scientists who have ever lived are alive today and, as you read this, they are busily involved in the search for facts.[4] Science is a body of knowledge which has been estimated to be the equivalent of some 10,000,000 books on science and applications. More important, this body of knowledge is increasing at a rate estimated to be about 1,000,000 book equivalents a year, or on the order of 100 books an hour. [5]

When prophesying of the time near Jesus' return, Daniel said:

✝ *...Many shall run to and fro, and knowledge shall increase* (Daniel 12:4 NKJV).

I believe this ever increasing explosion of knowledge is part of the end-time plan for people to be exposed to a greater intellectual understanding in order to better see God's role in the creation. Moreover, I believe that science without God in the equation will start coming to an end as scientists realize that the answers to the biggest scientific questions ultimately point to God. This is, of course, already the case on many points. Many of the assumptions that Godless science has used to explain the creation without God's involvement defy simple logic and ignore scientific evidence. What I'm suggesting is that it will become harder and harder to maintain this model as knowledge increases because more and more anti-God assumptions will be proven unquestionably wrong.

I believe the fact that the harvest cycles are getting shorter and shorter, as we grow closer to the endtimes, also has a planned purpose. Through it, God will provide the required physical resources and the acceleration of spiritual manifestations necessary for the Church to be able to reap a great end-time harvest. This truth should spur us on to act boldly on our faith. The good news is that our planted seeds will show a quicker return as we approach Christ's return.

In a spiritual and physical sense, this makes Robert Louis Stevenson's quote meaningful to me: "Don't judge each day by the harvest you reap, but by the seeds you plant."[6]

In Conclusion

Finally, consider this: the principle of Seed, Time, and Harvest is not something that God prepared just for you and me. Jesus said this about His death:

✟ *I tell you the truth, unless a kernel of wheat falls to the ground and dies, it remains only a single seed. But if it dies, it produces many seeds (John 12:24).*

God sowed *His* most precious possession, His only begotten Son, so that He could reap a harvest of sons and daughters. That's you and me.

MEDITATION POINT

The light of God exudes with power,
giving us the means for growth and multiplication.

Go to Chapter 1 in the Study Guide section on page 291.

ENDNOTES

1. Mario Murillo, *I am the Christian the Devil Warned You About* (Danville, CA: Fresh Fire Communications, 1996), 81-93.

2. Aristotle, *Quotation #29862* from *Classic Quotes* (www.quotationspage.com).

3. Daniel H. Johnston, *Lessons For Living: Simple Solutions for Life's Problems* (Macon, GA: Dagali Press, 2001), 72.

4. *Christian Science Monitor* January 23, 1971.

5. *Science News*, October 18, 1969.

6. Robert Louis Stevenson, www.quotesandpoem.com/quotes/slowquotes/author/Robert-louis-stevensen/25967.

Chapter 2

GIFT #8—INCREASE (PART 2)

HOW DO YOU GET THE GOOD KIND?

Before you begin to read, pray that the Holy Spirit will give you and all readers of this book understanding and application.

✠ *Do not be deceived, God is not mocked; for whatever a man sows, that he will also reap. For he who sows to his flesh will of the flesh reap corruption, but he who sows to the Spirit will of the Spirit reap everlasting life. And let us not grow weary while doing good, for in due season we shall reap if we do not lose heart* (Galatians 6:7-9 NKJV).

I have heard a story of a young Christian man who was about to graduate from college. For months he had admired a beautiful sports car in a dealer's showroom. Knowing that his father could afford it, he told him that the car was all he wanted for a graduation gift. As the day approached, the young man awaited signs that his father had purchased the car. Finally, on the morning of his graduation, his father called him into his private study. His father told him how proud he was to have such a fine son, and he told him how much he loved him. He handed his son a beautifully wrapped gift box. Curious, but somewhat disappointed, the young man opened the box and found a lovely leather-wrapped Bible. Angrily, he raised his voice at his father and said, "With all your money you gave me a Bible?" and stormed out of the house, leaving the "instruction book" behind.

Many years passed, and his life went as many "Christian" lives go—up and down, good and bad, like the ocean tides. He got married, had two kids, and started a business. The business had its ups and downs and never gave him the freedom he sought in life. The effort he put into the business detracted from his family relationships, and as a result, he got a divorce (like 35 percent of professing Christians). His son wound up in jail because of a drug habit, and his daughter never really forgave him for the divorce because, in her mind, he'd abandoned the family.

Sitting alone at home one day, he got a phone call letting him know that his father had passed away and that he would need to come home immediately to settle his father's estate. When he arrived, sudden sadness and regret filled his heart. He began to search through his father's important papers and saw the still-new Bible, just as he had left it 25 years earlier. With tears, he opened the Bible and began to turn the pages. As he read, a car key dropped from an envelope taped behind the Bible. It had a tag with a dealer's name, the same dealer who had the sports car he'd desired. On the tag was the date of his college graduation and the words, "Paid in full."

Are you expecting God to bring increase, blessings, and gifts the way *you* see fit? How often do we presume to know the way almighty God, the God who made the heavens and earth, should work? Honestly, as Christians, most of us know that Jesus is "the way, the truth, and the life" (see John 14:6), but when it comes to the way we actually live our lives, we still live by, "my way or the highway." What if your increase is embedded in a person, a mission, a teaching, or an encounter that you have yet to experience, that God has yet to give you, or that *you have yet to embrace*?

I found my increase in the midst of God profoundly exercising my faith; working *through* this process brought it about in a dramatic way. Remember that, just like the man in this story, your increase can only be *found* when, with faith in Him, you receive, unwrap, and then use the life-changing gift offered to you by your heavenly Father.

RECEIVING THE GIFT

Early in my Christian walk, I learned the significance of the opening verse of this chapter (Gal. 6:7-9); however, at the time I didn't realize that it would become the cornerstone of my testimony and would profoundly affect my faith. God punctuated this verse in my life in a very special way, since only He could know that I would eventually write this book.

In the summer of 1988, I was living well, and I was beginning to develop my personal relationship with Jesus Christ. However, I started getting into financial trouble. I lost my company, my money, my house, my car—it was a horribly painful series of events that seemed to snowball, leaving little behind. *Where was the God to whom I had just given my life? What was He doing with my life?* I couldn't help but wonder at times, *God, I've given you my life, now why are you trying to take it away—to destroy it?* Every time I thought it couldn't get any worse, it did.

At the time, I felt like my life was a really bad Christian witness. I dreaded people asking me to give my testimony. My story seemed so depressing—one people would want to avoid—so I wondered who could possibly be inspired or want to come to know Jesus after hearing it. On the other hand, in spite of my difficult experiences, my life, my relationships, and my outlook had changed for the better, and for the first time in my life, everything made sense in light of God's Word.

Yet, despite this profound clarity, I had lost nearly every one of my possessions. At one point, I thought it might be a virtue to be poor. This was taught in the church I attended as a young child; however, I couldn't find any support for it in the Bible. So what was happening in my life? Why did it seem like everything was falling apart?

Well, from the time I received Jesus, my wife and I had started praying diligently for faith. As we did, things seemed to get worse. How was that possible? As you recall, faith comes by trusting God—by acting in spite of what you see (see Heb. 11:1). The key here is the word *acting*. This is how we exercise our faith; this is how we grow—by *acting* on our hope *despite* what we *see* or *experience*. So, how does this work? Well, for my wife and me to have the opportunity to grow our faith, we had to initially see things for which we had *not* hoped, like losing all our possessions. So in our case, this exercise program wasn't a light jog—it was more of a boot camp.

So *praise* God. He *had* answered our prayers! God had instituted a faith-building exercise program using our finances, which was probably the easiest way for God to get and keep our attention. I was certainly very interested in that area of my life. Like most people, I was *too* interested. I can tell you, my flesh was not too thrilled about this faith exercise program, though God wanted me to be joyous about it.

This was the period of life when I discovered the principle of Seed, Time, and Harvest that you just read about in the previous chapter. As I mentioned, initially this principle seemed like bad news because, as a new Christian, so many of the seeds that I had sown were going to bear fruit that I didn't want. However, this principle and its supporting truths ultimately gave me a blueprint. It gave me hope and encouraged me to *work* my way out of the predicament that *I* had gotten *myself* into.

Unwrapping the Gift

The *first* step we took to begin living out this principle was to start *tithing*. *Tithe* means one-tenth. The first recorded tither was none other than the father of our faith, Abraham, who gave his king and priest the first *tenth* of everything that he received.

✟ [Melchizedek said,] *"And blessed be God Most High, who delivered your enemies into your hand." Then Abram **gave him a tenth of everything** (Genesis 14:20).*

Tithing later became part of the Mosaic Law for the Israelites, who were commanded to give the first tenth of their increase to God's priests the Levites.

✟ *A tithe of everything from the land, whether grain from the soil or fruit from the trees, belongs to the Lord; it is holy to the Lord* (Leviticus 27:30).

This verse indicates that this tenth *belongs* to the Lord and is holy. This would suggest that under the Mosaic Law, if they didn't pay their tithe, then they would essentially be stealing from God. The only place in the Bible where God challenges us to test Him is in relation to tithing.

✟ *"Bring all the tithes into the storehouse, that there may be food in My house, and **try Me now in this**," says the Lord of hosts, "**If** I will not open for you the windows of heaven and pour out for you such blessing that there will not be room enough to receive it"* (Malachi 3:10 NKJV).

Some Christians try to justify *not* tithing, saying, "These verses came from the Old Testament, which was a different spiritual season governed by the Law, and since we're now in a season of grace, tithing no longer applies." We have been *freed* from the law; however, I knew that it was still important to tithe, even in this season of grace. It was an offering of my obedience, faith, and surrender to God's work—to God's Kingdom and not humanity's—even in the midst of financial struggle (*especially* in the midst of financial struggle). Consider this important verse in Galatians that introduces the very principle of Seed, Time, and Harvest itself:

✢ *Anyone who receives instruction in the word* **must** *share all good things with his instructor. Do not be deceived: God cannot be mocked. A man reaps what he sows* (Galatians 6:6-7).

It was in the context of a discussion on giving (which is the main way that we support those who teach—our church pastors and staff) that God showed me the principle of Seed, Time, and Harvest. In this passage, God's use of the word *must* makes it crystal clear—we should support pastors, teachers, and those who preach God's Word *even in this season of grace.* Indeed, sometimes this will involve *more* than one-tenth of your income. Paul says that, in return, we will receive a reward for giving to God's work.

✢ *I planted, Apollos watered, but God gave the increase. So then neither he who plants is anything, nor he who waters, but God who gives the increase. Now he who plants and he who waters are one, and each will receive his own* **reward according to his own labor** (1 Corinthians 3:6-8 NKJV).

Watering a plant is what brings life to it. We see in the same way giving to God is how you bring the fullness of life to yourself that God desires for you. The same concept is presented in Proverbs:

✢ *Honor the Lord with your wealth, with the first fruits of all your crops; then your barns will be filled to overflowing, and your vats will brim over with new wine* (Proverbs 3:9-10).

As you might guess, the biggest problem with tithing is actually following through with it. Your faith *will* be tested on this point because of the time it takes for crops to grow and because of occasional crop failure. Mine was tested in a severe way many times. Of course, these tests will exercise your faith and build it up—which is ultimately a good thing.

ACTION & VISUALIZATION

Though it may be a challenge for you, start tithing regularly.

USING THE GIFT BY TITHING

When I accepted Christ, I was in the process of moving from a salaried position into commercial brokerage, where deal closings became my paydays. In commercial brokerage, you have the opportunity for big paydays, but these paydays can be irregular and are often spread far apart. Initially, my paydays weren't substantial, and they were spread very, very, *very* far apart. On top of that, I had built up a significant overhead from "better living days" that wasn't easy to get rid of. When I did get paid, it always seemed to be less than what I needed to make it to the next closing. Looking at the numbers, I could see that if I didn't give God His tithe, I *might* just make it if I got "lucky."

Due to the length of time it takes for a deal to close, I would typically know my dire financial picture months in advance. Yet, in spite of what I saw and the fear I felt, I chose to walk by faith and tithe anyway. Remember that faith is an action that pleases God. As a result, God would, at times, show me His hand operating in some very unusual ways. I admit that it was often a hair-raising period of life, as I was barely making enough to stay afloat. But in God's wisdom, He knew that this would cause me to hang tightly onto Him.

I lost all of my non-essential possessions in one physically and mentally painful event after another while I sank deeper and deeper into debt. I was eventually reduced to riding the bus and living in a *two-room* apartment. Not a two-bedroom apartment, but a *two-room* apartment. One room was our living room, kids' bedroom, kitchen, and dining room. The other was a bedroom for my wife and me as well as my office. Because I was in Hawaii, I had to get up at 3:00 A.M. to make calls to the East Coast.

I would sit on the corner of my bed all day, with files spread across it, occasionally staring out the one small window in the cinder block walls, thinking, *how will I get out of this hole?* As is the case with many Christians, my freedom to go places and do things was severely restricted because of my lack of financial increase. My life was clearly in a winter season.

Though I was unable to save, in debt, and barely providing for my family, I still knew that God was calling me to give, to tithe. Do you think that was challenging to my faith? Yes, *unbelievably* so. Yet, we did not lose heart, and we continued to tithe and give anyway, believing for a change of season. We were planting good seed; however, what we were experiencing was the truth that "due season" is something God determines, not us. I was still reaping the not-so-good fruit from the seeds I had planted before, and the *good* seeds I'd planted were not yet bearing fruit. God uses time to let us put our faith into *action*. My wife and I had to keep heart, and in faith, *continue* planting seed for the future in spite of the drought.

Of course, everytime things got worse, we prayed for *more* faith. (We didn't initially realize the intense exercise program we were putting into motion.) The apostles did something similar when they asked Jesus for more faith.

✝ *The apostles said to the Lord, "Increase our faith"* (Luke 17:5).

Only a short time later, their friend, teacher, and leader, Jesus, was *crucified*. Suddenly, everything they had dedicated their lives to was *gone*. Their world was *completely* and *forever* changed. Their faith was *severely* tested. Three days later, Jesus delivered on His promise by defeating death and rising from the dead. In *time* He will fulfill His promises to you and me too.

For my family, at our lowest point, we were living in Waikiki in our two-room apartment with no car. Our refrigerator was one of those tiny mini-bar refrigerators with no freezer, so my wife had to endure the adventure of riding the bus to purchase and then lug home food and ice *daily*.

Sometimes we would get a little extra money. My instinct was to buy a used car. However, my wife had a vision of a new green Nissan van. One day when she was walking in Waikiki, she saw one come around the corner, and it seemed to be moving in slow motion, glistening in the sun. She was convinced that it was God speaking to her in that circumstance. So we began trusting God for that Nissan van and nothing but the Nissan van. We were so sure of God's direction that we took any extra money—at first $1,000, then $5,000—and gave it to God beyond our tithes. This was "seed money" for the Nissan van. One July, it looked like I was going to close the biggest deal of my career, beyond my wildest expectations: *$800,000* in commissions.

However, it became clear that my co-broker, despite an agreement to the contrary, was going to double-cross me and keep the entire $1.6 million commission for himself. My client was sympathetic and agreed to pay me $100,000 directly. However, the $1.6 million went to the other broker. I was crushed, yet here again, it was another opportunity to *exercise* my heart and my faith.

I owed money to the IRS and other creditors, so after I paid the back taxes and old bills, there wasn't enough to get the Nissan van. In hopes of getting the van, I told the co-broker that, instead of taking him to court on the $800,000 he rightfully owed me, I would settle for just $25,000. He refused. You can imagine, given our situation, how *hard* this was to accept. I was heartbroken—all my hard work seemed wasted. As I struggled for understanding and direction about what to do next, my flesh wanted to kill the co-broker in some slow and torturous way. It was a very difficult decision—one I had to *work* at—but I wound up *not* suing him. I knew the long and costly process of litigation would keep anger burning in my heart. I don't know about you, but I am simply not spiritual enough to avoid letting anger get the best of me. My anger, justified or not, would *not* have been beneficial. Knowing that *my* heart is weak, I needed to protect it.

✠ *Keep your heart with all diligence, for out of it spring the issues of life* (Proverbs 4:23 NKJV).

Furthermore, Jesus had this advice for me:

✠ *...And from him who takes away your goods do not ask them back* (Luke 6:30 NKJV).

As much as I didn't want to admit it, I had not spiritually earned the money yet as all things are created in the spirit realm first.

✠ *To this John replied, "A man can receive only what is given him from heaven"* (John 3:27).

I can guarantee you that *nobody*, and I repeat, *nobody*, can take away what God intends for us. And no lawsuit was going to get for me what God hadn't yet intended for me. Only a *generous, forgiving* heart would help me receive what God was preparing.

✠ *Good will come to him who is generous...* (Psalm 112:5).

☩ *Give, and it will be given unto you. A good measure, pressed down, shaken together and running over, will be poured into your lap. For with the measure you use, it will be measured to you* (Luke 6:38).

God is not going to turn around, surprised, one day and say, "Oops, how did you get that $800,000 in your account?" Nor is He going to say, "Oops, what happened to that $800,000 I meant for you? Did someone cheat you out of it?"

USING THE GIFT BY GIVING

About a month after the deal closed, my wife, still without a car, was taking her Bible out of the nightstand to pray when a letter fell onto the floor. She had placed the envelope there a few days earlier without looking at it. Though it was clearly junk mail, God impressed on her that it was important. Inside was an offer to get a car financed with bad credit—this was a new concept at the time. I was leaving for Mexico the next morning, but because she felt so strongly about it, I made the call.

I quickly confirmed an arrangement to buy a new Dodge minivan—bad credit and all. Then it struck me, my wife's vision was for a green Nissan van *not* a Dodge. I called the Nissan dealership and asked if they had a similar bad credit loan program, and sure enough, they did. I went in and met with the representative from the lending company—who *happened* to be there that day. After everything was arranged, a man explained to me the surprising nature of this car deal: "*This is our first day of the bad credit loan program, and you're our first customer.*" Had I called even one day earlier, they would have said "no" because this lending program didn't exist! *And* because the lender was there setting up the program that first day, I got a *better deal*. I happily drove the glistening green Nissan van home that day, knowing that God was fulfilling His promise:

✠ *...To guide our feet into the way of peace* [contentment] (Luke 1:79 NKJV).

About six months after I bought the car, I received the largest commission I had ever received, $200,000. I had $100,000 left after paying current taxes, back taxes, and old debts. We had been praying for and trusting God for a home so that we could get out of the two-room apartment, but the remaining $100,000 was not enough for a house in Hawaii, especially given my credit problems. Additionally, we weren't hoping for just any house, we had high expectations!

✠ *...He who sows sparingly will also reap sparingly, and he who sows bountifully will also reap bountifully* (2 Corinthians 9:6 NKJV).

✠ *Now may He who supplies seed to the sower...**multiply** the seed you have **sown**...* (2 Corinthians 9:10 NKJV).

We knew that, if we wanted to get the kind of home we dreamed of, finding a way to *multiply* our money was the key. I could only get a 10 to 20 percent return from traditional investments. And even with $100,000, at those return rates it would take a long time to earn enough money for the home we wanted. I knew that because God is the God of *multiplication*, He could choose to give us a much greater return (increase) if I invested the money with Him.

Did my flesh and mind think this was a good idea? No! They *hated* the idea. I am sure a professional advisor would have also found fault with this investment concept. My natural mind thought it would be foolish to give away the most money that I'd ever had in our bank account. However, despite my natural mind's fears, I decided to walk in the Spirit and in faith.

Out of that original $200,000 commission, this is what I did: I gave $20,000 tithe; I paid off my debts and taxes with $100,000; I gave $50,000 as a gift to my church for their building program; I gave a gift of $25,000 to my former pastor so that he could put a down payment on a house in Denver; and I gave $5,000 to another church. I sowed everything I could, leaving nearly nothing in my bank account. With a warrior's spirit, I followed the lead of the widow with the two coins, and gave *all that I had* to God. *My spirit soared with expectations.*

My flesh and mind didn't stop working though. In fact, pride began to seep in when I calculated that the contribution that I had made to my church made up a noticeable amount of the entire building fund. Well, you guessed it; I still had more spiritual shaping up to do in the gym. A year went by and nothing happened—*still no harvest.*

God Surprises Us

Though very discouraged at times, I remained confident in the seeds I had planted, and a little more than a year later, while I was seeking a retail location for a ministry, I ran into an out-of-town commercial broker I knew. I'd met him previously while trying to sell a beautiful townhouse complex to a developer. At the time, I had actually hoped that I might be able to get one of the units in the complex if I sold the complex to a developer. Now two years later, the broker told me that the townhouses had all sold, except for one—a particularly nice unit—which was still personally owned by the developer. He thought the developer might be interested in selling.

Out of courtesy and curiosity, I made an appointment to look at it with the broker. Though it was *perfect* and even more wonderful than we expected, I didn't have enough for a down payment, nor could I qualify for a standard loan. I did *not* call him back again after the showing.

The next Sunday at church, I noticed the same broker sitting in the row in front of me. Interesting *coincidence*, don't you think? He turned out to be a fellow Christian who, when in Honolulu, would visit our church. After church, he asked me if I liked the townhouse. I said *yes* and then explained my problem. He said he thought he could do something to help. Ultimately, he was able to get the owner to hold a large second mortgage, which made getting a low-leverage first mortgage easy, even with my credit problem.

I was able to purchase the townhouse with almost no money down. One month later, the value went up by *more than $50,000*. God did what I thought was impossible. In that very same week, I found out that my former pastor had sold his house (the one he'd purchased a year earlier with my $25,000 gift) for a $70,000 profit. He then bought a bigger house that had room for his entire extended family. He was also, *that very same month*, taking advantage of a lower interest rate to pull $30,000 of equity out of his current house (without raising his payments) so that he could divide it between his three children (who were also in ministry) so that they could each get a condo. Amazingly, that *same month*, I was also placed in a position to help my current pastor acquire his dream house, giving me the same favor that I had given up a year earlier when I decided to help my former pastor instead.

The Surprising Increases

Wait! God wasn't finished yet. About a month later, I sold a $115 million portfolio of hotels, for which I received a $1.6 million commission (enough to pay off my new high-leverage mortgage). This showed me God's sense of humor. He was driving His point home in a very dramatic way: He could do the *impossible* with credit *or* cash. Remember the broker who double-crossed me for $800,000? This commission was double that amount!

✟ *If a man delivers to his neighbor money or articles to keep, and it is stolen out of the man's house, if the thief is found, he shall pay **double*** (Exodus 22:7 NKJV).

I believe this can apply to anything that the devil steals from you. This is illustrated in the Book of Job. After the season of trouble created by satan, God blessed Job by doubling the possessions that satan had taken and destroyed. Yes, you *really can* count it all joy when satan steals your possessions, because God can double what was stolen.

My harvest had begun, and it was beyond what I would have projected because it was clearly God's power at work. After a rapid series of other amazing examples of God's increase, I sold a $233 million resort hotel portfolio in Mexico. A month after that, I closed a $65 million joint venture hotel deal in Denver with the biggest hotel-buying company in the world. The seeds that I had been planting over the years were now bearing fruit in rapid succession.

✟ *He who goes out weeping, carrying seed to sow, will return with songs of joy, carrying sheaves with him* (Psalm 126:6).

Then the biggest hotel buying company asked if I could scout out European hotel chains that they could buy. What an incredible opportunity. Any intelligent businessperson would make time for a meeting with the world's largest hotel buying company. All I needed was a hotel owners' directory. I called and asked the presidents of the European hotel companies if they were interested in going to lunch with the director of real estate for the largest hotel buying company in the world. It was a no-brainer; who wouldn't say yes? God was orchestrating my increase, and it was clear to everyone around me—this was supernatural. God likes to show off in your life when you truly make room for Him to show up in it.

This particular fruit-bearing journey was not the result of hard work (though I always worked hard) or education (anyone could read a phone number, and I actually knew very little about hotels at the time). Instead, God was allowing me to operate well beyond my means, well beyond my high school education, and well beyond my intellect and abilities.

Some of you might be thinking, *I could never have that kind of faith, or, I could never give up everything like you did.* Both of those thoughts would be wrong. First, I was no spiritual superman. I made many, many errors—I still committed sins against God after I was saved. For those sins, I also reaped an unfruitful harvest in my life. Second, it may be that God gifted me initially with a large measure of faith, but *anyone* can build their faith with exercise. However, as I was soon to discover, keeping that faith strong takes continued exercise and commitment. Don't get lazy and avoid the gym.

Trusting God's Path

After my first wave of faith, I blinked. Yes, *blinked*. God had rewarded me financially with substantial increase. I had more money than I needed or could spend. My flesh—my mind and my body—*liked* having money in the bank. It felt good. It felt safe. But is it God's ultimate goal to make us feel good and safe? Yes, but only if He is our source and sustainer. God wanted me to feel good and safe *in Him*, even when money was going in and out of my bank account like the ocean's tide, because instability is part of a fallen world. He wanted me to trust in *Him*, not in my bank account, which of course is uncertain anyway.

✠ *Command those who are rich in this present world not to be arrogant, nor to put their hope in wealth, which is so uncertain, but to put their hope in God...* (1 Timothy 6:17).

✠ *The wealth of the rich is their fortified city; they **imagine** it an unscalable wall* (Proverbs 18:11).

I knew deep down that I was in for more spiritual training, but my mind made a convincing argument. With so much money in the bank, I could rely on traditional investments with lower returns. Maybe I didn't need to continue my aggressive faith-based investments into spiritual things, into His Kingdom's work. Making this mistaken rationalization, I changed strategies, and I stopped walking in pure aggressive faith. This new reliance on what I could see was, of course, not pleasing to God. I shrank back, and my flesh took over.

✠ *My righteous one will live by faith. And if he shrinks back, I will not be pleased with him* (Hebrews 10:38).

Admittedly, I had also become somewhat proud. I felt like, at my level of faith, I had "arrived" — I had reached faith's peak. Yet faith never reaches an end and becomes idle—there is no such thing as "coasting" with God. Instead, we should simply reach for new plateaus from which to launch into new and unknown territory. Unfortunately, my financial comfort led to less and less communication with God. I began to put my faith in bank statements rather than in His voice and His Word. It didn't take long for my new investment strategy to potentially wipe out much of God's increase in my life. Things went so bad in one investment that I wound up having to take out a $4 million business loan with my investing partners to cover the cash shortfall. The business was going so badly that it looked like I would soon be heading back to a two-room apartment. My, how chatty I can get with God during these kinds of circumstances. I sure became a better listener too. I don't know about you, but hanging over a boiling pit of grease by a thin thread causes me to be very communicative with God.

After I began listening to God, He led me back to my original investment strategy. Sure enough, things started to turn around again in amazing and miraculous ways.

I learned that when I was being obedient and following the leading of the Spirit—following the path God set before me—amazing God-driven things would come my way:

☩ *In the way of righteousness is life, and in its pathway there is no death* (Proverbs 12:28 NKJV).

☩ *...[God's] paths drip with abundance* (Psalm 65:11 NKJV).

This abundance does not necessarily mean material wealth (although it can)—it means experiencing all that God has offered you according to your unique destiny.

I also learned that, for our own good, God does not want us to place our love, trust, or hearts in the gifts that He gives us—instead of in Him. When we do, Jesus gives this corrective command:

☩ *Sell your possessions and give to the poor. Provide purses for yourselves that will not wear out, a treasure in heaven that will not be exhausted, where no thief comes near and no moth destroys. For where your treasure is, there your heart will be also* (Luke 12:33-34).

GOD'S PATH DRIPS WITH ABUNDANCE

In 1998, God took someone off of a flight from Honolulu to Chicago the day before my own flight to Chicago. The next day we were on the same red-eye flight, seated next to each other. As a result of a casual conversation, I sold him what many consider to be the best city hotel in the world *for $275 million*. He didn't own a hotel at the time, nor was he seeking to buy one. But God's path drips with abundance.

I ran into that *same* man in another "fluke" encounter at a mall in Oakbrook, Illinois. This encounter grew into a business relationship that has resulted in over *one billion dollars* in hotel sales as well as in an asset management assignment, which has provided me regular income for sometime.

About four years before meeting this man on the plane, I had met an investment banker on a red-eye flight to Mexico City. In 2005, I decided to introduce my two plane-encounter friends to each other, and this resulted in a mutually beneficial transaction for both of them as well as the largest loan placement I have ever done: *$425 million.*

Due to another "chance" encounter at the Tokyo Airport and another set of unusual circumstances, I entered into a distribution business in Japan for the man I originally met on the plane to Chicago. This allowed me while in Japan to assist in lining up a Japanese satellite for the first 24-hour Christian broadcasting network in Asia. I knew I was on destiny's path when I learned that the name of the satellite was JC3. This satellite now beams 24-hour Christian programming into over 7.5 million households in Asia. The network is responsible for many, many people receiving the Gospel and coming to know Jesus Christ. I consider this to be one of the most important things that God has allowed me to do in my life to date.

God's path *drips with abundance* and leads to your *destiny*. It starts with an *action* of faith. Are you willing to act by faith?

✟ *A gift opens the way for the giver. …* (Proverbs 18:16).

Your gifts will open ways and paths designated by God for you too. It's become clear to me in my own life experiences and through God's Word that He is *actively* involved in all aspects and details of my life's journey. The Bible says:

✟ *You enlarged my path under me; so my feet did not slip* (2 Samuel 22:37 NKJV).

✟ *Your word is a lamp to my feet and a light to my path* (Psalm 119:105 NKJV).

By walking in faith, through the actions of our heart, we are creating the circumstances that we will run into in our future. This is because we are constantly manufacturing things in the spirit realm that will *in due time* manifest in the physical realm.

I ran into the broker who cheated me out of an $800,000 commission again several years later. He had become the exclusive listing agent for a chain of hotels. Had I sued him, he would not have spoken to me. Instead, when I brought my client to look at his listings, he was very helpful and gave me an edge over other bidders in an effort to push things in my favor. As a result, I closed the deal, selling *more* hotels than ever before in one transaction. This is a great reminder for us to guard our hearts because our actions are setting into play our future circumstances.

✟ *Keep your heart with **all** diligence, for out of it spring the issues of* [your] *life* (Proverbs 4:23 NKJV).

My wife and I have chosen the path of relentless sowing. We've learned to continue on this path regardless of what we are seeing. This is the path with the greatest kind of rewards—eternal rewards.

ACTION & VISUALIZATION

Walk in faith and be consistent with the actions of your heart.

SEEK FIRST GOD'S KINGDOM

The Bible says in Matthew 6:33 that if you seek first the Kingdom of God, all things will be added unto you. Jesus paints this picture of the Kingdom of God:

✠ *He said, "To what shall we liken the kingdom of God? Or with what parable shall we picture it? It is like a mustard seed which, when it is sown on the ground, is smaller than all the seeds on earth; but **when it is sown**, it grows up and becomes greater than all herbs, and shoots out large branches, so that the birds of the air may nest under its shade"* (Mark 4:30-32 NKJV).

Now that my prior giving is returning a harvest, I am able to plant new seeds into people and ministries—going well beyond what would be possible from my own efforts. It is a blessing as a Christian to be able to make a positive impact on the world and to give to the Body of Christ.

For the past ten years, I have been able to provide funds for a number of ministries in ever-increasing amounts. I could only do this because I planted seeds that God grew into a towering oak tree, which now provides rest and shade for others. I could *not* have created these with my own efforts. There is indeed a *power beyond our own efforts* that can make a difference for the Kingdom—this is the power of faith, and it is evidenced in the principle of Seed, Time, and Harvest.

✝ *Wealth and honor come from You; You are the ruler of all things. In Your hands are strength and power to exalt and give strength to all* (1 Chronicles 29:12).

✝ *Therefore do not cast away your confidence, which has great reward* (Hebrews 10:35 NKJV).

ACTION & VISUALIZATION

Seek God first by confidently sowing into His Kingdom. Then you will be rewarded with the fullness of His power, releasing freedom in your life.

THE IMPORTANCE OF GENEROSITY

God wants His Body on earth to be a blessing to the world and to other Christians in need. God needs Christians who will be *open conduits* through whom He can pour out His provisions and gifts. We are blessed when increase and gifts come to us, but we create further blessings when we allow them to flow *through* us. God blesses those who trust Him to use them for His purposes. It is good and right to become a blessing to others in this way. The Scriptures are full of verses about the importance of generosity:

✝ *...Freely you have received, freely give* (Matthew 10:8).

✝ *Each man should give what he has decided in his heart to give, not reluctantly or under compulsion, for God loves a cheerful giver (2 Corinthians 9:7).*

✝ *...remembering the words the Lord Jesus Himself said: "It is more blessed to give than to receive" (Acts 20:35).*

✝ *He who is kind to the poor lends to the Lord, and He will reward him for what he has done (Proverbs 19:17).*

✝ *A generous man will prosper; he who refreshes others will himself be refreshed (Proverbs 11:25).*

✝ *A generous man will himself be blessed, for he shares his food with the poor (Proverbs 22:9).*

For me, the harvest keeps coming, and I am able to re-sow the seeds in order to give more back to God. Remember the pastor to whom I gave $25,000 that returned $70,000 then later $30,000 more? The last time I spoke to him, he said that he was able to refinance his house yet *again*. With that money, he was able to build a Bible college in Burma and a home for the director of an orphanage—all for $25,000! Shortly after that, his uncle gave him his house, worth over $400,000.

Why was all this happening to him? He told me that, when he moved to take the pastoral job where I met him, he had sowed the equity from his house—valued at approximately $25,000. The very day that I originally called him to tell him that I was going to give him $25,000 for a house, he and his wife had spent the afternoon looking at houses they couldn't afford. His wife had asked him, "Do you think we will ever be able to afford a house again?" Before he could answer, he received my call and the $25,000 gift. So you see, *the seed you sow* can reap a harvest beyond your imagination, and it can continue multiplying itself like a ripple in a pond. It all *begins* when you toss your pebble of faith into the water.

God wants us to focus on giving because it's a fundamental principle in how the Kingdom of God works. Jesus tells a parable in Luke about a very successful man who was rich:

The ground of a certain rich man produced a good crop. He thought to himself, "What shall I do? I have no place to store my crops." Then he said, "This is what I'll do. I will tear down my barns and build bigger ones, and there I will store all my grain and my goods. And I'll say to myself, 'You have plenty of good things laid up for many years. Take life easy; eat, drink and be merry.'" But God said to him, "You fool! This very night your life will be demanded from you. Then who will get what you have prepared for yourself?" **This is how it will be with anyone who stores up things for himself but is not rich toward God** (Luke 12:16-21).

Despite the rich man's apparent worldly success, Jesus called him a *fool* because he was *not* generous toward God. Being rich, even famously so, is not synonymous with being wise. I am sure you can think of some examples who are in the media today. It's interesting that the rich man's wealth came from crops—a profession in which the increase clearly comes from God. Did you notice that the rich man's favorite word in the parable is *my*? The fact is, our money, talents, intellect, abilities, power, and authority all come from God, and we should generously give of them to help His other children. And you should also be giving back to God for the blessings and gifts that He gives to you:

✠ *Each of you **must** bring a gift in proportion to the way the Lord your God has blessed you* (Deuteronomy 16:17).

The apostle Paul wrote this encouragement to the Corinthians who had been supporting God's work through giving to his ministry:

✠ *Now... [God] will also supply and increase your store of seed and will enlarge the harvest of your righteousness. You will be made rich in every way **so that you can be generous** on every occasion...* (2 Corinthians 9:10-11).

ACTION & VISUALIZATION

Be a generous giver.

YOUR GIFT IS YOUR SWORD

In the Old Testament there is a story of God calling Gideon to save Israel from the Midianites who were preparing to attack Israel. Gideon not feeling he was physically qualified for this calling and he answered God this way:

✠ *"But Lord," Gideon asked, "How can I save Israel?" My clan is the weakest in Manasseh, and I am the least in my family"* (Judges 6:15).

In preparation for this great battle, Gideon prepares an offering of meat and *bread* to God (see Judges 6:16-21). So that God could clearly show that the battle would be won in His power and not by the strength of Gideon's army (from the weakest clan) God moved Gideon through several events paring his army down from 30,000 to 300 men (see Judges 7:1-8). Then Gideon, with just his 300 remaining men, was on the hill above the camp of Midianites and Amalekites. Once there God instructed Gideon to go down and ambush the enemy's encampment. Just prior to their attack, God instructed Gideon and his servant to sneak into the enemy's camp so they could listen to what his enemy was saying about him.

☦ *The Midianites, the Amalekites and all the other eastern peoples had settled in the valley, thick as locusts. Their camels could no more be counted than the sand on the seashore. Gideon arrived just as a man was telling a friend his dream. "I had a dream," he was saying. "A round loaf of barley* **bread** *came tumbling into the Midianite camp. It struck the tent with such force that the tent overturned and collapsed. His friend responded, "This can be nothing other than the* **sword** *of Gideon son of Joash, the Israelite. God has given the Midianites and the whole camp into his hands (Judges 7:12-14).*

Gideon's offering of *bread* had become his *sword* powerful enough to defeat his seemingly undefeatable enemy. You, too, by wielding the weapon of your offerings, can find victory even when the odds are against you.

Action & Visualization

Remember when your enemy is encamped around you your offering to God can be your sword—make sure it is a powerful one that can take down any enemy.

Not Just Money

I want to point out here that, while I have primarily focused on the ways in which God provided increase to my finances, this is certainly not the only way in which God applies the principle of Seed, Time, and Harvest. I highlight the financial aspect only to show how God used this area to teach me (He knew it would most effectively catch my attention). So, what is God using to catch your attention? Where do you need to plant seeds? Where are you seeking increase?

The gift of giving is also my calling and the area where He knew I could serve Him best. But as I expressed in the previous chapter, when we sow good seeds of *any* kind, God will use them and provide a *rich* harvest.

Indeed, sowing grace and mercy has had the most tangible and impactful harvest in my life. Since I am imperfect, the one thing I need the most in my relationships with others is grace. When I judge people for their actions, I am sowing judgment, and I will reap judgment in my own earthly relationships. However, if I sow grace, I will reap that much-needed grace from others. Just like sowing financially, you may have to sow over and over again in faith, but eventually you will receive a crop of grace and mercy in your life.

✟ *Blessed are the merciful, for they will be shown mercy* (Matthew 5:7).

Another great example of sowing is in missionary work. When Mother Teresa began sowing her kindness and care to the unwanted in Calcutta, she was one of only 12 who were called to serve that community. Today, the order she founded has more than 4,000 members, each dedicated to giving sacrificially to help those in need. Her seed of faith multiplied into other workers while bringing countless others to faith in Christ.

You will always have seeds of some kind to sow into someone's life. When you step out and sow with your faith into others' lives, you will bring a harvest of faith into your own. You have read my testimony. You now know what I know. You have read God's words, and if you act on what you have read and if you sow, this Gift of Increase will set you free from the restrictions of this world. There is one thing you can count on:

As long as the earth endures, seedtime and harvest, cold and heat, summer and winter, day and night will never cease (Genesis 8:22).

MEDITATION POINT

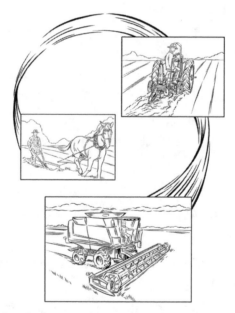

Seed, time, and harvest will never cease.

Go to Chapter 2 in the Study Guide section on page 299.

Chapter 3

Gift #9—Gifts of the Spirit (Part 1)
How do your gifts bring life to your life?

Before you begin to read, pray that the Holy Spirit will give you
and all readers of this book understanding and application.

✟ [God's] *intent was that now, through the church* [you and me], *the
manifold wisdom of God should be made known to the rulers and
authorities in the heavenly realms* (Ephesians 3:10).

Holding your own newborn child is an amazing experience. Your
heart is flooded with love and affection for this precious life. As a
new dad or mom, you realize that life is beyond you, is bigger than
just your own personal needs. You now have another life that is dependent
on you, and your attention and focus change dramatically. At first, parent-
hood is awkward; your sleep, meals, and lifestyle are turned upside-down.
Then you begin to see life through new eyes—the eyes of a mother or
father—and your vision is permanently altered.

So what about our new life in Christ? What new responsibilities do we
have that will shift our vision, desires, goals, and lifestyle? How do we
adjust and walk into those changes, into that new life? God has given us the
Holy Spirit, who offers each of us certain gifts, for this very reason. This
chapter is devoted to explaining the new responsibilities of life in Christ

and the ways that these Gifts of the Spirit will assist you in fulfilling those responsibilities and living an abundant life.

Look again at the verse at the beginning of the chapter. Wow! What an awesome responsibility. We live in this world, and the other spirit (heavenly) realm exists around us. Activities in one affect the other and vice versa. This passage says that God will make known His manifold wisdom *through us* to both realms. In the Book of Hebrews, when speaking of the prior patriarchs of the Bible who showed great faith, it says that their acts still live as a witness in the atmosphere (see Hebrews 11:4). Your acts of faith will live on beyond you.

☦ *Therefore, since we are* **surrounded by such a great cloud of witnesses** *[actions of faith by Old Testament patriarchs], let us throw off everything that hinders and the sin that so easily entangles, and let us run with perseverance the race marked out for us* (Hebrews 12:1).

When I first read these verses, I marveled at their implications. You may be asking, *how do I do this? How do I make God known to the spirit realm? How do I create an eternal witness? I have enough trouble just looking after the earthly realm.* And yet, these passages say that life is more than feeding ourselves, caring for our families, or pursuing our careers. We all will not be full-time apostles, pastors, evangelists, etc., yet even through our earthly jobs we are working for Him—fulfilling His greater plan.

☦ *Whatever you do, work at it with all your heart, as working for the Lord, not for men, since you know that you will receive an inheritance from the Lord as a reward. It is the Lord Christ you are serving.* (Colossians 3:23-24).

You see no matter what we do for a living we all have simultaneous goals to attain as it relates to the *spiritual realm*. Let's examine how we can partner with the Holy Spirit to accomplish these and our other responsibilities as Christians.

GOD REVEALS HIMSELF

Before beginning our discussion of the Gifts of the Spirit, I want to emphasize one of their key purposes. Through them, God reveals Himself in you to the world. And this is one of our key responsibilities as Christians. As you read about the many ways that God reveals Himself, remember that He has chosen you to be a part of His revelation.

✠ *We are therefore Christ's ambassadors, as though God were making His appeal through us* (2 Corinthians 5:20).

As you manifest the Gifts of the Spirit you reveal His power and presence on earth. You will find in the church that Christians and Pastors can sometimes overly rely on words to try and persuade people of God's existence and love for them. The Apostle Paul said this about his preaching to others.

✠ *'My message and my preaching were **not** with wise and persuasive **words**, but with a demonstration of the Spirit's power, so that your faith might not rest on men's wisdom, but on God's power* (1 Corinthians 2:4-5).

Having a close intimate relationship with God like the Apostle Paul will strengthen God's Spirit within you—His Spirit working through you is far more persuasive and powerful than any human words or sermon.

Since the beginning of the world God has revealed His divine truth to His creation in many different ways. He reveals His truth through nature:

✠ *The heavens declare the glory of God; the skies proclaim the work of His hands* (Psalm 19:1).

✠ *For since the creation of the world God's invisible qualities—His eternal power and divine nature—have been clearly seen, being understood from what has been made, so that men are without excuse* (Romans 1:20).

God reveals His truth through man's conscience:

✠ *They show that the requirements of the law are written on their hearts, their consciences also bearing witness, and their thoughts now accusing, now even defending them* (Romans 2:15).

He wrote the truth on stone tablets:

✠ *The Lord said to Moses, "Come up to me on the mountain and stay here, and I will give you tablets of stone, with the law and commands I have written for their instruction"* (Exodus 24:12).

God spoke the truth through Jesus Christ, the living Word:

✠ *The Word became flesh and made His dwelling among us. We have seen His glory, the glory of the One and Only, who came from the Father, full of grace and truth* (John 1:14).

He revealed the truth in all of Scripture:

✠ *For everything that was written in the past was written to teach us, so that through endurance and the encouragement of the Scriptures we might have hope* (Romans 15:4).

God writes His truth on man's new heart through the Holy Spirit:

✠ *This is the covenant I will make with the house of Israel after that time, declares the Lord. I will put my laws in their minds and write them on their hearts...* (Hebrews 8:10).

✠ *I will give you a new heart and put a new spirit in you; I will remove from you your heart of stone and give you a heart of flesh. And I will put my Spirit in you and move you to follow my decrees and be careful to keep my laws* (Ezekiel 36:26-27).

And finally, God writes His truth through your very life and testimony:

✠ *You yourselves are our letter, written on our hearts, known and read by everybody. You show that you are a letter from Christ, the result of our ministry, written not with ink but with the Spirit of the living God, not on tablets of stone but on tablets of the human hearts* (2 Corinthians 3:2-3).

✠ [God's] *intent was that now, through the church* [you], *the manifold wisdom of God should be made known to the rulers and authorities in the heavenly realms* (Ephesians 3:10).

What a privilege—God wants to reveal Himself through you! Are you wondering how you can express God's wisdom and truth in your life, how you can create your personal testimony? God offers us the many Gifts of the Spirit to assist us.

The Gifts Have a Purpose

God has woven the Church together by His Spirit into one Body. As parts of that Body, we are the only physical representation of God on earth. Each member of the Body is designed to serve a unique function that will ultimately benefit the whole. To achieve His plan, God offers different gifts in varying amounts to each member of the Church Body—to you and me.

Each of us is given specific gifts, some in greater measure, some that grow in time, and one that may be primary and dominate. In the course of your life, you will have opportunities to use your gifts. In fact, it is critical. If you don't use and exercise your gifts, the entire Body can't function properly, and you won't fulfill your purpose. As with the other gifts, we must receive, unwrap, and use them if we want them to benefit us and others.

Proper Gift-Wrapping

In this chapter, I want to remind you of the proper context (wrapping) for the Gifts of the Spirit. The Gifts of the Spirit ignite when they are wrapped in the fruit of the Spirit. This wrapping is crucial if we want them to be properly received and opened by others. If they are *not* wrapped in the fruit of the Spirit, then the gifts are *not* likely to be received well. The gifts must be exercised with character and maturity, which is what the fruit of the Spirit is all about: *love, joy, peace, patience, kindness, goodness, faithfulness, gentleness, and self control* (see Galatians 5:22-23). Are you exhibiting these traits as you manifest the gifts of the Spirit given you?

Think of yourself as a tree. Each limb is a Gift of the Spirit. As you read the following verses, you will understand that those limbs are only useful when they bear fruit—in our case, the fruit of the Spirit.

The Gifts

Let's examine the passages that reveal the 21 primary Gifts of the Spirit. In the next chapter, we will look at each gift in depth in order to help you locate your specific gifting—which will be given to you in larger measure by the Holy Spirit. Before doing that we will examine the proper way to operate in the gifts. Though the following passages are long, I choose to quote them in their entirety because they demonstrate the right context (healthy Body life) in which the gifts belong. Using them in the right context is what makes them powerful and effective for the fulfillment of God's purpose.

Paul, in his letter to the Ephesian church, identifies five positions (the five-fold ministry) needed by a church in order to begin and maintain both its spiritual and physical growth.

✠ *As a prisoner for the Lord, then, I urge you to live a life worthy of the calling you have received. Be completely humble and gentle; be patient, bearing with one another in love. Make every effort to keep the unity of the Spirit through the bond of peace. There is one body and one Spirit—just as you were called to one hope when you were called— one Lord, one faith, one baptism; one God and Father of all, who is over all and through all and in all. But to each one of us grace has been given as Christ apportioned it* [in various degrees]... *It was He who gave some to be **apostles**, some to be **prophets**, some to be **evangelists**, and some to be **pastors** and **teachers**, to prepare God's people for works of service, so that the body of Christ may be built up until **we all reach unity in the faith and in the knowledge of the Son*** *of God and become mature, **attaining to the whole measure of the fullness of Christ.** Then we will no longer be* [spiritual] *infants, tossed back and forth by the waves, and blown here and there by every wind of teaching and by the cunning and craftiness of men in their deceitful scheming. Instead, speaking the truth in love, we will in all things* [spiritually] *grow up into Him who is the Head, that is, Christ. From Him the whole body, joined and held together by every supporting ligament, grows and builds itself up in love, as each part* [you and I] *does its work. So I tell you this, and insist on it in the Lord, that you must no longer live as the Gentiles do, in the futility of their thinking. They are darkened in their understanding and separated from the life of God because of the ignorance that is in them due to the hardening of their hearts. Having lost all sensitivity, they have given themselves over to sensuality so as to indulge in every kind of impurity, with a continual lust for more* [walking in the flesh and not in the Spirit]. *You, however, did not come to know Christ that way. Surely you heard of Him and were taught in Him in accordance with the truth that is in Jesus. You were taught, with regard to your former way of life, to put off your old self, which is being corrupted by its deceitful desires; to be made new in the attitude of your minds; and to put on the new self, created to be like God in true righteousness and holiness. Therefore each of you must put off falsehood and speak truthfully to his neighbor* [in your words and deeds, despite possible resulting persecution], *for we* [Believers] *are all members of one body. "In your anger do not sin": Do not let the sun go down while you are still angry, and do not give the devil a foothold. He who has been stealing must steal no longer, but must work, doing something useful with his own hands, that he may have something to share with those in need. Do not let any unwholesome talk come out of your mouths, but only what is helpful for building others up according to their needs, that it may benefit those who listen. And do not grieve the Holy Spirit of God, with whom you were sealed for the day of redemption. Get rid of all bitterness, rage and anger, brawling and* *slander, along with every form of malice. Be kind and compassionate to one another, forgiving each other, just as in Christ God forgave you* (Ephesians 4:1-7, 11-32).

In Romans Chapter 12, Paul speaks about the qualities and characteristics of a faithful follower of Christ, attributes that are required for the Church Body to function. These are a second wave of gifts which, when used, will show God to the world through you!

*Therefore, I urge you, brothers, in view of God's mercy, to offer your bodies as living sacrifices, holy and pleasing to God—this is your spiritual act of worship. Do not conform any longer to the pattern of this world, but be transformed by the renewing of your mind. Then you will be able to test and approve what God's will is—His good, pleasing and perfect will. For by the grace given me I say to every one of you: Do not think of yourself more highly than you ought, but rather think of yourself with sober judgment, in accordance with the measure of faith God has given you. Just as each of us has one body with many members, and these members do not all have the same function, so in Christ we who are many form one body, and each member belongs to all the others. We have different gifts, according to the grace given us. If a man's gift is **prophesying**, let him use it in proportion to his faith. If it is **serving**, let him serve; if it is **teaching**, let him teach; if it is **encouraging**, let him encourage; if it is contributing to the needs of others, let him **give** generously; if it is **leadership**, let him govern diligently; if it is showing **mercy**, let him do it cheerfully. Love must be sincere. Hate what is evil; cling to what is good. Be devoted to one another in brotherly love. Honor one another above yourselves. Never be lacking in zeal, but keep your spiritual fervor, serving the Lord. Be joyful in hope, patient in affliction, and faithful in prayer. Share with God's people who are in need. Practice **hospitality**. Bless those who persecute you; bless and do not curse. Rejoice with those* *who rejoice; mourn with those who mourn. Live in harmony with one another. Do not be proud, but be willing to associate with people of low position. Do not be conceited. Do not repay anyone evil for evil. Be careful to do what is right in the eyes of everybody. If it is possible, as far as it depends on you, live at peace with everyone. Do not take revenge, my friends, but leave room for God's wrath, for it is written: "It is mine to avenge; I will repay," says the Lord. On the contrary: "If your enemy is hungry, feed him; if he is thirsty, give him something to drink. In doing this, you will heap burning coals on his head." Do not be overcome by evil, but overcome evil with good* (Romans 12:1-21).

Finally, Paul lists additional gifts that the overall Church Body needs to exhibit to become life-giving and effective in our witness of God.

✠ *Now about spiritual gifts, brothers, I do not want you to be ignorant. You know that when you were pagans, somehow or other you were influenced and led astray to mute idols. Therefore I tell you that no one who is speaking by the Spirit of God says, "Jesus be cursed," and no one can say, "Jesus is Lord," except by the Holy Spirit. There are different kinds of gifts, but the same Spirit. There are different kinds of service, but the same Lord. There are different kinds of working, but the same God works all of them in all men. Now to each one the manifestation of the Spirit is given for the common good. To one there is given through the Spirit the message of* **wisdom**, *to another the message of* **knowledge** *by means of the same Spirit, to another* **faith** *by the same Spirit, to another gifts of* **healing** *by that one Spirit, to another* **miraculous** *powers, to another* **prophecy**, *to another distinguishing* [**discernment**] *between spirits, to another speaking in different kinds of* **tongues**, *and to still another the* **interpretation** *of tongues. All these are the work of one and the same Spirit, and He gives them to each one* [of us], *just as He determines. The body is a unit, though it is made up of many parts; and though all its parts are* *many, they form one body. So it is with Christ. For we were all baptized by one Spirit into one body—whether Jews or Greeks, slave or free—and we were all given the one Spirit to drink. Now the body is not made up of one part but of many. If the foot should say, "Because I am not a hand, I do not belong to the body," it would not for that reason cease to be part of the body. And if the ear should say, "Because I am not an eye, I do not belong to the body," it would not for that reason cease to be part of the body. If the whole body were an eye, where would the sense of hearing be? If the whole body were an ear, where would the sense of smell be? But in fact God has arranged the parts in the body, every one of them, just as He wanted them to be. If they were all one part, where would the body be? As it is, there are many parts* [each of us uniquely different for the function we are made to perform], *but* [working together as] *one body. The eye cannot say to the hand, "I don't need you!" And the head cannot say to the feet, "I don't need you!" On the contrary, those parts of the body that seem to be weaker are indispensable, and the parts that we think are less honorable we treat with special honor. And the parts that are unpresentable are treated with special modesty, while our presentable parts need no special treatment. But God has combined the members of the body and has given greater honor to the parts that lacked it, so that there should be no division in the body, but that its parts should have equal concern for each other. If one part suffers, every part suffers with it; if one part is honored, every part rejoices with it. Now you are the body of Christ, and each one of you is a part of it. And in the church God has appointed first of all apostles, second prophets, third teachers, then workers of miracles, also those having gifts of healing, those able to help others, those with gifts of administration, and those speaking in different kinds of tongues* (1 Corinthians 12:1-28).

We see in these passages that the Gifts of the Spirit, within the context of mature and healthy relationships, enable us to display the manifold wisdom of God in our lives. And even beyond His wisdom, these passages offer us the supernatural power of God's Spirit. So how do we locate and utilize the Gifts of the Spirit meant for us? Those specific gifts meant for us would, of course, be the greater gifts for us. Paul in First Corinthians Chapter 12 goes on to instruct us on how to start finding and utilizing them.

> But **eagerly desire** the greater gifts. And now I will show you the most excellent way (1 Corinthians 12:31).

Finding and utilizing your specific gifting will *begin* with your *heart*. The strength and intensity of your desire will translate into the outpouring and display of the Spirit's gifts in your life.

THE CHURCH BODY

These three passages, which provide Scripture's main discussion of the Gifts of the Spirit, each discuss in detail the importance of Body life. As a Christian, you are part of a larger Body, and you are expected to coordinate with the other members to enact God's overall plan. This is a *major* purpose in each of our lives. This concept is simple to understand. All who have accepted Jesus into their hearts and have received the Holy Spirit have become part of a greater Body. The Holy Spirit could be compared to the Body's central nervous system. Jesus Christ is the head, and we are the Body—together we work to accomplish God's will:

> For the husband is the head of the wife as Christ is the head of the church, His body, of which He is the Savior. Now as the church submits to Christ, so also wives should submit to their husbands in everything (Ephesians 5:23-24).

✝ *And God placed all things under His feet and appointed Him* [Jesus] *to be head over everything for the church* (Ephesians 1:22).

✝ *Consequently, you are no longer foreigners and aliens, but fellow citizens with God's people and members of God's household, built on the foundation of the apostles and prophets, with Christ Jesus Himself as the chief cornerstone. In Him the whole building is joined together and rises to become a holy temple in the Lord. And in Him you too are being built together to become a dwelling in which God lives by His Spirit* (Ephesians 2:19-22).

✝ *As you come to* [Jesus], *the living Stone—rejected by men but chosen by God and precious to Him—you also, like living stones, are being built into a spiritual house to be a holy priesthood, offering spiritual sacrifices acceptable to God through Jesus Christ* (1 Peter 2:4-5).

Moreover, Paul says that the gifts play a major role in bringing maturity and wholeness to the Body. That is one of their key purposes:

✝ *...to prepare God's people for works of service, so that the body of Christ may be built up until* **we all reach unity** *in the faith and in the knowledge of the Son of God and become mature,* **attaining to the whole measure of the fullness of Christ** (Ephesians 4:12-13).

✝ *Now I rejoice in what was suffered for you, and I fill up in my flesh what is still lacking in regard to Christ's afflictions, for the sake of His body, which is the church. I have become its servant by the commission*

God gave me to present to you the word of God in its fullness.... We proclaim Him, admonishing and teaching everyone with all wisdom, so that we may present everyone perfect in Christ. To this end I labor, struggling with all His energy, which so powerfully works in me [to show Himself through me] (Colossians 1:24-25;28-29).

Finally, the apostle Paul makes two important points about the Body of Christ. First, he says that God alone chooses who receives what gift and how we all fit together as a whole:

God has arranged the parts in the body, every one of them, just as He wanted them to be (1 Corinthians 12:18).

All these [gifts] are the work of one and the same Spirit, and He gives them to each one, just as He determines (1 Corinthians 12:11).

Second, he says that we must both suffer and rejoice together. We must stand with each other, even when we have different gifts and callings, because that is what a Body does:

If one part suffers, every part suffers with it; if one part is honored, every part rejoices with it (1 Corinthians 12:26).

Yes, we have the lead role in our own life—and are fully responsible for it—but we also have a role to play in the overall Body. We are accountable to both believers and non-believers alike—and this is a great responsibility.

[God said,] "And for your lifeblood I will surely demand an accounting. I will demand an accounting from every animal. And from each

*man, too, I will demand an accounting for the life of his **fellow man**"* (Genesis 9:5).

✠ *The entire law is summed up in a single command: "Love your neighbor as yourself"* (Galatians 5:14).

It's no wonder that we are told to love our neighbors as ourselves because we were intended to be part of the same Body. Jesus Himself gives this important command:

✠ *Love one another. As I have loved you, so you must love one another. By this all men will know that you are my disciples, if you love one another"* (John 13:34-35).

Remember that the kind of love Jesus had for His disciples led Him to the Cross. That's a tall order that we cannot attain on our own. It is only through the power of the Holy Spirit flowing in us that we can live that kind of love.

Our purpose is to create a Heaven-like experience for everybody on earth (for Christians and non-Christians alike). If we want them to receive this heavenly experience, we need to exude God's love (His will and essence) to everybody. This means, through the Holy Spirit, working in concert with all of the other parts of the Body—*eliminating* collision and friction between the parts.

The brain and central nervous system keep all of your body parts working in unison without bumping into each other. This is what Christ (the Head) and the Holy Spirit (the Central Nervous System) do for the Church. Only through submission to God will the parts of the Church Body coordinate and operate in unison. This is why we all need to accept Christ as our head and follow the leading of the Spirit daily. Indeed without reliance on the power of the Holy Spirit within us, we falter in producing God's kind of love, especially in the face of trying circumstances and people.

In this life we will fail at times; so this is why we all need to be purified and perfected before we begin our actual Heaven experience. God's plan is that Heaven will be a perfect, trouble-free experience, which of course *cannot* happen if we are *not* all operating in God's love and will. Indeed, this is what creates the prerequisite of voluntarily being born again to get to Heaven and knowingly allowing God to conform us to His image and likeness. Otherwise, Heaven as described in the Bible, couldn't exist.

ACTION & VISUALIZATION

Submit yourself to Christ's headship and the leading of the Holy Spirit so that you can be a functioning member of His Body.

BEARING FRUIT

A major part of participating with the Body in unity is bearing fruit. Without fruit, we will experience only friction and division. But, if we are operating in the leading and fullness of the Holy Spirit, we will bear fruit. Wherever the Holy Spirit is, fruit grows. However, when we attempt to exercise our gifts through the logic of our own minds, out of duty, or out of mindless repetition, the fruit of the Spirit is absent. When this happens, our gifts cannot bear fruit and they will receive a poor reception from others because their purpose is only to build up the Church Body in both size and spiritual strength.

✝ *...since you are zealous for spiritual gifts, let it be for the edification of the church that you seek to excel* (1 Corinthians 14:12).

God did *not* give you specific Gifts of the Spirit for bragging rights or because you earned them. Rather, He gave you these gifts when He originally designed you because He knew they would enable you to complete *your* purpose in His plan. As parts of the Body of Christ, we have an *individual* purpose, and when *united together*, we are also working toward a *corporate goal*.

Our individual purpose can be completed with the specific gifts that we have been offered. But from a corporate standpoint, we must work interdependently with other Christians and their gifts in order to accomplish God's overall purpose. This interdependence helps us keep our pride in check. Avoid the temptation of pride in your gifts at all cost, for it is Satan's ultimate snare for believers.

When we use our gifts with humility, the distribution of different gifts to specific members orchestrates a beautiful and complete Body—a Body that is working together *using* our Gifts of the Spirit. Each part may be individually weak, but when we work together in unity, the result is a masterpiece of God's design.

THREE THINGS TO GIVE

Your ability to complete your individual and corporate purpose boils down to having a close relationship with God. We see in Peter's relationship with Jesus that he had to take three major steps before he could fulfill his purpose. You too will have to take these steps before you can fulfill yours.

Initially, Peter had a mental recognition or revelation of who Jesus is:

✝ *Simon Peter answered, "You are the Christ; the Son of the living God." Jesus replied, "Blessed are you, Simon son of Jonah, for this was not revealed to you by man, but by my Father in heaven"* (Matthew 16:16-17).

The Holy Spirit gave you a revelation of who Jesus is when you were saved. Let your revelation of Him be complete as you fully embrace His nature and intentions for you so that you can also fully embrace His purpose for your life. In other words, you must give your *mind* to Him:

✠ *Do not conform any longer to the pattern of this world, but be transformed by the renewing of your mind. Then you will be able to test and approve what God's will is—His good, pleasing and perfect will* (Romans 12:2).

Later, Peter had to give Jesus his *heart*:

✠ *When they had finished eating, Jesus said to Simon Peter, "Simon son of John, do you truly love me more than these?" "Yes, Lord," he said, "you know I love you." Jesus said, "Feed my lambs." Again Jesus said, "Simon son of John, do you truly love me?" He answered, "Yes, Lord, you know I love you." Jesus said, "Take care of my sheep." The third time he said to him, "Simon son of John, do you love me?" Peter was hurt because He asked him the third time, "Do you love?" He said, "Lord, you know all things; you know that I love you." Jesus said,* **"Feed my sheep"** (John 21:15-17).

The way Jesus asks for Peter's love shows Peter and us that He desires a kind of love that is more than spoken love. Jesus desires us to have a living love for Him that manifests itself through our demonstration of God's love to His children. Whatever God calls us to do for the Body should not be simply a job. We should strive to model our attitude for ministry after Jesus, to take ownership, to be passionate, and pursue a full heartfelt commitment.

✠ *I am the good Shepherd. The good Shepherd lays down His life for the sheep. The hired hand is not the shepherd who owns the sheep. So when he sees the wolf coming, he abandons the sheep and runs away. Then the wolf attacks the flock and scatters it* (John 10:11-12).

Jesus knows that we will be attacked by our enemy when we try to care for people. If our hearts aren't committed, we will flee when the inevitable trouble comes.

At this point, Peter has now given Jesus his head and heart; however, there is still one thing required to bring that relationship to full life. He must give Jesus his *hands*. Do you remember the story in Book One of John and Peter running into the lamb beggar as they passed through the gate called Beautiful?

✠ *Then Peter said, "Silver or gold I do not have, but what I have I give you. In the name of Jesus Christ of Nazareth, walk." Taking him by the* **hand**, *he helped him up and instantly the man's feet and ankles became strong* (Acts 3:6-7).

To bring Jesus' living love alive in the world, we must give our minds and hearts to Him, and we must be His hands on earth. By so doing, we are at the same time enlivening our relationship with God—because everything in the creation is interconnected through Him.

ACTION & VISUALIZATION

Follow the three steps Peter took in his relationship with Jesus.
Give Him your head, heart, and hands.

Be Fruitful with Love

As we said earlier, the effective Christian life requires the fruit of the Spirit. So how do love and the other fruit of the Spirit mix? How do they truly become real, effective, and alive? This is how Paul continued his discussion of the Gifts of the Spirit in First Corinthians:

✝ *...And now I will show you the most excellent way. If I speak in the tongues of men and of angels, but have not love, I am only a resounding gong or a clanging symbol. If I have the gift of prophecy and can fathom all the mysteries and all knowledge, and if I have a faith that can move mountains, but have **not love**, **I gain nothing**.... Love is patient, love is kind. It does not envy, it does not boast, it is not proud. It is not rude, it is not self-seeking, it is not easily angered, it keeps no record of wrongs. Love does not delight in evil but rejoices with the truth. It always protects, always trusts, always hopes, always perseveres. **Love never fails**...* (1 Corinthians 12:31-13:4-8).

This is a passage to read over and over again. God's definition of love should be committed to memory (create a reminder card and post it around your house if necessary). Apply it to all aspects of your life. If you do, your life will be different in ways that you can't even imagine. Love is the binding, vital force to all of our virtue.

✝ *Therefore, as God's chosen people, holy and dearly loved, clothe yourselves with compassion, kindness, humility, gentleness and patience. Bear with each other and forgive whatever grievances you may have against one another. Forgive as the Lord forgave you, and over all these virtues put love, which binds them all together in perfect unity* (Colossians 3:12-14).

Love is the primary fruit out of which all other gifts grow. Pride about how well our gifts work is dangerous, particularly if we begin to think our gifts are somehow more important or have a greater impact. Another danger is using our gifts for personal gain—for applause, money, love, favor, or other self interests. We are then seeking glory for ourselves, not the Giver of the gifts—and our gifts will become powerless in our lives and ineffective in the Body. His gifts are designed to be delivered in love, not out of pride or greed.

✟ *...God is love. Whoever lives in love lives in God, and God in him. In this way, love is made complete among us so that we will have confidence on the day of judgment, because in this world we are **like Him*** (1 John 4:16-17).

And again if we are to be **like Him** in this world what is He?

✟ *...God is love* (1 John 4:8).

We live in a created world that is full of objects so our tendency is to think of God as an object; however, this verse is describing God as an *action*—the action of *love*. His *physical* presence is the *living action of love*—patient, kind, humble, sensitive, gentle, compassionate, forgiving, truthful and yet merciful. Ponder on this for a minute. Is this you? If we are going to be *like Him* our actions are what's important—not how we look. Indeed it is our actions that are supposed to give life to the creation itself—to bring it alive in splendor and beauty. Remember the three-step process Peter went through that will help us in achieving His likeness here on earth. We should use all aspects of our personal physical creation in concert with God's Spirit within us to manifest real love to the world—true love, *God Himself.*

ACTION & VISUALIZATION

Memorize each attribute of God's love. Rely on the Holy Spirit to assist you in manifesting them in all aspects of your daily life.

LOVE FULFILLS THE LAW

When you act in love, you become like the Source of love, you grow closer to Him, and your confidence in salvation grows (see 1 John 4:17). Indeed when you exude love, you are actually fulfilling the Law by fulfilling a higher law.

☦ *Let no debt remain outstanding, except the continuing debt to love one another, for he who loves his fellowman has **fulfilled** the law (Romans 13:8).*

☦ *The entire law is summed up in a single command: "Love your neighbor as yourself" (Galatians 5:14).*

You are fulfilling the Law because, at that moment, you are becoming the image and likeness of God.

☦ *No one has ever seen God; but if we love one another, God lives in us and His love is made complete in us (1 John 4:12).*

When Adam was created, he had the Spirit of God (the source of love) in him, but he did not have the knowledge of good and evil. He was created to do everything through God—through love—so that God could manifest Himself in His creation through man. However, when Adam ate from the tree of the knowledge of good and evil, he lost his eternal guidance system. He had the illusion that he could guide himself—but he was no longer in sync with God's will, and God's love no longer freely flowed in and through him. Because humans lost their eternal guidance-by-love system, they projected their broken fallen selves into the Creation to bring all kinds of evil into it through their misguided actions. So God had to institute the Law.

The Law is an imperfect definition of love. Real love is a complex and living thing and cannot fully be defined by words. For example, real love is kind and knows how to find the proper balance between mercy and truth. Finding this balance in love is what allows truth's full benefits to be recognized. Because the Law is an attempt to define love, love itself fulfills the Law.

Jesus' eternal purpose was to fulfill the Law through simply loving, in addition to providing our salvation. By following His Father's leading, who is love, He automatically fulfilled the Law—indeed Jesus went beyond the Law because God's essence is perfect love, which is *higher* than the Law. We also should follow Jesus' example and be guided by the Father's love, through the Holy Spirit:

✝ *If you are led by the Spirit, you are not under the law* (Galatians 5:18).

✝ *...he who loves his fellowman has fulfilled the law* (Romans 13:8).

✝ *The fruit of the Spirit is love, joy, peace, patience, kindness, goodness, faithfulness, gentleness and self-control. Against such things there is no law* (Galatians 5:22-23).

Therefore, *any* action done in God's love fulfills the Law, even if it seems to contradict the letter of the Law. What determines the difference between *real* love and those things that masquerade as love? God's love comes to you through His Spirit and is manifested from your heart, and only God knows what is in a man's heart.

✝ *All a man's ways seem innocent to him, but motives are weighed by the Lord* (Proverbs 16:2).

You must be careful not to stretch this truth—love fulfills the Law. Some have used this as a justification to kill abortion doctors who are killing unborn babies. What these people miss is that the *whole truth* of the Word that embodies God's wisdom makes love. You can't merely take a piece of that truth to justify your actions. True love gives us a different plan of attack for stopping the senseless killing of babies. Consider these passages:

✝ *Submit yourselves for the Lord's sake to every authority instituted among men: whether to the king, as the supreme authority, or to governors, who are sent by him to punish those who do wrong and to commend those who do right* (1 Peter 2:13-14).

✝ *For our struggle is not against flesh and blood, but against the rulers, against the authorities, against the powers of this dark world and against the spiritual forces of evil in the heavenly realms.... And pray in the Spirit on all occasions with all kinds of prayers and requests...* (Ephesians 6:12,18).

✠ *A wise man attacks the city of the mighty and pulls down the stronghold in which they trust* (Proverbs 21:22).

Perhaps the wisest, most loving, and most effective way to stop this slaughter is for God's people to pray and, thereby, change the heart of the nation.

✠ *If **My** people, who are called by **My** name, will humble themselves and pray and seek My face and turn from their wicked ways, then I will hear from heaven and will forgive their sin and will **heal** their land* (2 Chronicles 7:14).

God does not hold the non-believers responsible to change what is happening in our country. He holds *believers*—who should be operating by the Spirit (in love)—responsible for making spiritual changes that can then manifest as changes in the physical realm. Hear this warning to us from the Lord:

✠ *Son of man, I have made you a watchman for the house of Israel; so hear the word I speak and give them warning from me. When I say to a wicked man, "You will surely die" and you do not warn him or speak out to dissuade him from his evil ways in order to save his life, that wicked man will die for his sin, and I will hold **you** accountable for his blood. But if you do warn the wicked man and he does not turn from his wickedness or from his evil ways, he will die for his sin; but you will have **saved yourself*** (Ezekiel 3:17-19).

There are two principles I want to call to your attention. First, we must warn those who live in sin—using *love*, of course. Second, once we have done this, we are *not* required by God to *physically* stop them. Remember,

God gave us *all* freedom and independence to choose. Taking things into our own hands preempts God and doesn't allow the offender time to repent. It also *distracts* us from using our spiritual weapons—the weapons that have *real* power to make changes in both the spiritual and natural worlds. By aligning our will with His will we allow Him to work through us.

Instead of using our individual physical efforts, together we can work in one accord with God to pull down the spiritual strongholds of evil. As we covered in the previous books, strongholds are thoughts, mindsets, actions, habits, forces, etc. (individual or corporate) that are not in the will of God. These strongholds are our real enemy; and we should be unified in fighting against *them*, not against each other. Many strongholds are too powerful for you alone to bring down, particularly ones established by a collective action, thinking or belief by a group of people. That's why God intends us to all join together as one Body to work with Him in pulling them down. I believe that no stronghold is more powerful than a unified Body of Christ on earth.

✠ *And the Lord said, "Indeed the people **are one**...now nothing that they propose to do will be withheld from them"* (Genesis 11:6 NKJV).

Remember from Book One that God originally gave Adam and Eve authority over earth (see Genesis 1:28) and that would now be collectively the case for humankind—we are gifted with the authority of God.

POWER IN UNITY

Clearly, because of this power in collective authority, the Church should be unified against all strongholds and operate in *one accord*. We should unite ourselves under the banner of love—the very nature and purpose of God. Jesus Himself prayed for our unity:

✠ [I pray] *that all of them* [believers] *may be **one**, Father, just as You are in Me and I am in You...* (John 17:21).

In speaking to the Body of believers, Paul said:

✠ *I appeal to you, brothers, in the name of our Lord Jesus Christ, that all of you agree with one another so that there may be no divisions among you and that you may be perfectly united in mind and thought* (1 Corinthians 1:10).

Remember from Book Two that the early church had a supernatural power of God manifesting through their unity.

✠ *All the believers were one in heart and mind...* (Acts 4:32).

✠ *The apostles performed many miraculous signs and wonders among the people...* (Acts 5:12).

This same power is available to us today if we follow their example.

✠ *So continuing daily with **one accord** in the temple, and breaking bread from house to house they ate their food with gladness and **simplicity of heart*** (Acts 2:46 NKJV).

Notice they were not caught up with arguments over doctrine. Rather, they built unity around the simplicity of His message—*love from the heart.* If we want Him with us in our efforts then as the apostle Paul says:

✠ *Accept him whose faith is weak [or you may perceive as weak], without passing judgment on disputable matters* (Romans 14:1).

✠ *... avoid foolish controversies and genealogies and arguments and quarrels about the law, because these are unprofitable and useless* (Titus 3:9).

✠ *...Aim for perfection, listen to my appeal, be of **one mind** and live in **peace**. And the God of love and peace will be with you* (2 Corinthians 13:11).

In unity of spirit, God's Spirit will empower our collective agreement. With His Spirit, we as a united body have added power to do miraculous wonders and pull down the strongest of strongholds allowing us to give people a most convincing case for God's presence and love for them.

One of the ways we are called to demonstrate unity is through our response to our earthly authorities:

✠ *Everyone must submit himself to the governing authorities, for there is no authority except that which God has established. The authorities that exist have been established by God* (Romans 13:1).

While submitting in obedience to authorities, we can pull down strongholds and (through that act of submission) release punishment for acts of disobedience to Christ. For example, in our response to abortion, we should be praying against the deceiving spirit that makes people believe that abortion is not murder. We should be praying against the spirit of lust that leads to unintended pregnancies. And we should be praying that our leaders and politicians would see the wisdom of God. Rather than acting in illegal ways (like attacking abortion doctors or burning down clinics), we must submit ourselves to the laws of our government, and with God bring change through appropriate means like prayer and fasting (as well as other forms of petition and communication allowed by our government). If we want to change the direction of our nation, it is most important to also change the hearts of the people (and not just the laws) because people will break the laws. Indeed, all people break even God's laws—including Christians.

When you use your Gifts of the Spirit, as a member of the unified Body who operates in love (and the rest of the fruit of the Spirit), you will show God's wisdom to the world and the spiritual principalities. Attacking evil powers in the spirit realm while loving their victims in the physical realm will give you great success. If *all* followers of Christ join together in this effort, then God's plan surely will be carried out.

ACTION & VISUALIZATION

Unite with other believers, even across denominational lines, so that you can bring down the strongest of strongholds.

WHY THEN THE LAW?

God gave us the law because we lost relationship with Him; yet, we have already learned that we cannot get back into relationship with God through the Law because:

✝ *All have sinned and fall short of the glory of God* (Romans 3:23).

So why did God give us the Law? These verses provide some insight:

✛ *Therefore no one will be declared righteous in His sight by observing the law; rather, through the law we become conscious of sin* (Romans 3:20).

✛ *What shall we say, then? Is the law sin? Certainly not! Indeed I would not have known what sin was except through the law. For I would not have known what coveting really was if the law had not said, "Do not covet"* (Romans 7:7).

The Law brought us face to face with our sin—showed us how we fell short of His image and likeness—how we fell short of our intended purpose. The Law made us conscious of the fact that we had rejected God's will and that we needed a Redeemer. Because our flesh was too weak—to live in love and to fulfill the law—we needed a Redeemer.

✛ *For what the law was powerless to do in that it was weakened by the sinful nature, God did by sending His own Son in the likeness of sinful man to be a sin offering...* (Romans 8:3).

✛ *The former regulation* [the law] *is set aside because it was weak and useless (for the law made nothing perfect), and a better hope* [Jesus] *is introduced, by which we draw near to God* (Hebrews 7:18-19).

✛ *What, then, was the purpose of the law? It was added because of transgressions until the Seed* [Jesus] *to whom the promise referred had come...* (Galatians 3:19).

✛ *So the law was put in charge to lead us to Christ that we might be justified by faith. Now that faith has come, we are no longer under the supervision of the law* (Galatians 3:24).

Allow me to clarify; we were originally created to be in an eternal intimate relationship with God. The Law could only lead us to this relationship but not replace the relationship. It is our faith in Jesus that both replaces the Law and re-establishes our relationship with God. Jesus describes eternal life we've been given this way:

✛ *Now this is eternal life: that they may know You* [know as in have an intimate relationship with], *the only true God, and Jesus Christ, whom You have sent* (John 17:3).

If you look at the Law (the Ten Commandments, in Exodus 20:1-17, are God's most important laws), you will see that they define right and wrong in a way that attempts to express this loving relationship that we are to have first with God and then also with His other children on earth. The problem is, relationships and love are dynamic—they cannot be expressed adequately on paper or stone tablets. Additionally, no one using human efforts alone can keep every law perfectly. Can you also see how a constant attempt to keep every letter of the law would keep you a slave in your efforts to perform it?

So instead God needed to change our imperfect, stone hearts into living hearts so that we could understand and live out the same living love that God offered us when He sent His son to die on the Cross for our sins.

✛ *I will give them one heart, and I will put a new spirit within them, and take the stony heart out of their flesh, and give them a heart of flesh* (Ezekiel 11:19 NKJV).

Now it is simply a matter of actually using our new spirit and heart. It is by God's will that we operate in love so that we can be free from adherence to the Law. This freedom comes to us through *faith* in our Redeemer, whose perfect adherence to the Law freed us from slavery to it. This *faith* in our Redeemer then frees us from the bondage of the Law by allowing God's Spirit to reside in us again.

✠ *Before this faith came we were held prisoners by the law, locked up until faith should be revealed* (Galatians 3:23).

Once lead back to God we in *faith* are given His Spirit. It is the Holy Spirit that gives us freedom to conform to His likeness, which in turn enhances our relationship.

✠ *Now the Lord is Spirit, and where the Spirit of the Lord is, there is **freedom**. And we, who with unveiled faces all reflect the Lord's glory, are being transformed into His likeness with ever-increasing glory, which comes **from** the Lord, who is the Spirit.* (2 Corinthians 3:17-18).

JESUS FULFILLS THE LAW

As you have seen, it is through Jesus we are again allowed to have an eternal relationship with God. So, how did Jesus do it? How did He overcome the Law of sin and death?

✠ *Christ redeemed us from the curse of the law by becoming a curse for us, for it is written, "Cursed is everyone who is hung on a tree"* (Galatians 3:13).

Does this mean that Jesus' actions got rid of the Law? No, rather Jesus' action of love *fulfilled* the Law. As He said:

✠ *Do not think that I have come to abolish the Law or the Prophets; I have not come to abolish them but to fulfill them* (Matthew 5:17).

By becoming both fully man and fully God, Jesus lived a perfect life, fulfilling the Law so that, when He went to the Cross, He could pay for our sins. Only someone who had not sinned could fulfill the Law.

✠ *Through Christ Jesus the law of the Spirit of life set me free from the law of sin and death. For what the law was powerless to do in that it was weakened by the sinful nature, God did by sending His own Son in the likeness of sinful man to be a sin offering. And so He condemned sin in sinful man, in order that the righteous requirements of the law might be fully met in us, who do not live according to the sinful nature but **according to the Spirit*** (Romans 8:2-4).

While Jesus came to earth as a man, Paul notes that He still had the fullness of God within Him:

✠ *For God was pleased to have His **fullness** dwell in Him* [Jesus] *and through Him to **reconcile** to Himself **all things**, whether things **on earth** or things **in heaven**, by making peace through His blood, shed on the cross* (Colossians 1:19-20).

Because Jesus was fully man and fully God, He could fuse man and the Spirit back together through His life and His death:

✠ *For* [Jesus] *Himself is our peace, who has made the **two one** and has* *destroyed the barrier, the dividing wall of hostility, by abolishing in His flesh the law with its commandments and regulations. His purpose was to create in Himself one new man out of the two, thus making peace, and in this one body to reconcile both of them to God through the cross, by which He put to death their hostility* (Ephesians 2:14-16).

Through this fusion process Jesus abolished the Law for us so that it could not condemn us or enslave us in the future.

✠ [Jesus] *having canceled the written code, with its regulations, that was against us and that stood opposed to us; He took it away, nailing it to the cross. And having disarmed the powers and authorities, He made a public spectacle of them, triumphing over them by the cross* (Colossians 2:14-15).

We too should *not* walk according to our flesh, but according to the Spirit of God within us.

✠ *It is for freedom that Christ has set us free. Stand firm, then, and do not let yourselves be burdened again by a yoke of slavery* (Galatians 5:1).

Be clear on this point because it might be the most important one I make in this book. The yoke of slavery is the Law; as a child of God don't ever let yourself become a slave to it. You will see in your walk of faith that both Christians and Christian leaders, much of the time, lose sight of this *very important* point. We were not created to adhere to a Law that would enslave us. We were created to be in relationship, to freely react to life's situations in God's love, according to our own unique personality. If we only had a standardized legal requirement to perform in every situation, then why would we need a living relationship with God?

Your own religious precepts or even religious leaders will at times lead you back into the slavery of the Law even though Jesus has set us free from the Law. Religiosity can keep you busy with a bunch of do's and don'ts but relationship is all about finding *intimacy* and *oneness*. Driving for that oneness is our only true goal. However, this does not mean that we should use our new freedom for selfish reasons.

✠ *You, my brothers, were called to be free. But do not use your freedom to indulge the sinful nature; rather, serve one another in love* (Galatians 5:13).

We should utilize the Gifts of the Spirit that He offers to bring down strongholds in the spiritual realm and to make public spectacles of them in both the physical realm and the heavenly places. The strong presence of the Holy Spirit working through you can help keep you free as well as assist in setting others free, because wherever the Spirit is there is real freedom.

✠ *Now the Lord is Spirit, and where the Spirit of the Lord is, there is freedom* (1 Corinthians 3:17).

ACTION & VISUALIZATION

Develop a most intimate relationship with God in you so that He can better make spiritual statements through you.

Fruit-Bearing Condition

When preparing to use our Gifts of the Spirit, it's important to be in good fruit-bearing condition. To do this, we must walk in the Spirit.

☩ *But now, by dying to what once bound us, we have been released from the law so that we serve in the new way of the Spirit, and not in the old way of the written code* (Romans 7:6).

To sum it all up, the best way to operate in this world is by walking by the Spirit, by being in fruit-bearing condition. This truly contradicts the ways of the world; however, through God's power, will, and nature, you will be able to convincingly show the world the way they should go. Walking in contradiction to the world when you're not in fruit-bearing condition will only be a bruising experience for you and others.

We previously explored what it means to be fruit-bearing. Here I want to summarize what I believe is the four-step process for fruit bearing.

The first step is to maintain a receptive spirit and heart at all times.

☩ *But the one who received the seed that fell on **good soil** is the man who hears the word and understands it. He produces a crop, yielding a hundred, sixty or thirty times what was sown* (Matthew 13:23).

The second step is to die to your old life, which allows God's life in you to flourish.

☩ *I tell you the truth, unless a kernel of wheat falls to the ground and dies, it remains only a single seed. But if it dies, it produces many seeds* (John 12:24).

The third step is to remain open to the inevitable and valuable cutting or pruning process.

✠ [God] **cuts off** *every branch in me that bears no fruit, while every branch that does bear fruit He **prunes** so that it will be even more fruitful* (John 15:2).

Finally, the fourth step is to abide in Christ at all times.

✠ *I am the vine; you are the branches. If a man remains **in Me** and I in him, he will bear much fruit; apart from Me you can do nothing* (John 15:5).

Clearly, your Gifts of the Spirit will be in the best fruit-bearing condition when you are operating in the fruits of the Spirit.

ACTION & VISUALIZATION

Work the four-step fruit-bearing process into your everyday life.

CULTIVATE YOUR GIFTS

God has endowed you with the right measure of gifts to accomplish what He wants you to do.

✠ *For we are God's workmanship, created in Christ Jesus to do good works, which God prepared in advance for us to do* (Ephesians 2:10).

God gave you specific gifts according to your function in life. But your performance is not automatic. Just as preparation for a race requires exercising your muscles, so too your God-given gifts need exercise if you want to perform your calling well. Jesus illustrated this in a parable:

✠ *Again, it will be like a man going on a journey, who called his servants and entrusted his property to them. To one he gave five talents of money, to another two talents, and to another one talent, each according to his ability. Then he went on his journey. The man who had received the five talents went at once and put his money to work and gained five more. So also, the one with the two talents gained two more. But the man who had received the one talent went off, dug a hole in the ground and hid his master's money. After a long time the master of those servants returned and settled accounts with them. The man who had received the five talents brought the other five. "Master," he said, "you entrusted me with five talents. See, I have gained five more." His master replied, "well done good and faithful servant! You have been faithful with a few things; I will put you in charge of **many things**. Come and share your master's happiness"* (Matthew 25:14-21).

We share in our Master's happiness by receiving, unwrapping, and using the gifts He gives. By doing this, we are giving God a gift in return that He will surely receive, unwrap, and use, perhaps to craft the Gift of Increase for you.

If you are going to live out the full potential that God offers you, then you must recognize and utilize His gifts. If we do not use them, we may find ourselves getting the same sort of treatment given to the man who, in Jesus' parable, did *not* invest what God had given him.

✠ [His master replied,] *"Take the talent from him and give it to the one* who has the ten talents. For everyone who has will be given more, and he will have abundance. Whoever does not have, even what he has will be taken from him. And throw that worthless servant outside, into the darkness, where there will be weeping and gnashing of teeth" (Matthew 25:28-30).

When we use our gifts, they will increase; however, when we don't, we will lose them. Paul exhorted Timothy this way:

✝ **Do not neglect your gift,** *which was given you through a prophetic message when the body of elders laid their hands on you* (1 Timothy 4:14).

The Bible suggests that the laying on of hands can be a possible catalyst to manifest your gifts.

✝ *For this reason I remind you to fan into flame the gift of God, which is in you through the laying on my hands* (2 Timothy 1:6).

✝ *When Paul placed his hands on them, the Holy Spirit came on them, and they spoke in tongues and prophesized* (Acts 19:6).

Remember that you were baptized in the Holy Spirit, perhaps even by the laying on of hands by an elder. From that point on, it's important for you to seek revelation about your Gifts of the Spirit. You may not discover them right away, but if you are seeking, the knowledge will come. You may receive a prophetic word from a prophet or from God directly. Perhaps you or others will simply notice your exceptional abilities. It is important as you read about each of these gifts to pray for discernment. A Website that contains a lot of good information on the Gifts of the Spirit (including spiritual gift tests to assist you in determining which gifts God may have given you) can be found at www.buildingchurch.net. When you know what gifts God has offered to you, start using them. Paul told Timothy (when talking about using his gifts) to be bold and to step out in faith.

For God did not give us a spirit of timidity, but a spirit of power, of love and of self-discipline (2 Timothy 1:7).

We need to be diligent in self-discipline and focused on building our gifts in order to succeed in the race we are running. You and God are in this for the long haul. Review your gifts and start fanning the flame that God has deposited in you. No matter your age, look for new gifts. I did not know that I had the gift of teaching until I wrote this book series in my 50s, almost 20 years after I was saved. Always be open to new things because some gifts develop as you grow and, therefore, may not be noticeable when you first begin looking. Of course, they all become stronger as you use them. The gift of teaching within me grew substantially in the three years of completing these books.

Lessons From Elisha

To further cultivate your gifts, you will need to stay close to your teacher and mentor—the Holy Spirit. The Old Testament includes the story of Elisha—to whom God gave the gift of prophecy. Elisha sought a double-portion of the gift of prophecy that his teacher and mentor, the great prophet Elijah, had. Just prior to the time when Elijah was taken to Heaven, he told Elisha that he was going to *Bethel* and actually asked Elisha to not come with him (he was testing him). What's important to note here is that the name Bethel means "house of God." The city received its name approximately 700 years earlier from Jacob, who had a vision from God in which angels were ascending and descending in that location (see Genesis 28:10-22). But Elisha responded to Elijah, "I will not leave you" (see 2 Kings 2:2). Likewise, your gifts will be cultivated in the house of God.

Once Elijah and Elisha reached Bethel, Elijah again asked Elisha to stay behind while he went on to Jericho. Jericho, of course, as you know from Book One, represents the strongholds in your life that need to come down for you to fully inhabit your Promised Land. Again Elisha responded, "I will not leave you" (see 2 Kings 2:4). Likewise, you need to bring down the strongholds in your life in order to increase your gifts.

Finally, Elijah said that he was going to the Jordan River, and he asked Elisha to not come with him. Of course, as you learned in Book One, the crossing of the Jordan River represents the baptism of the Holy Spirit. And once again, Elisha responded, "I will not leave you" (see 2 Kings 2:6). Likewise, you need to follow the leading of the Spirit to receive and increase your gifts.

We, too, have a choice everyday. Will we follow, or will we be led astray from our teacher and mentor, the Holy Spirit? Following Him into the house of worship, into battle against our strongholds, and into our Promised Land across the Jordan will cultivate our gifts and enable them to grow in exponential ways.

The Bible describes the handing over of Elijah's mantel to Elisha in this way:

✟ *Fifty men of the company of the prophets went and stood at a distance, facing the place where Elijah and Elisha had stopped at the Jordan. Elijah took his cloak, rolled it up and struck the water with it. The water divided to the right and to the left, and the two of them crossed over on dry ground.* [The Israelites had originally gone across the same river to enter their Promised Land.] *When they had crossed, Elijah said to Elisha, "Tell me, what can I do for you before I*

*am taken from you?" "Let me inherit a double portion of your spirit,"
Elisha replied. "You have asked a difficult thing," Elijah said, "yet **if
you see me when I am taken from you, it will be yours**—otherwise
not." As they were walking along and talking together, suddenly a
chariot of fire and horses of fire appeared and separated the two of
them, and Elijah went up to heaven in a whirlwind. Elisha saw this
and cried out, "My father! My father! The chariots and horsemen of
Israel!" And Elisha saw him no more. Then he took hold of his own
clothes and tore them apart. He picked up the cloak that had fallen
from Elijah and went back and stood on the bank of the Jordan. Then
he took the cloak that had fallen from him and struck the water with
it. "Where now is the Lord, the God of Elijah?" he asked. When he
struck the water, it divided to the right and to the left, and he crossed
over* (2 Kings 2:7-14).

Elisha saw God working in his circumstances—he had *insight* about
what was happening in the spiritual realm while living in the physical
world. Because of this *insight*, he was granted (or you might say, *he automatically had access to*) a double portion of his gift. When you keep an eye
on the spirit realm and how it interplays with your daily life, then your gifts
will automatically have more impact in the physical realm.

It is interesting that Elijah and Elisha were almost like twins. They lived
similar lives, and the miracles they performed were similar. But they had
differences too. Elijah was more of a loner, one who was in an unavailing
struggle against the evils of the time. He suffered serious bouts of depres-
sion. On the other hand, Elisha's double portion of the gift allowed him to
live a more triumphant life. He was more involved with the people of his
time. There is no record of him ever fleeing from his enemy, complaining,
or losing courage as Elijah did from time to time. You too can have this
same increased manifestation of the gifts in your life if you will learn to see
what is happening in the spiritual realm when you look at your physical
circumstances.

The first miracle that Elisha performed after receiving the double portion of his gift has an important message in it, if we choose to unwrap it:

✠ *The men of the city said to Elisha, "Look, our lord, this town is well situated, as you can see, but the water is bad and the land is unproductive." "Bring me a new bowl," he said, "and put salt in it." So they brought it to him. Then he went out to the spring and threw the salt into it, saying, "This is what the Lord says: 'I have healed this water. Never again will it cause death or make the land unproductive.'" And the water has remained wholesome to this day, according to the word Elisha had spoken* (2 Kings 2:19-22).

The message is clear—we must have salt in our lives (water represents life) if we want to be productive, if we want to become salt in the world, healing it and stopping death's increase. Our lives are salted when our gifts are manifested in *love*.

Now that I have shared with you this additional perspective (God's perspective) on exercising your gifts in love, I would like to return to the original passages that you read from Romans. This time, I would ask you to pause and meditate on each point that emphasizes the application of love as it applies to the different aspects of your life. Take your time and talk with God about it.

✠ *Love must be sincere. Hate what is evil; cling to what is good. Be devoted to one another in brotherly love. Honor one another above yourselves. Never be lacking in zeal, but keep your spiritual fervor, serving the Lord. Be joyful in hope, patient in affliction, faithful in prayer. Share with God's people who are in need. Practice hospitality. Bless those who persecute you; bless and do not curse. Rejoice with those who rejoice; mourn with those who mourn. Live in harmony with one another. Do not be proud, but be willing to associate with* *people of low position. Do not be conceited. Do not repay **anyone** evil for evil. Be careful to do what is right in the eyes of everybody. If it is possible, as far as it depends on you, live at peace with everyone. Do not take revenge, my friends, but leave room for God's wrath, for it is written: "It is mine to avenge; I will repay," says the Lord. On the contrary: "If your enemy is hungry, feed him; if he is thirsty, give him something to drink. In doing this, you will heap burning coals on his head." Do not be overcome by evil, but overcome evil with good* (Romans 12:9-21).

Yes, transforming your attitude will not be easy because you will be giving up your human attitude for God's attitude—indeed His very essence, love. Of course, we can only grow in love by getting closer to it's true source—God. And really, that is our primary goal. It is only by God's love that we are saved, and through that expression of love, we become His intimate sons and daughters.

Action & Visualization

Operating in your gifts, start exuding love whenever and wherever you can.

MEDITATION POINT

The rulers and authorities of the heavenly realms look on to see
the wisdom of God manifest through you.

Go to Chapter 3 in the Study Guide section on page 309.

Chapter 4

GIFT #9—GIFTS OF THE SPIRIT (PART 2)
HOW DO YOU FIND YOUR GIFTS?

Before you begin to read, pray that the Holy Spirit will give you
and all readers of this book understanding and application.

✠ *His intent was that now, through the church, the manifold wisdom of
God should be made known to the rulers and authorities in the heavenly realms, according to His eternal purpose which He accomplished
in Christ Jesus our Lord* (Ephesians 3:10-11).

If you've ever been to the symphony, you're familiar with the warm-up
that happens before the conductor comes out. Each member tunes up
his or her instrument—the violins playing in different keys, the drums
banging, and the horns blasting out random notes. It doesn't sound so
enjoyable, and in fact, it might sound like fingernails across a chalkboard
to some. However, when the conductor comes out and raises his arms, the
individual instruments are hushed and then—*perfect harmony*. They are
unified in rhythm, pitch, and volume, sounding beautiful together and creating a *moving* experience for the listener. Each individual part plays and
complements the others.

You have read about the 21 Gifts of the Spirit that Paul lays out for us
as disciples of Christ. Because you are God's follower, God has fashioned

you with gifts to ring out in harmony within the Body of Christ. In essence, you are instrumental in God's orchestra, His Church, whose mandate is to create a moving experience for the world to hear. This chapter is dedicated to finding and tuning the gifts He has given you—gifts that, when used to their fullest potential, will complement the whole and bring joy and fulfill-ment to your life and to others.

So, what part does God want you to play in the Body? What gifts did He specifically give to you in good measure? You may not know for sure until you try some out, experiencing each gift through trial and error. Perhaps, when you were a child, your parents exposed you to different sports, music, and arts, in order to discover areas in which you are gifted. In that case, it was up to your parents to expose you, and it was up to you to sharpen your gifts once they were found. In this case, I'm going to lay out all of God's gifts for you to choose which ones you will pursue and sharpen. If you try teaching and notice everybody sleeping, then move on to the next, and so on; however, if you get a little positive response on one gift, then stay with it awhile. Remember, gifts gain strength with exercise.

As you read these verses, remember that we're all members of one Body (Jesus' Body on earth) and that each member is called to do his or her part for the greater good of the whole Body. If all parts perform well, then the whole—the Church—can have a powerful impact on the world. But if the parts don't perform well, then the whole Body suffers, and so does the world.

As I said in the last chapter, it's important that we are led by the Spirit and are flowing in love when exercising these gifts. This is what helps hold the Body of Christ together. Actions performed in love can have a greater impact than the most persuasive words of wisdom delivered without it. Also, if our motivation becomes pride or self-interest, the gift backfires, falling flat because it is void of God's power.

✟ *If I speak in the tongues of men and of angels, but have not love, I am only a resounding gong or a clanging symbol. If I have the gift of prophecy and can fathom all mysteries and all knowledge, and if I have a faith that can move mountains, but have not love, I am nothing. If I give all I possess to the poor and surrender my body to the flames, but have not love, I gain nothing. Love is patient, love is kind. It does not envy, it does not boast, it is not proud. It is not rude, it is not self-seeking, it is not easily angered, it keeps no record of wrongs. Love does not delight in evil but rejoices with the truth. It always protects, always trusts, always hopes, always perseveres. Love never fails...* (1 Corinthians 13:1-8).

ADMINISTRATION

The gift of *administration*, when used in love, gives you the skills to identify goals and to organize people to accomplish them.

✠ *And in the church God has appointed...those with gifts of **administration**...* (1 Corinthians 12:28).

✠ *Suppose one of you wants to build a tower. Will he not first sit down and estimate the cost to see if he has enough money to complete it? For if he lays the foundation and is not able to finish it, everyone who sees it will ridicule him, saying, "This fellow began to build and was not able to finish"* (Luke 14:28-30).

✠ *The reason I left you in Crete was that you might straighten out what was left unfinished and appoint elders in every town, as I directed you* (Titus 1:5).

Apostolic Ministry

The gift of *apostolic ministry*, when used in love, gives you the ability to exercise skillful leadership over several churches.

✝ *And in the church God has appointed first of all* **apostles**... (1 Corinthians 12:28).

✝ *It was He who gave some to be* **apostles**... (Ephesians 4:11).

✝ *Truly the signs of an apostle were accomplished among you with all perseverance, in signs and wonders and mighty deeds* (2 Corinthians 12:12 NKJV).

✝ *Consequently, you are no longer foreigners and aliens, but fellow citizens with God's people and members of God's household, built on the foundation of the* **apostles** *and prophets, with Christ Jesus Himself as the chief cornerstone* (Ephesians 2:19-20).

Discernment

The gift of *discernment*, when used in love, gives you the ability to identify the root cause of someone's actions—whether their actions are inspired divinely, humanly, or satanically. This is an important gift because determining the source of someone's actions allows you to react correctly in your efforts to help them and the overall Church Body.

✠ *...to another* [there is given] ***distinguishing between spirits...***
(1 Corinthians 12:10).

✠ *From that time on Jesus began to explain to His disciples that He must go to Jerusalem and suffer many things at the hands of the elders, chief priests and teachers of the law, and that He must be killed and on the third day be raised to life. Peter took Him aside and began to rebuke Him. "Never, Lord!" he said. "This shall never happen to you!" Jesus turned and said to Peter, "Get behind me, satan! You are a stumbling block to Me; you do not have in mind the things of God, but the things of men"* (Matthew 16:21-23).

✠ *"But what about you?"* [Jesus] *asked. "Who do you say I am?" Simon Peter answered, "You are the Christ, the Son of the living God," Jesus replied, "Blessed are you, Simon son of Jonah, for this was not revealed to you by man, but by My Father in heaven"* (Matthews 16:15-17).

✠ *"Sir,"* the [Samaritan] *woman said, "I can see that You* [Jesus] *are a prophet"* (John 4:19).

✠ *Dear friends, do not believe every spirit, but test the spirits to see whether they are from God, because many false prophets have gone out into the world. This is how you can recognize the Spirit of God: Every spirit that acknowledges that Jesus Christ has come in the flesh is from God, but every spirit that does not acknowledge Jesus is not from God. This is the spirit of the antichrist, which you have heard is coming and even now is already in the world. You, dear children, are from God and have overcome them, because the one who is in you is greater than the one who is in the world. They are from the world and therefore speak from the viewpoint of the world, and the world listens to them. We are from God, and whoever knows God listens to us; but whoever is not from God does not listen to us. This is how we recognize the Spirit of truth and the spirit of falsehood* (1 John 4:1-6).

✝ *The man without the Spirit does not accept the things that come from the Spirit of God, for they are foolishness to him, and he cannot understand them, because they are spiritually discerned* (1 Corinthians 2:14).

✝ *But solid food is for the mature, who by constant use have trained themselves to distinguish good from evil* (Hebrews 5:14).

EVANGELISM

The gift of *evangelism*, when used in love, gives you the special ability to present the Gospel to unbelievers in ways that have a great effect.

✝ *It was He who gave...some to be **evangelists**...* (Ephesians 4:11).

✝ *Leaving the next day, we reached Caesarea and stayed at the house of Philip the **evangelist**...* (Acts 21:8).

✝ *Philip went down to a city in Samaria and proclaimed the Christ there. When the crowds heard Philip and saw the miraculous signs he did, they all paid close attention to what he said* (Acts 8:5-6).

✝ *They preached the good news in that city and won a large number of disciples. Then they returned to Lystra, Iconium and Antioch...* (Acts 14:21).

✝ *But you, keep your head in all situations, endure hardship, do the work of an **evangelist**, discharge all the duties of your ministry* (2 Timothy 4:5).

EXHORTATION

The gift of *exhortation*, when used in love, is the God-given ability to administer words of meaningful, life-changing encouragement, growth, or warning.

✝ *...if* [a man's gift] *is **encouraging**, let him encourage...* (Romans 12:8).

✝ *Each of us should please his neighbor for his good, to build him up* (Romans 15:2).

✠ *Let us not give up meeting together, as some are in the habit of doing, but let us **encourage** one another—and all the more as you see the Day approaching* (Hebrews 10:25).

✠ *[They returned,] strengthening the disciples and **encouraging** them to remain true to the faith. "We must go through many hardships to enter the kingdom of God," they said* (Acts 14:22).

✠ *He must hold firmly to the trustworthy message as it has been taught, so that he can **encourage** others by sound doctrine and refute those who oppose it* (Titus 1:9).

✠ *And we urge you, brothers, warn those who are idle, **encourage** the timid, help the weak, be patient with everyone. Make sure that nobody pays back wrong for wrong, but always try to be kind to each other and to everyone else* (1 Thessalonians 5:14-15).

✠ *I long to see you so that I may impart to you some spiritual gift to make you strong—that is, that you and I may be mutually **encouraged** by each other's faith* (Romans 1:11-12).

FAITH

The gift of *faith*, when used in love, is an extraordinary confidence that moves you to act on what you believe but can't yet see.

✠ *Now* **faith** *is being sure of what we hope for and certain of what we do not see. This is what the ancients were commended for. By faith we understand that the universe was formed at God's command, so that what is seen was not made out of what was visible. By faith Abel offered God a better sacrifice* [a sacrifice of shed blood, which represented a sacrifice of one's own life] *than Cain did. By faith he was commended as a righteous man, when God spoke well of his offerings. And by faith he still speaks, even though he is dead. By faith Enoch was taken from this life, so that he did not experience death; he could not be found, because God had taken him away. For before he was taken, he was commended as one who pleased God. And without faith it is impossible to please God, because anyone who comes to Him must believe that He exists and that He rewards those who earnestly seek Him. By faith Noah, when warned about things not yet seen, in holy fear built an ark to save his family. By his faith he condemned the world and became heir of the righteousness that comes by faith. By faith Abraham, when called to go to a place he would later receive as his inheritance, obeyed and went, even though he did not know where he was going. By faith he made his home in the promised land like a stranger in a foreign country; he lived in tents, as did Isaac and Jacob, who were heirs with him of the same promise.* **For he was looking forward** *to the city with foundations, whose architect and builder is God. By faith Abraham, even though he was past age—and Sarah herself was barren—was enabled to become a father because he considered Him faithful who had made the promise. And so from this one man, and he as good as dead, came descendants as numerous as the stars in the sky and as countless as the sand on the seashore. All these people were still living by faith when they died. They did not receive the things promised; they only saw them and welcomed them from a distance. And they admitted that they were aliens and strangers on earth. People who say such things show that they are looking for a country of their own. If they had been thinking of the* *country they had left, they would have had opportunity to return. Instead, they were **longing for a better country**—a heavenly one. Therefore God is not ashamed to be called their God, for He has prepared a city for them. By faith Abraham, when God tested him, offered Isaac as a sacrifice. He who had received the promises was about to sacrifice his one and only son, even though God had said to him, "It is through Isaac that your offspring will be reckoned." Abraham reasoned that God could raise the dead, and figuratively speaking, he did receive Isaac back from death.... By faith Moses' parents hid him for three months after he was born, because they saw he was no ordinary child, and they were not afraid of the king's edict. By faith Moses, when he had grown up, refused to be known as the son of Pharaoh's daughter. He chose to be mistreated along with the people of God rather than to enjoy the pleasures of sin for a short time. He regarded disgrace for the sake of Christ as of greater value than the treasures of Egypt, because **he was looking ahead** to his reward. By faith he left Egypt, not fearing the king's anger; he persevered because he saw Him who is invisible. By faith he kept the Passover and the sprinkling of blood, so that the destroyer of the firstborn would not touch the firstborn of Israel. By faith the people passed through the Red Sea as on dry land; but when the Egyptians tried to do so, they were drowned. By faith the walls of Jericho fell, after the people had marched around them for seven days.... And what more shall I say? I do not have time to tell about Gideon, Barak, Samson, Jephthah, David, Samuel and the prophets, who through faith conquered kingdoms, administered justice, and gained what was promised; who shut the mouths of lions, quenched the fury of the flames, and escaped the edge of the sword; whose weakness was turned to strength; and who became powerful in battle and routed foreign armies. Women received back their dead, raised to life again. Others were tortured and refused to be released, so that they might gain a better resurrection. Some faced jeers and flogging, while still others were chained and put in prison. They were stoned; they were sawed in two; they* *were put to death by the sword. They went about in sheepskins and goatskins, destitute, persecuted and mistreated—the world was not worthy of them. They wandered in deserts and mountains, and in caves and holes in the ground. These were all commended for their faith, yet none of them received what had been promised. God had planned something better for us so that only together with us would they be made perfect* (Hebrews 11:1-17, 23-30, 32-40).

✠ *Against all hope, Abraham in hope believed and so became the father of many nations, just as it had been said to him, "So shall your offspring be." Without weakening in his **faith**, he faced the fact that his body was as good as dead—since he was about a hundred years old—and that Sarah's womb was also dead. Yet he did not waver through unbelief regarding the promise of God, but was strengthened in his faith and gave glory to God, being fully persuaded that God had power to do what He had promised* (Romans 4:18-21).

✠ *In the same way, **faith** by itself, if it is **not** accompanied by **action**, is **dead*** (James 2:17).

GIVING

The gift of *giving*, when used in love, is the ability to give generously and to receive satisfaction in doing so.

✠ *...if* [a man's gift] *is contributing to the needs of others, let him **give** generously...* (Romans 12:9).

Jesus sat down opposite the place where the offerings were put and watched the crowd putting their money into the temple treasury. Many rich people threw in large amounts. But a poor widow came and put in two very small copper coins, worth only a fraction of a penny. Calling His disciples to Him, Jesus said, "I tell you the truth, this poor widow has put more into the treasury than all the others. They all gave out of their wealth; but she, out of her poverty, put in everything— all she had to live on" (Mark 12:41-44).

The disciples, each according to his ability, decided to provide help for the brothers living in Judea (Acts 11:29).

*And now, brothers, we want you to know about the grace that God has given the Macedonian churches. Out of the most severe trial, their overflowing joy and their extreme poverty welled up in rich generosity. For I testify that they **gave** as much as they were able, and even beyond their ability. Entirely on their own, they urgently pleaded with us for the privilege of sharing in this service to the saints. And they did not do as we expected, but they gave themselves first to the Lord and then to us in keeping with God's will. So we urged Titus, since he had earlier made a beginning, to bring also to completion this act of grace on your part. But just as you excel in everything—in faith, in speech, in knowledge, in complete earnestness and in your love for us—see that you also excel in this **grace of giving*** (2 Corinthians 8:1-7).

HEALING

The gift of *healing*, when used in love, gives you the ability to share God's healing power with others and to cure them of various infirmities—whether they are physical, emotional, or spiritual.

✠ *And in the church God has appointed... also those having **gifts of healing**...* (1 Corinthians 12:28).

✠ [Jesus] *called His twelve disciples to Him and gave them authority to drive out evil spirits and to **heal** every disease and sickness* (Matthew 10:1).

✠ [In Jesus' name,] *they* [believers] *will pick up snakes with their hands, and when they drink deadly poison, it will not hurt them at all; they will place their hands on sick people, and they will get well* (Mark 16:18).

✠ *The apostles performed many miraculous signs and wonders among the people. And all the believers used to meet together in Solomon's Colonnade. No one else dared join them, even though they were highly regarded by the people. Nevertheless, more and more men and women believed in the Lord and were added to their number. As a result, people brought the sick into the streets and laid them on beds and mats so that at least Peter's shadow might fall on some of them as he passed by. Crowds gathered also from the towns around Jerusalem, bringing their sick and those tormented by evil spirits, and all of them were **healed*** (Acts 5:12-16).

HELPS

The gift of *helps*, when used in love, gives you the ability to help others in a variety of practical ways.

✠ *And in the church God has appointed... those able to* **help** *others...* (1 Corinthians 12:28).

✠ *Some women were watching from a distance. Among them were Mary Magdalene, Mary the mother of James the younger and of Joses, and Salome. In Galilee these women had followed Him and cared for His needs. Many other women who had come up with Him to Jerusalem were also there* (Mark 15:40-41).

✠ *In reply Jesus said: "A man was going down from Jerusalem to Jericho, when he fell into the hands of robbers. They stripped him of his clothes, beat him and went away, leaving him half dead. A priest happened to be going down the same road, and when he saw the man he passed by on the other side. So too, a Levite, when he came to the place and saw him, passed by on the other side. But a Samaritan, as he traveled, came where the man was; and when he saw him, he took pity on him. He went to him and bandaged his wounds, pouring on oil and wine. Then he put the man on his own donkey, took him to an inn and took care of him. The next day he took out two silver coins and gave them to the innkeeper. 'Look after him,' he said, 'and when I return I will reimburse you for any extra expenses you may have.' Which of these three do you think was a neighbor to the man who fell into the hands of the robbers?" The expert in the law replied, "The one who had mercy on him." Jesus told him, "Go and do likewise"* (Luke 10:30-37).

HOSPITALITY

The gift of *hospitality*, when used in love, is the ability God gives you to be unusually welcoming to those in need of food or lodging.

✠ *Love must be sincere. Hate what is evil; cling to what is good. Be devoted to one another in brotherly love. Honor one another above yourselves. Never be lacking in zeal, but keep your spiritual fervor, serving the Lord. Be joyful in hope, patient in affliction, faithful in prayer. Share with God's people who are in need. Practice* **hospitality** (Romans 12:9-13).

✠ *One of those listening was a woman named Lydia, a dealer in purple cloth from the city of Thyatira, who was a worshiper of God. The Lord opened her heart to respond to Paul's message. When she and the members of her household were baptized, she invited us to her home. "If you consider me a believer in the Lord," she said, "come and stay at my house." And she persuaded us* (Acts 16:14-15).

✠ *Keep on loving each other as brothers. Do not forget to* **entertain** *strangers, for by so doing some people have entertained angels without knowing it* (Hebrews 13:1-2).

✠ *Offer* **hospitality** *to one another without grumbling* (1 Peter 4:9).

Intercession

The gift of *intercession,* when used in love, is the ability to pray on behalf of others with unusual intensity as the Holy Spirit leads.

In the same way, the Spirit helps us in our weakness. We do not know what we ought to pray for, but the Spirit Himself intercedes for us with groans that words cannot express (Romans 8:26).

Therefore [Jesus] *is able to save completely those who come to God through Him, because He always lives to* **intercede** *for them* (Hebrews 7:25).

When [Peter realized he had been rescued], *he went to the house of Mary the mother of John, also called Mark, where many people had gathered and were praying* (Acts 12:12).

Is any one of you sick? He should call the elders of the church to pray over him and anoint him with oil in the name of the Lord. And the prayer offered in faith will make the sick person well; the Lord will raise him up. If he has sinned, he will be forgiven. Therefore confess your sins to each other and pray for each other so that you may be healed. The prayer of a righteous man is powerful and effective (James 5:14-16).

I urge, then, first of all, that requests, prayers, intercession and thanksgiving be made for everyone—for kings and all those in authority, that we may live peaceful and quiet lives in all godliness and holiness (1 Timothy 2:1-2).

KNOWLEDGE

The gift of *knowledge*, when used in love, is the ability God gives you to know things that you would have no other way of knowing except through the Spirit.

✠ *...to another* [there is given] **the message of knowledge** *by means of the same spirit...* (1 Corinthians 12:8).

✠ *The Lord told* [Ananias], *"Go to the house of Judas on Straight Street and ask for a man from Tarsas named Saul, for he is praying. In a vision he has seen a man named Ananias come and place his hands on him to restore his sight"* (Acts 9:11-12).

✠ *While Peter was still thinking about the vision, the Spirit said to him, "Simon, three men are looking for you. So get up and go downstairs. Do not hesitate to go with them, for I have sent them"* (Acts 10:19-20).

✠ *He told* [the Samaritan woman], *"Go call your husband and come back," "I have no husband," she replied. Jesus said to her, "You are right when you say you have no husband. The fact is, you have had five husbands, and the man you now have is not your husband. What you have just said is quite true"* (John 4:16-18).

✠ *My purpose is that they may be encouraged in heart and united in love, so that they may have the full riches of complete understanding, in order that they may know the mystery of God, namely, Christ, in whom are hidden all the treasures of wisdom and* **knowledge** (Colossians 2:2-3).

✠ *I* [Paul] *may not be a trained speaker, but I do have* **knowledge**. *We have made this perfectly clear to you in every way* (2 Corinthians 11:6).

LEADERSHIP

The gift of *leadership*, when used in love, is the ability God gives you to lead others in accomplishing God's will.

✠ *...if* [a man's gift] *is* **leadership**, *let him govern diligently...* (Romans 12:8).

✠ *Then I heard the voice of the Lord saying, "Whom shall I send? And who will go for Us?" And I said, "Here am I. Send me"* (Isaiah 6:8).

✠ [God] *rescued him from all his troubles. He gave Joseph wisdom and enabled him to gain the goodwill of Pharaoh king of Egypt; so he made him ruler over Egypt and all his palace* (Acts 7:10).

✠ *As they traveled from town to town, they delivered the decisions reached by the apostles and elders in Jerusalem for the people to obey. So the churches were strengthened in the faith and grew daily in numbers* (Acts 16:4-5).

✝ *The elders who direct the affairs of the church well are worthy of double honor, especially those whose work is preaching and teaching* (1 Timothy 5:17).

✝ *Whoever wants to be first must be your slave—just as the son of man* [Jesus, our best example of leadership] *did not come to be served, but to serve...* (Matthew 20:27-28).

MERCY

The gift of *mercy*, when used in love, enables you to have an unusual compassion for those who are hurting.

✝ *...if* [a man's gift] *is showing **mercy**, let him do it cheerfully...* (Romans 12:8).

✝ *Blessed are the **merciful**, for they will be shown mercy* (Matthew 5:7).

✝ *At that hour of the night the jailer took them and washed their wounds; then immediately he and all his family were baptized. The jailer brought them into his house and set a meal before them; he was filled with joy because he had come to believe in God—he and his whole family* (Acts 16:33-34).

✠ *Then Peter came to Jesus and asked, "Lord, how many times shall I forgive my brother when he sins against me? Up to seven times?" Jesus answered, "I tell you, not seven times, but seventy-seven times. Therefore, the kingdom of heaven [God] is like a king who wanted to settle accounts with his servants. As he began the settlement, a man who owed him ten thousand talents was brought to him. Since he was not able to pay, the master ordered that he and his wife and his children and all that he had be sold to repay the debt. The servant fell on his knees before him. 'Be patient with me,' he begged, 'and I will pay back everything.' The servant's master took pity on him, canceled the debt and let him go. But when that servant went out, he found one of his fellow servants who owed him a hundred denarii. He grabbed him and began to choke him. 'Pay back what you owe me!' he demanded. His fellow servant fell to his knees and begged him, 'Be patient with me and I will pay you back.' But he refused. Instead, he went off and had the man thrown into prison until he could pay the debt. When the other servants saw what had happened, they were greatly distressed and went and told their master everything that had happened. Then the master called the servant in. 'You wicked servant,' he said, 'I canceled all that debt of yours because you begged me to. Shouldn't you have had* **mercy** *on your fellow servant just as I had on you?' In anger his master turned him over to the jailers to be tortured, until he should pay back all he owed. This is how My heavenly Father will treat each of you unless you forgive your brother from your heart"* (Matthew 18:21-35).

✠ *...And what does the Lord require of you? To act justly and to love* **mercy** *and to walk humbly with your God* (Micah 6:8).

✠ *Be **merciful**, just as your Father is merciful* (Luke 6:36).

MIRACLES

The gift of *miracles*, when used in love, gives you God's power to change circumstances in supernatural ways.

✠ *...to another* [is given] ***miraculous powers...*** (1 Corinthians 12:10).

✠ *...This salvation, which was first announced by the Lord, was confirmed to us by those who heard Him. God also testified to it by signs, wonders, and various **miracles**, and gifts of the Holy Spirit distributed according to His will* (Hebrews 2:3-4).

✠ *Everyone was filled with awe, and many wonders and **miraculous signs** were done by the apostles* (Acts 2:43).

✠ *Now Stephen, a man full of God's grace and power, did great wonders and **miraculous signs** among the people* (Acts 6:8).

✠ *I* [Paul] *will not venture to speak of anything except what Christ has accomplished through me in leading the Gentiles to obey God by what I have said and done—by the power of signs and **miracles**, through the power of the Spirit...* (Romans 15:18-19).

✝ *The things that mark an apostle—signs, wonders and* **miracles**—*were done among you with great perseverance* (2 Corinthians 12:12).

Pastoral Ministry

The gift of *pastoring* or *shepherding,* when used in love, is the ability and willingness to assume the personal responsibility for a group of Christians' spiritual development and welfare.

✝ *It was He who gave...some to be* **pastors**... (Ephesians 4:11).

✝ *Then I will give you* **shepherds** *after My own heart who will lead you with knowledge and understanding* (Jeremiah 3:15).

✝ *To the elders among you, I appeal as a fellow elder, a witness of Christ's sufferings and one who also will share in the glory to be revealed: Be* **shepherds** *of God's flock that is under your care, serving as overseers—not because you must, but because you are willing, as God wants you to be; not greedy for money, but eager to serve; not lording it over those entrusted to you, but being examples to the flock* (1 Peter 5:1-3).

✝ *Here is a trustworthy saying: If anyone sets his heart on being an overseer* [**pastor**], *he desires a noble task. Now the overseer must be above reproach, the husband of but one wife, temperate, self-controlled, respectable, hospitable, able to teach, not given to* *drunkenness, not violent but gentle, not quarrelsome, not a lover of money. He must manage his own family well and see that his children obey him with proper respect. (If anyone does not know how to manage his own family, how can he take care of God's church?) He must not be a recent convert, or he may become conceited and fall under the same judgment as the devil. He must also have a good reputation with outsiders, so that he will not fall into disgrace and into the devil's trap* (1 Timothy 3:1-7).

PROPHECY

The gift of *prophecy*, when used in love, is the ability to receive and communicate God's message to others.

✝ *...to another [there is given]* **prophecy***...* (1 Corinthians 12:10).

✝ *...If a man's gift is* **prophesying***, let him use it in proportion to his faith* (Romans 12:6).

✝ *It was He who gave some...to be* **prophets***...* (Ephesians 4:11).

✝ *Judas and Silas, who themselves were* **prophets***, said much to encourage and strengthen the brothers* (Acts 15:32).

✝ *He [Philip] had four unmarried daughters who* **prophesied***. After we* *had been there a number of days, a **prophet** named Agabus came down from Judea. Coming over to us, he took Paul's belt, tied his own hands and feet with it and said, "The Holy Spirit says, 'In this way the Jews of Jerusalem will bind the owner of this belt and will hand him over to the Gentiles'"* (Act 21:9-11).

✠ *I will pour out My Spirit on all people. Your sons and daughters will **prophesy**, your old men will dream dreams, your young men will see visions* (Joel 2:28).

✠ *In the past God spoke to our forefathers through the **prophets** at many times and in various ways, but in these days He has spoken to us by His Son, who He appointed heir of all things, and through whom He made the universe* (Hebrews 1:1-2).

SERVICE

The gift of *service*, when used in love, is the God-given heart to help meet people's needs by serving them sacrificially.

✠ *If* [a man's gift] *is **serving**, let him serve...* (Romans 12:7).

✠ *In those days when the number of disciples was increasing, the Grecian Jews among them complained against the Hebraic Jews because their widows were being overlooked in the daily distribution of food. So the Twelve gathered all the disciples together and said, "It would not be right for us to neglect the ministry of the word of God in order to wait on tables. Brothers, choose seven men from among you who are known to be full of the Spirit and wisdom. We will turn this responsibility over to them and will give our attention to prayer and the ministry of the word." This proposal pleased the whole group. They chose Stephen, a man full of faith and of the Holy Spirit; also Philip, Procorus, Nicanor, Timon, Parmenas, and Nicolas from Antioch, a convert to Judaism. They presented these men to the apostles, who prayed and laid their hands on them. So the word of God spread. The number of disciples in Jerusalem increased rapidly, and a large number of priests became obedient to the faith* (Acts 6:1-7).

✠ *May the Lord show mercy to the household of Onesiphorus, because he often refreshed me and was not ashamed of my chains. On the contrary, when he was in Rome, he searched hard for me until he found me. May the Lord grant that he will find mercy from the Lord on that day! You know very well in how many ways he helped me in Ephesus* (2 Timothy 1:16-18).

✠ *Carry each other's burdens, and in this way you will fulfill the law of Christ* (Galatians 6:2).

✠ *Therefore, as we have opportunity, let us do good to all people, especially to those who belong to the family of believers* (Galatians 6:10).

Teaching

The gift of *teaching*, when used in love, is the ability God gives you to effectively communicate truth in such a way that brings others closer to God.

✟ *And in the church God has appointed...third* **teachers**... (1 Corinthians 12:28).

✟ *It was He who gave... some to be pastors and* **teachers**... (Ephesians 4:11).

✟ *...if* [a man's gift] *is* **teaching**, *let him teach* (Romans 12:7).

✟ *Meanwhile a Jew named Apollos, a native of Alexandria, came to Ephesus. He was a learned man, with a thorough knowledge of the Scriptures. He had been instructed in the way of the Lord, and he spoke with great fervor and* **taught** *about Jesus accurately, though he knew only the baptism of John. He began to speak boldly in the synagogue. When Priscilla and Aquila heard him, they invited him to their home and explained to him the way of God more adequately. When Apollos wanted to go to Achaia, the brothers encouraged him and wrote to the disciples there to welcome him. On arriving, he was a great help to those who by grace had believed. For he vigorously refuted the Jews in public debate, proving from the Scriptures that Jesus was the Christ* (Acts 18:24-28).

✠ *You know that I have not hesitated to preach anything that would be helpful to you but have **taught** you publicly and from house to house. I have declared to both Jews and Greeks that they must turn to God in repentance and have faith in our Lord Jesus* (Acts 20:20-21).

✠ *Therefore go and make disciples of all nations, baptizing them in the name of the Father and of the Son and of the Holy Spirit, and **teaching** them to obey everything I have commanded you...* (Matthew 28:19-20).

✠ *Not many of you should presume to be **teachers**, my brothers, because you know that we who teach will be judged more strictly* (James 3:1).

TONGUES

The gift of *tongues*, when used in love, is the ability God gives you to speak in a heavenly language to help your spirit discern and accomplish God's will.

✠ *...to another* [there is given] *speaking in **different kinds of tongues**...* (1 Corinthians 12:10).

✠ *When the day of Pentecost came, they were all together in one place. Suddenly a sound like the blowing of a violent wind came from heaven and filled the whole house where they were sitting. They saw what seemed to be tongues of fire that separated and came to rest on* *each of them. All of them were filled with the Holy Spirit and began to speak in **other tongues** as the Spirit enabled them. Now there were staying in Jerusalem God-fearing Jews from every nation under heaven. When they heard this sound, a crowd came together in bewilderment, because each one heard them speaking in his own language. Utterly amazed, they asked: "Are not all these men who are speaking Galileans? Then how is it that each of us hears them in his own native language? Parthians, Medes and Elamites; residents of Mesopotamia, Judea and Cappadocia, Pontus and Asia, Phyrgia and Pamphylia, Egypt and the parts of Libya near Cyrene; visitors from Rome (both Jews and converts to Judaism); Cretans and Arabs—we hear them declaring the wonders of God in our own tongues!" Amazed and perplexed, they asked one another, "What does this mean?" Some, however, made fun of them and said, "They have had too much wine"* (Acts 2:1-13).

✠ *While Peter was still speaking these words, the Holy Spirit came on all who heard the message. The circumcised believers who had come with Peter were astonished that the gift of the Holy Spirit had been poured out even on the Gentiles. For they heard them **speaking in tongues** and praising God* (Acts 10:44-46).

✠ *For then I will restore to the peoples a pure language, that they may all call on the name of the Lord, to serve Him with one accord* (Zephaniah 3:9 NKJV).

✠ *For anyone who **speaks in a tongue** does not speak to men but to God. Indeed, no one understands him; he utters mysteries with his spirit* (1 Corinthians 14:2).

Interpretation of Tongues

The gift of *interpretation of tongues*, when used in love, is given to you to be able to hear tongues in a corporate or group setting and to interpret them for the benefit and nourishment of others.

✠ *...to still another* [there is given] *the* **interpretation of tongues** (1 Corinthians 12:10).

✠ *What then shall we say, brothers? When you come together, everyone has a hymn, or a word of instruction, a revelation, a tongue or an* **interpretation***. All of these must be done for the strengthening of the church. If anyone speaks in a tongue, two—or at the most three— should speak, one at a time, and someone must* **interpret***. If there is no interpreter, the speaker should keep quiet in the church and speak to himself and God* (1 Corinthians 14:26-28).

Wisdom

The gift of *wisdom*, when used in love, is the ability to receive insight and spiritually meaningful knowledge from God that allows you to become supernaturally solid in your walk of faith—creating a powerful testimony for others.

✠ *To one there is given through the Spirit the message of* **wisdom***...* (1 Corinthians 12:8).

*And He said to man, "The fear of the Lord—that is **wisdom**, and to shun evil is understanding"* (Job 28:28).

*Therefore everyone who hears these words of Mine and puts them into practice is like a **wise** man who built his house on the rock* (Matthew 7:24).

*Bear in mind that our Lord's patience means salvation, just as our dear brother Paul also wrote you with the **wisdom** that God gave him. He writes the same way in all his letters, speaking in them of these matters. His letters contain some things that are hard to understand, which ignorant and unstable people distort, as they do the other Scriptures, to their own destruction* (2 Peter 3:15-16).

*If any of you lacks **wisdom**, he should ask God, who gives generously to all without finding fault, and it will be given to him. But when he asks, he must believe and not doubt, because he who doubts is like a wave of the sea, blown and tossed by the wind* (James 1:5-6).

Truly, the Gifts of the Spirit are the tools that God gives us in order that we might show Him and His intentions to the world—we are His Body on earth. So we are called by God not only to identify our gifts, but also to use them in their fullness, to exercise them correctly. This is the key. Indeed, to the extent that we can, we are to use them in love wherever opportunities arise. Paul eloquently describes the *attitude* we should have as we use these gifts, as members within the Body of believers, the Church:

☩ *My purpose is that they may be encouraged in heart and united in love, so that they may have the full riches of complete understanding, in order that they may know the mystery of God, namely, Christ, in whom are hidden all the treasures of wisdom and knowledge* (Colossians 2:2-3).

ACTION & VISUALIZATION

Locate and use the Gifts of the Spirit that God has given you, in love, wherever opportunities arise.

FINDING ALL THE GIFTS

Since the gifts are all used to build up the Body of Christ and you are part of the Body, once you have determined what gifts you have been given in good measure, then you need to locate and expose yourself to people gifted in the *other* areas. It is important to have exposure to *all* of the gifts (especially the gifts of prophet, pastor, and teacher), whether through yourself, a friend, or a church leader. We need each other's gifts to reach perfect maturity:

☩ *It was He who gave some to be apostles, some to be prophets, some to be evangelists, some to be pastors and teachers, to prepare God's people for works of service, so that the body of Christ* [including you] *may be built up until we all reach unity in the faith and in the knowledge of the Son of God and become mature, attaining to the whole measure of the fullness of Christ* (Ephesians 4:11-13).

He who walks with the wise grows wise... (Proverbs 13:20)

ACTION & VISUALIZATION

Expose yourself to all of the Gifts of the Spirit so that you can become mature and perfected into the image of Christ.

MEDITATION POINT

Alone you may not make moving music,
but in concert with others it will have a beautiful, powerful impact.

Go to Chapter 4 in the Study Guide section on page 317.

Chapter 5

GIFT #10—RELATIONSHIP

HOW DO RELATIONSHIPS COMPLETE YOU AND YOUR DESTINY?

Before you begin to read, pray that the Holy Spirit will give you and all readers of this book understanding and application.

Two are better than one, because they have a good return for their work: If one falls down, his friend can help him up. But pity the man who falls and has no one to help him up! Also, if two lie down together, they will keep warm. But how can one keep warm alone? Though one may be overpowered, two can defend themselves. A cord of three strands is not quickly broken (Ecclesiastes 4:9-12).

The government recently calculated the cost of raising one child from birth to age 18: $249,180![1] Imagine what kind of exotic vacation, sports car, or boat you could buy with that kind of money. Looking at it strictly from an economic position, one might wonder if the best financial advice would be to avoid having children altogether. If you're a parent, though, I suspect you can attest to the truth that the money you've invested in your children has given you a truly rich return. At all stages— from the loss of their first tooth to their high school graduation, from their first step to their first day driving a car—children are priceless.

Yet parents, friends, husbands, and wives are prone to ignore the kinds of returns that we can receive when we relentlessly invest in a relationship. How often do we think about what we can take from our marriage or our friendships? Do we sometimes just think about what we will lose or gain? With Christ as our example, true relationship—the richest relationship— seeks to pour our lives into others. For our Savior, this sort of relationship took Him to the Cross so that He could offer us an eternal relationship. How do we live this out as parents, friends, husbands, wives, sons, and daughters?

If we break it down, we see that God offers us two kinds of relationship: a relationship with Himself and relationships with others here on earth, which is the subject of this chapter. We will discuss our relationship with God in Chapter 7. Though you will see that our relationship with other people is both a part of our relationship with God and a vehicle to help us achieve a deeper relationship with God.

God offers us earthly relationships for many reasons. Companionship, of course, is one of the most important. Imagine what life would be like if you had nobody to talk to or share things with. Relationships also help us complete our destiny—giving us the critical support that we need to help us execute our calling and, thereby, impact the world. Imagine our world without the relationships of parents, teachers, pastors, mentors, spouse, children, or friends. What would fill us with information, instruction, life's joyful moments and most importantly love? We would be empty without relationships.

Just as we needed parents to raise and provide for us when we were young, so too as adults we need relationships to strengthen, support, and encourage us throughout life. Not only do we find personal support, but we also give support; our earthly relationships enable us to help one another in times of trouble. This is another way we find purpose in life.

God has created us for synergy with others. We can see this even at the most basic levels. Have you ever scooted close to someone just to stay warm? That shared body heat is a wonderful, physical example of a spiritual truth. In challenging times or when under attack, two or more have a better chance than one of fending off the attack or persevering through the trial. Together we create something each one of us individually doesn't have alone.

Spiritually speaking, we find incredible power in a prayer of agreement with others—in joining our faith together as one. We are each uniquely gifted, as we've already explored in previous chapters. So another benefit of human relationships is that we can team up with those who are strong where we are weak. This happens in business partnerships all the time, and it can be a wonderful truth in married life as well.

✙ *The Lord God said, "It is not good for the man to be alone. I will make*
a helper suitable for him" (Genesis 2:18).

Perhaps this seems obvious, but the very truth that the continuation of civilization requires the union of man and woman (through the living out of a God-ordained human relationship in marriage) is evidence of the value and necessity of relationship.

There is another wonderful phenomenon that comes about as a result of relationships. Each of us was created uniquely different and we each have different positions and areas of interest (parent, teacher, pastor, mentor, spouse, child, sibling, friend, servant, boss, entertainer, etc.). As two people interact to create a relationship, they draw out of each other and react to each other in their own unique ways; thereby making every relationship unique! What an interesting life God gives us, an opportunity where no two relationships are the same. Parents can even tell you that the relationships with each of their children have a different give-and-take component, thereby manifesting a unique relationship.

In Book One I make the analogy that we are each like crystals that create a unique pattern of colors when God's light shines through us. So likewise when we line up in relationship and God's light shines through us there is yet another pattern of colors created by our relationship—one that matches no other.

Now let me pause for a moment and remind you that much of what has already been explored in this series of books is all about relationships. Jesus' ministry, the work of the Spirit and the heart of God is focused around relationship with you and me—in turn, we affect the world because of our relationship with Him. So, the other Gifts of Freedom are aimed to impact the way you relate to friends, family, co-workers, and even strangers. You have already learned how God uses your relationship with other believers (the Body of Christ) to accomplish His greater purpose. Now let's take it a step deeper. I'd like to highlight a few of the reasons why all kinds of relationships are vital to our spiritual growth. Applying these truths will enhance and enrich your earthly relationships as well as your relationship with God.

FOR SELF IMPROVEMENT

Relationships can help us improve ourselves in ways that make success in all areas easier and likelier:

✝ *As iron sharpens iron, so one man sharpens another* (Proverbs 27:17).

✝ *If the ax is dull and its edges unsharpened, more strength is needed…* (Ecclesiastes 10:10).

✝ *Where there is no counsel, the people fall; but in a multitude of counselors there is safety* (Proverbs 11:14 NJKV).

✝ *Plans fail for lack of counsel, but with many advisors they succeed* (Proverbs 15:22).

It's important to have someone in your life who will hold you accountable for your Christian walk and the goals that you set for yourself. This person (or people) should be someone who knows you and someone you are free to be honest with—to discuss your trials, your victories, and your defeats. We have spiritual blind spots, and accountability partners give us perspective—which can help reveal these blind spots if we are open to it.

We will all face times when we need others' help. We may need physical help or prayer or encouragement or a rediscovery of the right perspective when the schemes of satan get us turned around. Their presence can create both a physical and a spiritual synergy to help keep us "warm." Also you just learned in the last two chapters that all believers possess different gifts that are meant to build up the whole Body and bring us to a greater revelation of Christ. And don't forget that there is a special kind of power in praying in agreement with others—in combining your faith with them. This is just a few of many reasons why it's good to be part of a Christian fellowship where you can regularly *give* and *receive* support.

Outward Focus

Paul exhorts us to have the same attitude as Jesus when it comes to making friends. When you focus on others' needs, you forget what you are lacking. And when you forget about what you're lacking, you give God room to deal with it. But, as Paul addresses in this passage, it's not always easy to be a good friend. Listen to his definition:

> *Then make my joy complete by being like-minded, having the same love, being one in spirit and purpose. Do nothing out of selfish ambition or vain conceit, but in humility consider others better than yourselves. Each of you should look not only to your own interests, but also to the interest of others. Your attitude should be the same as that of Christ Jesus: who, being in very nature God, did not consider equality with God something to be grasped, but made Himself nothing, taking on the very nature of a servant, being made in human likeness. And being found in appearance as a man, He humbled Himself and became obedient to death* [of His self-interest]*—even death on a cross!* **Therefore** *God exalted Him to the highest place and gave Him the name that is above every name* (Philippians 2:2-9).

You will be tempted to set yourself above others in situations because of power, authority, money, or even a gift that you have received that would seem to make you "better" than another. In these situations, Jesus is our example. He certainly could have set Himself above mere humans. Instead, Jesus elected to be equal and, indeed, to be a servant to His brothers and sisters— even though by human standards He would have been considered better. We, too, are called not to set ourselves above other people but to serve them.

> *Whoever wants to be first must be your slave—just as the Son of Man* [Jesus] *did not come to be served, but to serve…* (Matthew 20:27-28).

> [Jesus said,] *"For who is greater, the one who is at the table or the one who serves? Is it* **not** *the one who is at the table? But I am among you as one who serves"* (Luke 22:27).

SERVANTHOOD

Jesus showed us how to be a servant by washing the feet of the disciples. Jesus also said:

✝ *...whoever wants to become great among you must be your servant, and whoever wants to be first must be slave of all* (Mark 10:43-44).

When you are serving, you will be given stronger friends. Strong friends will help you become the person that God intends you to be. The Bible includes a number of stories about strong friendships. One of the most familiar is David and Jonathan.

✝ *After David had finished talking with Saul, Jonathan became one in spirit with David, and he loved him as himself. From that day Saul kept David with him and did not let him return to his father's house. And Jonathan made a covenant with David because he loved him as himself. Jonathan took off the robe he was wearing and gave it to David, along with his tunic, and even his sword, his bow and his belt* (1 Samuel 18:1-4).

In the end, Jonathan laid down his own *right* to the throne and instead helped David become the king that God wanted him to be. The way you become a strong and serving friend is by putting others' interests and needs before your own. Jesus teaches that this loving service is second in importance only to your relationship with God (the first commandment).

✝ [Jesus said] *"The second is this: 'Love your neighbor as yourself.' There is no commandment greater than these'"* (Mark 12:31).

In a conversation with an expert in the law, Jesus described what the act of loving your neighbor as yourself looks like:

☦ *In reply Jesus said, "A man was going down from Jerusalem to Jericho, when he fell into the hands of robbers. They stripped him of his clothes, beat him and went away leaving him half dead. A priest happened to be going down the same road, and when he saw the man, he passed by on the other side. So too, a Levite, when he came to the place and saw him, passed by to the other side. But a Samaritan, as he traveled, came where the man was; and when he saw him, he took pity on him. He went to him and bandaged his wounds, pouring on oil and wine. Then he put the man on his own donkey, took him to an inn and took care of him. The next day he took out two silver coins and gave them to the innkeeper. 'Look after him,' he said. 'And when I return, I will reimburse you for any extra expense you may have.' Which of these three do you think was a neighbor to the man who fell into the hands of robbers?" The expert in the law replied, "The one who had mercy on him." Jesus told him, "Go and do likewise"* (Luke 10:30-37).

In this parable, Jesus offers clear instructions about how to respond when we meet people with *physical* needs. However, Jesus is *also* giving us clear instruction about how to care for each other's *spiritual* needs. We are not to leave people by the side of the road to spiritually die.

Re-read this passage, but look at it from a spiritual perspective. Assume that the robbers are satan and satanic forces. The priest and Levite are religious leaders who portray themselves as caring for the spiritually sick, but in this story, they're wrapped up in their own interests (the playground where satan likes to keep our attention). Who is the Samaritan? He is an example of who we are called to be. With oil (the Holy Spirit) and wine (the Blood of Jesus), we can minister to a spiritually sick person. It's important to remember that it is up to the man to work out his own salvation. This is why you are to put him back on his own donkey. We are only asked to pour on the oil and wine.

Now look at the innkeeper. In our spiritual re-thinking of the story, the innkeeper represents the pastor of a local church who can care spiritually for the injured man. We aren't finished when we drop the man at the church, though. Jesus asks us to financially support those churches that are caring spiritually for people. We are also to return and make sure that they're healthy. Now with that in mind, imagine yourself in life *going and doing likewise* as Jesus ordered.

FULFILLING THE LAW

Paul said that the very act of friendship fulfills the Old Testament Law and Christ's command:

✠ *Let no debt remain outstanding, except the continuing debt to love one another, for he who **loves** his fellowman has **fulfilled** the law* (Romans 13:8).

✠ *Carry each other's burdens, and in this way you will **fulfill** the law of Christ* (Galatians 6:2).

Friendship fulfills the Law because becoming a true friend is an act of loving, and loving is serving (just as Jesus served). Cultivating good friendships through serving can create stronger relationships, even beyond those within your own family.

✝ *Do not forsake your friend and the friend of your father, and do not go to your brother's house when disaster strikes you—**better a neighbor nearby than a brother far away*** (Proverbs 27:10).

✝ *A man of many companions may come to ruin, but **there is a friend who sticks closer than a brother*** (Proverbs 18:24).

✝ *A friend loves at all times, and a brother is born for adversity* (Proverbs 17:17).

✝ *A wise servant will rule over a disgraceful son, and will share the inheritance as one of the brothers* (Proverbs 17:2).

HOW TO WIN FRIENDS

So how do we find meaningful friendships and people we can rely on? Well, as you already know, they don't just appear. The answer to this question is a familiar one: we reap what we sow. If you want friends, offer friendship to others. If you want a strong friendship, you must be a strong friend. The degree in which you sow and plant unselfishly within relationships will be revealed in the harvest of strong friendships. Jesus, of course, is the ideal model for this:

✝ *Greater love has no one than this, that he lay down his life for his friends* (John 15:13).

We did not deserve His friendship, but He invested Himself in becoming our friend.

*You see, at just the right time, when we were still powerless, Christ died for the ungodly. Very rarely will anyone die for a righteous man, though for a good man someone might possibly dare to die. But God demonstrates His own love for us in this: While we were **still** sinners* [not yet friends], *Christ died for us* (Romans 5:6-8).

Paul instructed us to imitate Christ in this way:

I try to please everybody in every way. For I am not seeking my own good but the good of many, so that they may be saved (1 Corinthians 10:33).

Do nothing out of selfish ambition or vain conceit, but in humility consider others better than yourselves. Each of you should look not only to your own interests, but also to the interests of others (Philippians 2:3-4).

This means that you may have to show friendship to people who are not being friendly to you. That is why Paul says the following:

Do not repay anyone evil for evil. Be careful to do what is right in the eyes of everybody (Romans 12:17).

We should also actively seek to do good both for those who deserve it and for those who are not able to help themselves.

✠ *Do not withhold good from those who deserve it, when it is in your power to act. Do not say to your neighbor, "Come back later; I'll give it tomorrow"—when you now have it with you* (Proverbs 3:27-28).

✠ *Blessed is he who has regard for the weak; the Lord delivers him in times of trouble. The Lord will protect him and preserve his life; He will bless him in the land and not surrender him to the desire of his foes* (Psalm 41:1-2).

Essentially, as you, like Christ, reach out in love to others, many faithful and strong friends will be attracted to you. And as you become closer to the image and likeness of God, you will attract friends who will reflect that *light* back to you—making them the best kind of friend to have.

ACTION & VISUALIZATION

Be a friend to others in faith and love.

MARRIAGE: THE ULTIMATE EARTHLY RELATIONSHIP

The strongest earthly relationship that God offers to us is that between a *man* and a *woman* in marriage. Through this relationship, that of a parent and child can also grow. I could fill a few books on the topic of what makes a great marriage. Thankfully, there are plenty of great books that teach what a biblically-based marriage ought to look like. But because this is such an important aspect of the Gift of Relationship, I wanted to be sure to introduce here some of the *key* concepts that make a marriage flourish.

Marriage is the ultimate expression of companionship, as two are spiritually tied together in such a way that they practically become *one person*. This combining of two is also a simple model of the ultimate relationship that God desires to spiritually have with us—a combining into one—Him in us and us in Him. Let's start at the beginning, in order to understand the marriage relationship.

✢ *...But for Adam no suitable helper was found* [among the creation]. *So the Lord God caused the man to fall into a deep sleep; and while he was sleeping, he took one of the man's ribs and closed up the place with flesh. Then the Lord God made a woman from the rib he had taken out of the man, and he brought her to the man. The man said, "This is now bone of my bones and flesh of my flesh; she shall be called 'woman,' for she was taken out of the man." For this reason a man will leave his father and mother and be united to his wife, and they will become* **one flesh** (Genesis 2:20-24).

TWO UNIQUE ROLES

God created man and woman to have interlocking abilities and weaknesses which, when combined in marriage, can help them accomplish their combined God-given purpose. Likewise, spiritually speaking they also interlock to become one.

Let's look first at God's intent for each in creation.

✢ *...*[Man] *is the image and glory of* **God**; *but the woman is the glory of* **man** (1 Corinthians 11:7).

This does not imply in any way that men are more important than women—of course not. It merely tells us that each has a distinctly different purpose and role. It's like asking what's better, the light bulb or the socket it fits in? Neither. They both require the electricity to function as one. Marriage is the same. The two in the marriage require each other, as well as God's power, to give the marriage life and proper function. Spiritually, men and women are equal in God's eyes; He doesn't play favorites. His love reaches out to both genders, encouraging us to seek His purpose for our lives—oneness.

✝ *There is neither...male nor female, for you are one in Christ Jesus* (Galatians 3:28).

Indeed *both* are *equally* needed to accomplish God's purpose, and in the case of married couples, the Bible tells us they become "one flesh" in God's eyes anyway (see Genesis 2:24). It is helpful, though, to look at the differences between men and women so that we can better understand God's individual plan for each as He intended them to complement one another.

Role of Men

Men were designed primarily for function. God talks about this function immediately after The Fall:

✝ *To Adam [God] said, "Because you listened to your wife and ate from the tree about which I commanded you, 'You must not eat of it,' "Cursed is the ground because of you; through painful toil you will eat of it all the days of your life. It will produce thorns and thistles for you, and you will eat the plants of the field. By the sweat of your brow you will eat your food until you return to the ground, since from it you were taken; for dust you are and to dust you will return"* (Genesis 3:17-19).

This description of a man's role is not unlike that of a workhorse. Think of a heavy-duty truck used for hauling—the kind that you see at construction sites. For *thousands* of years, history has demonstrated that we naturally grade a man on his ability to *perform*, because that is what we intuitively *know* he was designed to do.

✠ *If anyone does not provide for **his** relatives, and especially for his immediate family, **he** has denied the faith and is worse than an unbeliever* (1 Timothy 5:8).

Regardless of the increased number of women into the workplace, men are still primarily responsible to be the providers for their families. Another verse, directed at women, further describes the man's role in spiritual matters:

✠ *...Your desire will be for your husband, and he will rule over you* (Genesis 3:16).

For the man, this might at first seem like the "best" position to hold, the position with all of the "glory" and power so to speak. But *think about it*: in business, who is responsible when something goes wrong? The person who is in charge. God gives men authority, but also the responsibility that goes with it. If things go wrong, God holds the man *responsible* for his actions and the leadership direction to those under his authority.

Some men may be thinking that, because God put them in charge, they must have all the answers. Men, in order for you to have the right perspective, I think it's worth reviewing the sobering words that God used when He looked at the man He had made:

✝ *And the Lord God said, "It is not good that man should be alone. I will make him a **helper** comparable to him"* (Genesis 2:18 NKJV).

Yes, God knew in His infinite wisdom that men could not make it alone. All men, like Adam, are lacking and need help.

Role of Women

God gave a very different role to women. One of the key differences, as we all know, is that she is the sole child-bearer and primary child-care provider.

✝ *To the woman [God] said, "I will greatly increase your pains in child-bearing; with pain you will give birth to children..."* (Genesis 3:16).

But the Bible also says that women are the glory of men. Instead of that heavy-duty truck, think of a beautiful, unique sports car—the sort of car that you take great pride in, that you take great care of, and that you like to take out for Sunday drives. As the glory of man, her sheer beauty shines from the *inside out*, much like that sports car, glistening in the light from the sun.

The truck has a rather straightforward method to perform its function. You just turn on the ignition switch and drive. But the sports car requires more attention, more finesse. All of those switches, gauges, dials, and buttons have to be just right for it to perform at its optimum level.

Even our symbols for marriage—the rings—reflect these distinct differences. The simpler design of the husband's ring conveys, in a straightforward, no fanfare way, the fact that he is married, while the wife's more intricate wedding ring reflects the beauty that the husband feels for and through her.

Celebrate Your Differences

The differences in the way that God made men and women help them each to fulfill their roles within their relationship. Man alone was incomplete—lacking. So women were made with *differences* that, when combined with men, complete them—*together* they can achieve God's perfect plan.

Consider this: if we were designed exactly alike, how could one possibly help the other's weakness? How would it make sense that we could combine and become one? It can be tempting to blur those differences and attempt to conform one to the other. However, instead we should celebrate those *differences*. Indeed isn't it those very *differences* that make the marriage relationship interesting? Think about it.

Let's look at some of these differences. According to one understanding of the science behind gender differences, during the eight weeks in development within the womb a man receives more of a testosterone wash in his brain that causes the brain to suffer a kind of damage. (Of course, my wife tells me that she knew that all along.) Simply put, this results in men having fewer nerve cells than women that connect the brain. The basic effect of this is that women are much more physically connected to the world and to their bodies. Information from the senses (sight, sound, touch, and taste) are being processed in the brain in greater quantity all the time. Moreover the area of the brain that handles language in a woman is better connected to the right hemisphere allowing it to pitch in on language.[2]

As a result of this, women generally have the ability to simultaneously notice and process more of what's happening around and to them. They have an acute sense of their surroundings—their radar is fine-tuned far beyond men's. They are also wired for communication. This natural gift of communication is fed by a *desire* to communicate the information they are receiving; indeed women are fulfilling a God-given purpose when they pursue this desire. This is why their need to know that their communication is being received is so *vital* and *fulfilling*.

My wife is enviably more communicative than I am. Substantially so! I have read books and articles that compare the number of words a woman speaks to that of a man in an average day. While the findings differ from one study to the next, all I have read seem to agree that women speak many more words than men—twice as many or more. When I told my wife this, she said, "Of course! We have to repeat everything twice for you men to hear!" While this may not always be true, it is interesting and significant that many women do believe it to be true. Regardless of the actual difference in words spoken, the average man clearly comes up short in communication skills—according to many women, most men either don't listen or don't *properly* acknowledge that they were listening.

Men, on the other hand, having less exterior information to process, tend to be more cerebral than women in their approach to the world—more detached. This is a result of having more white matter in the brain allowing men to be superior at spatial reasoning.[3] They process information in a different manner, conceptualizing and strategizing life into linear goals. In conversation, they are more likely to leap right to "the point" and skip over an explanation of the bigger more detailed picture—usually requiring fewer words. This habit of leaping right to the point without first properly acknowledging a woman's input can leave her feeling that her input wasn't heard at all, thereby making her feel *incomplete* and *unfulfilled*.

Let's look at an example of how these different views play out in everyday life. When my wife and I are heading to the mall so that she can buy a new pair of shoes, I am thinking about the layout of the mall and the best place to park. I'm doing this so that I might get home in time for the next game on TV. She, on the other hand, is enjoying the ride and the nice day out as she seeks to engage me in conversation about some relational issue with our kids. After she has finished a vivid blow-by-blow of the issue, she waits for my comments, and of course, I respond with a quick (and thereby probably unsatisfying) "yes" as I'm trying to figure out, based on traffic at the mall that day, whether it is worth driving closer or not in hopes of getting a better parking spot.

When we get into the mall, my attention is still on the practical: the hunt for shoes. My goal is to find them, grab them, bag them, and go. She on the other hand is enjoying the walk though the mall, the window-shopping, the people watching, the smells, the sounds, the sights. Indeed she stops in front of a display window looking at a pretty dress that caught her attention.

"I thought we came for shoes," I say in protest of this distraction from our original objective. In the end, she doesn't find any shoes she likes, so we head for home. For her, the whole shopping experience was stimulating and enjoyable and, therefore, *complete*. I on the other hand experience a sense of incompleteness. Something is missing: where are the shoes we came to buy?

Understanding these basic differences can help us as we attempt to relate to one another. Instead of seeing our differences as a point of conflict, we can learn from each other. For example, the man can learn more about the world around him through her senses, and the woman can learn interesting ways to navigate through that world. When we respect and honor these differences, we allow the other to complete us—equipping us to complete God's plan.

The *key* to enjoying these differences is *allowing* each partner to be who he or she is. Compromise is important, but acknowledging that we're not going to change the other person from what God intended him or her to be is also vital to a healthy relationship. We must work in tandem, balancing one another, viewing our individual differences as a means to growth, not as a point of conflict.

Combination Makes Whole

The abilities and characteristics that God gave men and women allow them to combine into one flesh, fulfilling a family's needs. Man is designed to provide for the family and will generally feel some level of incompleteness when he is not successful at doing this.

The man is also designed to be the head of the family.

☩ *Now I want you to realize that the head of every man is Christ, and the head of the woman is man, and the head of Christ is God* (1 Corinthians 11:3).

From a purely biological sense, this seems logical. A mind primarily focused on strategy and survival would be critical to the success of a family. But the role of the woman is no less important in the process. The body gives the mind *critical* feedback that it *needs* to properly perform its function. A woman's feedback and insight can give critically needed information and light to the man's strategic and linear thinking. Simply put, when God said, "It's not good for man to be alone," He knew what He was talking about.

This brings up a point that I need to emphasize to the men reading this book. Please listen well to your wife and acknowledge that you're listening. Remember that a woman's sense of completeness is based on being heard, as well as being taken seriously for the thoughts that she offers. If you surveyed married couples at any point in history, you'd find that the most common problem is a "communication problem." Usually this means that either the man isn't listening, or he isn't doing a very good job of acknowledging that he's listening, or both. When this happens, there will be a lack of completeness in the marriage, leading to relational problems.

And don't miss this: what she offers is of *great* value. Women tend to detect non-verbal information better than men. This is particularly the case when it comes to feelings. God created woman to be sensitive and nurturing, knowing, for example, what a baby needs simply by the sound of his or her cry. Because of this, she is usually best at seeing and responding to family fractures. Indeed many women weave themselves into the entire experience of the family relationship, and that broader experience of "family" becomes a significant part of their identity. This is why she may feel that you're criticizing or attacking her personally when you identify things that you may feel are shortcomings with the house or family. Remember the heightened, fine-tuned radar allows her to incorporate the greater experience of house and family into her self in such a way that the line between where one ends and the other begins is less defined. So choose your words carefully and seek to be an encourager to your wife. When you do so, she will respond positively, like a plant being watered.

I want to reiterate that God doesn't see either role as more important than the other—*just as different*. Both the man and woman need each other in marriage to be *complete*. When you think about it, you realize that God has made marriage a beautiful circle. Woman originally came from man, but man comes from woman; and it takes the union of them both, as one flesh, to plant the seed to create a new life. And God designed that very union of planting the seed to be the most satisfying and unifying experience that a husband and wife can share.

ACTION & VISUALIZATION

Acknowledge and enjoy your differences in the gift of marriage that God offers you.

A Word to Husbands

Your role as the head of the family should never be exercised by physical force, mental leveraging, or even by the exertion of God-given spiritual leadership. Your role is to *inspire* your wife to *follow* your lead as you travel down the path of life. If you are behind her, pushing her down the path, then you are not inspiring her (or perhaps you are not listening enough). To instill this trust, you need to have an open dialogue. You will successfully inspire her if you have the same attitude as Christ.

☦ *Husbands, love your wives, just as Christ loved the church and* **gave Himself up for her**... (Ephesians 5:25).

☦ *In this same way, husbands ought to love their wives as their own bodies. He who loves his wife loves himself. After all, no one ever hated his own body, but he feeds and cares for it, just as Christ does the church...* (Ephesians 5:28-30).

☦ *Husbands, in the same way be considerate as you live with your wives, and treat them with respect as the weaker partners and as heirs with you of the gracious gift of life, so that nothing will hinder your prayers* (1 Peter 3:7).

Look at the similarity between this passage and what I wrote earlier. Your role as leader in the marriage relationship is that of a servant leader. Let's go a little deeper with this. First, consider this Scripture:

☦ *Wives, submit to your husbands as to the Lord. For the husband is the head of the wife as Christ is the head of the church, His body, of which*

He is the Savior. Now as the church submits to Christ, so also wives should submit to their husbands in everything. Husbands, love your wives, **just as Christ loved the church and gave Himself up for her to make her holy,** *cleansing her by the washing with water through the word, and to present her to Himself as a radiant church, without stain or wrinkle or any other blemish, but holy and blameless. In this same way, husbands ought to love their wives as their own bodies.* **He who loves his wife loves himself.** *After all, no one ever hated his own body, but he feeds and cares for it, just as Christ does the church— for we are members of His body. "For this reason a man will leave his father and mother and be united to his wife, and the two will become one flesh." This is a profound mystery—but I am talking about Christ and the church. However, each one of you also must love his wife as he loves himself, and the wife must respect her husband* (Ephesians 5:22-33).

The first thing to note here is that God created a structure where everyone is submitted to someone else: wife to husband, husband to Christ, and Christ to God. Your success as a husband will be directly proportional to your submission to Christ and your willingness to follow His example. Indeed, if you are not already married, keep in mind that one of the most attractive qualities to Christian women is a humble and contrite spirit—as demonstrated through your obedience to God.

The second thing to note in the above passage is that the better we treat our wives, the better our wives will be. If you treat your wife meanly, you will probably have an unhappy and spiteful wife. What you put *in* her you will get *out* of her, so be *wise* and *invest wisely.*

ACTION & VISUALIZATION

Men, respect your God-given role in your marriage.

A WORD TO WIVES

God created the world to have order and structure. Unfortunately, mankind has brought chaos to that order. If you are married, you decided to join together with a man to drive down the highway of life. There's only one steering wheel in the car. You can strive for relational equality, but in the *end*, when a turn has to be made, to avoid disaster, only *one* person can drive. God has clearly designed and designated this position for man. Considering the differences between men and women, this makes sense, doesn't it?

Because of your design, being so strongly connected to your senses, it is important that you do not let them sway you from spiritual realities as happened with Eve.

✠ *Then the Lord God said to the woman, "What is this you have done?" The woman said, "The serpent **deceived** me, and I ate"* (Genesis 3:13).

✠ *But I am afraid that just as Eve was **deceived** by the serpent's cunning, your minds may somehow be led astray from your sincere and pure devotion to Christ* (2 Corinthians 11:3).

In some ways, because of your design, you have the tougher road to go in holding your spiritual ground. Knowing this, God holds men more responsible for their actions than He does women. Even though the Bible says that the woman sinned *first*, God held the man *responsible* for *headship*—it was actually *not* her sin but *his* sin that brought sin into the world. The woman was *deceived*, but the man *disobeyed* God.

✠ *...Sin entered the world through one **man**, and death through sin, and in this way death came to all men, because all sinned* (Romans 5:12).

It is, therefore, important that you do not allow yourself to be deceived about what your real priorities are in life and marriage. Outer beauty and worldly pursuits should not be your primary goal; your spiritual development and obedience to God should be.

✠ *Your beauty should not come from **outward** adornment, such as braided hair and the wearing of gold jewelry and fine clothes. Instead, it should be that of your **inner** self, the unfading beauty of a gentle and quiet spirit, which is of great worth in God's sight. For this is the way the holy women of the past who put their hope in God used to make themselves **beautiful**. They were submissive to their own husbands, like Sarah, who obeyed Abraham and called him her master. You are daughters if you do what is right and do not give way to fear* (1 Peter 3:3-6).

If you are an unmarried woman, remember that your most attractive quality to Christian men will be your inner beauty that shines God's love out of you.

ACTION & VISUALIZATION

Women, respect your God-given role in marriage.

MARRY A BELIEVER

If you are not currently married, it is critical for you to only consider marrying another Christian. The Bible is clear on this:

✠ *Do **not** be yoked together with unbelievers. For what do righteousness and wickedness have in common? Or what fellowship can light have with darkness? What harmony is there between Christ and Belial?*

What does a believer have in common with an unbeliever? What agreement is there between the temple of God and idols? For we are the temple of the living God... (2 Corinthians 6:14-16).

It is particularly important for a woman to have a believing husband because of his spiritual leadership in their marriage (as noted in the previous section). His submission to Christ should be your main concern if you want to enjoy a lifelong and prosperous marriage. Indeed it is through your husband that you and your family will obtain your spiritual covering in the battles that you are sure to face in this fallen world. Men, you need to marry a strong Christian girl who shows God's image and likeness from the inside out so that she will be your glory.

✝ *A wife of noble character is her husband's crown...* (Proverbs 12:4).

However, for wives who already are married to an unbelieving husband, the Bible offers the following course of action:

✝ *Wives, in the same way be submissive to your husbands so that, if any of them do not believe the word, they may be won over without words by the behavior of their wives, when they see the purity and reverence of your lives* (1 Peter 3:1-2).

Staying the Course

Paul, who was not married, expressed his belief that those who did not get married could fully dedicate themselves to the Lord and His work. There is certainly great value in this truth. However, he also cautioned that, because of the weakness of the flesh to sexual sin, it is better in most cases to get married if you don't possess the God-given gift of celibacy. Due to our shared sexual weakness, Paul exhorts us to give our bodies exclusively to each other in marriage to eliminate the temptation for sexual or emotional satisfaction outside of this sacred union.

Now for the matters you wrote about: It is good for a man not to marry. But since there is so much immorality, each man should have his own wife, and each woman her own husband. The husband should fulfill his marital duty to his wife, and likewise the wife to her husband. The wife's body does not belong to her alone but **also to her husband**. *In the same way, the husband's body* [including his ears and mouth] *does not belong to him alone but* **also to his wife**. *Do not deprive each other except by mutual consent and for a time, so that you may devote yourselves to prayer. Then come together again so that satan will not tempt you* [with inappropriate emotional or sexual relations] *because of your lack of self-control. I say this as a concession, not as a command. I wish that all men were as I am. But each man has his own gift from God; one has this gift, another has that* (1 Corinthians 7:1-7).

Today, primarily because of so many women entering the work place, there is an epic shift in the way sexual infidelity is mutating before our very eyes. Traditionally for men, love is one thing and sex is …well, sex. Now, men as well as women are forming deep emotional attachments before they even slip into an extramarital bed together. It often happens as they work long hours together in the office. This kind of an affair, where emotional attachments are involved, is more likely to end in divorce, as it can bind two people together way beyond a sexual encounter.[4] You need to be alert and careful in setting boundaries where you have extensive interaction with the opposite sex whether it's at work, church, or any other setting. Be wise about the sharing of intimate things meant strictly for your spouse.

Most affairs begin as seemingly honest, innocent conversations between two people that grow into inappropriate emotional attachments.

Paul in his discourse on marriage goes on to give other relevant advice on the subject.

✠ *Now to the unmarried and the widows I say: It is good for them to stay unmarried, as I am. But if they cannot control themselves, they should marry, for it is better to marry than to burn with passion. To the married I give this command (not I, but the Lord): A wife must not separate from her husband. But if she does, she must remain unmarried or else be reconciled to her husband. And a husband must not divorce his wife. To the rest I say this (I, not the Lord): If any brother has a wife who is not a believer and she is willing to live with him, he must not divorce her. And if a woman has a husband who is not a believer and he is willing to live with her, she must not divorce him. For the unbelieving husband has been sanctified through his wife, and the unbelieving wife has been sanctified through her believing husband. Otherwise your children would be unclean, but as it is, they are holy. But if the unbeliever leaves, let him do so. A believing man or woman is not bound in such circumstances; God has called us to live in peace. How do you know, wife, whether you will save your husband? Or, how do you know, husband, whether you will save your wife? Nevertheless, each one should retain the place in life that the Lord assigned to him and to which God has called him. This is the rule I lay down in all the churches* (1 Corinthians 7:8-17).

MARRIAGE'S ULTIMATE PURPOSE

We learned that marriage can benefit and bless us in many ways. But is marriage just about our comfort and happiness in this world, or is it about something greater? Does it have an eternal purpose?

Adam and Eve related to God in tandem, and in His image and likeness they exuded God's love into the world. Then came The Fall. Man and woman became full of sin and their perspectives were distorted by sin. Their focus became more on self—not on God, not on others. Marriage, from that point forward, would become difficult (at times) for men and women. However, God embedded an opportunity in those difficulties.

Remember, within every wrong path that we choose to walk, God has embedded signs that point us back to Him. Marriage, though we have distorted it with sin, has the call of God embedded within its very nature. It reflects our intended relationship with Him—one of ultimate love, trust, and sacrifice—a holy union of two into one.

Because you are a fallen person, married to a fallen spouse, marriage will at some point challenge your character in a profound way. My wife and I can certainly attest to this. Becoming successful at marriage requires you to become Christ-like—to become forgiving, selfless, and serving (as she has learned and I am learning to be). You will face moments of "sink or swim" as you develop and strengthen your character through the exercise of marriage. It is a *molding* and *shaping* experience *if* you seek to do it as God instructs. The intensity of a close relationship 24/7 will exercise your *faith* and *heart* because *selflessness* is a requirement for a healthy marriage relationship.

Our problem is that we have a selfish approach to marriage—we want to know what we can get out of it. God meant marriage to be a place where we practice our relationship with Him. We need not worry about our needs getting met, but must focus instead on satisfying our spouse's needs (sowing seeds). Then and only then will we reap satisfaction in some very surprising ways. Marriage gives us real opportunity to practice subjecting our will to another's. Throughout Scripture, our relationship with Christ is compared to a marriage, and earthly marriage is one main way that we make ourselves ready for our ultimate marriage with Him.

✟ *...For the wedding of the Lamb has come, and His bride* [you and me] *has made herself ready* (Revelation 19:7).

A healthy earthly marriage will help prepare you for an eternal wedding, an everlasting union.

Most believers miss the eternal and spiritual benefits of marriage—the enhancing of their relationship with God while they are molded into a better person. Instead, most are merely seeking happiness or romance. We already know from Book One that happiness can't be maintained in this world because it is temporal. Likewise, our spouses will eventually make us unhappy. This then puts too much weight on something temporal and will leave us susceptible to wanting a new spouse when the happiness in the current relationship can't be maintained. If we are basing our marriage solely on happiness, then our marriage is doomed to fail.

And how about romance? How many times have we heard "there's no romance left in our marriage"? What are they saying? What exactly is romance?

The tricky thing about romance is that it's subjective; it means different things to different people. Our definitions of romance also tend to *change* as we grow. You will have problems in your marriage if it's based on movie-theater romance. Don't blame your lack of romance on your marriage partner (which is what the world does). Instead, if you want more romance in your marriage, plant seeds of romance. *Sow it!* The beautiful part of this concept is that you can sow the exact type of romance that you desire. Just like sowing anything else, it may take some time for those seeds to grow, and you may suffer crop failure at times. But if you don't lose heart and if you keep on sowing, you will eventually harvest what you sow. If you want romance in your marriage, it is *your* responsibility to create it.

Another problem with basing a marriage on romance is that, like happiness, it is only temporal. Some people attach that fluttering feeling of infatuation to romance. I have heard people suggest that this is the feeling of love that God gives us. In my case, I felt that toward more than one woman before I was married. Does that mean that God wanted me to have more than one wife? Of course not. Indeed, I think we all have experienced, at some time, even after we were married, that same fleeting feeling toward someone else. Does that mean that God wanted us to get a divorce and marry another person? Of course not:

✠ *"I hate divorce," says the Lord God of Israel...* (Malachi 2:16).

So what is that feeling that we get sometimes? In my case, this has happened less and less as my marriage has matured and as I've grown closer to God. Perhaps it is simply a warning system. Much like when you start moving your hand close to a fire and it starts getting warm, signaling you to be cautious about your approach. I am not saying that this feeling is always a warning away from someone at the first signs of attraction. What I am saying is that, because there is a natural attraction to this particular person, which could lead to desire, God has provided a warning system for you.

If you are single, approach carefully and be alert; don't let yourself fall into temptation. If you are married, stop and reverse course. If you live as if this concept is true, you will be better off. It is certainly true that such romantic feelings will not sustain a marriage. Just like fear, which can momentarily be an exciting feeling for those who like roller coasters or scary movies, trying to sustain these romantic feelings will be unsatisfying and ultimately impossible to sustain—a long-term healthy marriage requires much more.

The marriage relationship is built on love, not love that is a feeling, but that is a decision to serve the other—a decision to sow ourselves into the relationship with steadfast *perseverance* as we deal with the inevitable ups and downs of a shared life between two imperfect people.

✝ *Therefore encourage one another and build each other up...* (1 Thessalonians 5:11).

✝ *May the Lord direct your hearts into God's love and Christ's persever-ance* (2 Thessalonians 3:5).

To err is human, but to forgive is the nature of God; so a happy marriage is the union of two good forgivers operating in the Spirit of God. That Spirit also leads us into servanthood and putting the other first.

✝ *Doing nothing out of selfish ambition or vain conceit, but in humility consider others better than yourselves* [whether or not you think they are]. *Each of you should look not only to your own interests, but also to the interests of others. Your attitude should be the same as that of Christ Jesus* (Philippians 2:3-5).

What was the nature of Jesus? He had a servant's attitude, washing the feet of His disciples, including the one who would betray Him, Judas. Jesus died for us while we were still sinners so that He could have an eternal relationship with us. Your spouse is also a sinner, and you will have to die to yourself at times so that you can bring life to the relationship.

✝ *We always carry around in our body the death of Jesus, so that the life of Jesus may also be revealed in our body* (2 Corinthians 4:10).

This death to ourselves allows us to enter into and take possession of our Promised Land. Christians must be obedient and commit to their marriage vows, which are made before God, by acting selflessly in love. Indeed,

Jesus says that we are to love our enemies, so we are certainly to love our spouses too (see Matthew 5:44). No matter how wonderful your spouse is, he or she is still infected with sin, which will lead to selfish actions at times. This will stretch your ability to love—and that is a good thing.

ACTION & VISUALIZATION

Take every opportunity to approach your spouse in a selfless, serving way.

UNTIL DEATH DO YOU PART

God holds the marriage union between two believers as sacred. In times of trouble, remember that God does not want you to divorce and change to another spouse. Most likely, He wants you to *change yourself and trust in Him*; this puts your faith into action, and it will eventually change the spouse that you already have. It is through marriage that you, your spouse, and your children will find life and freedom to the fullest.

Satan brings chaos into our world and will try everything he can to tear you away from your marriage union through fleshly and emotional temptations, as well as through your pride. You must remain focused on giving yourself to your marriage wholeheartedly. Don't let the enemy distract or discourage you. For good reason, God sets a high goal for you to stand by:

✝ *Some Pharisees came and tested* [Jesus] *by asking, "Is it lawful for a man to divorce his wife?" "What did Moses command you?" He replied. They said, "Moses permitted a man to write a certificate of divorce and send her away." "It was because your hearts were hard that Moses wrote you this law," Jesus replied. "But at the beginning of creation God 'made them male and female.' 'For this reason a man will leave his father and mother and be united to his wife, and the two* *will become one flesh'. So they are no longer two, but one. Therefore what God has joined together, let man **not** separate." When they were in the house again, the disciples asked Jesus about this. He answered, "Anyone who divorces his wife and marries another woman commits adultery against her. And if she divorces her husband and marries another man, she commits adultery"* (Mark 10:2-12).

The sanctity of marriage is important to God. But what if you fail? This does not mean that you lose your eternal salvation. However, it does mean that you will not have the most abundant life possible while on earth. Holding onto your relationship may involve fighting in spiritual warfare and pulling down strongholds. It might mean swallowing your pride or seeing your faith tested beyond what you ever expected. If you are with an abusive spouse, healing may require time apart. A successful marriage will involve much prayer and trust in God. It will often involve offering forgiveness. And it will always require actions of faith to last until "death do you part."

I want to say here, though, that if you are divorced, you shouldn't lose heart. God may hate divorce, but He loves those who have been through divorce. He offers you forgiveness and hope.

Action & Visualization

Respect and honor your marriage.
Base it on obedience to God so that it will stand the unavoidable storms.

Marriage Benefits Your Children

God created the relationship of marriage not only for your benefit but also for the benefit of your children. God's plan was that children would have both a father and a mother through whom they would experience the attributes of God. Divorce, therefore, distorts children's perception of God. God holds both parents responsible for providing for, nurturing, training, and sculpting their children because it takes both parents to fully complete the job in the way that God intends. Statistics show us that a break up in a marriage causes a breakdown in the fulfillment of these God-given responsibilities. The results show that their children will not be as likely to fulfill their purpose. In fact a study shows that 75 percent of youth suicides are from homes where a parent has been absent.[5]

One study shows that children of divorce are *twice* as likely to drop out of school, *three* times as likely to have babies out of wedlock, *five* times more likely to be in poverty, and *twelve* times more apt to become incarcerated.[6]

Teach Your Children

Of course, there's more to good parenting than simply avoiding divorce. Listen to what the Word of God has to say about our responsibility as parents. The Bible says that training your children will produce a good result, even though it may not seem so at the time:

Train a child in the way he should go, and when he is old he will not turn from it (Proverbs 22:6).

A parent is responsible to know, believe, and execute God's Word. And parents must also teach God's Word to their children:

Fix these words of Mine in your hearts and minds; tie them as symbols on your hands and bind them on your foreheads. **Teach them to your children,** *talking about them when you sit at home and when you walk along the road, when you lie down and when you get up.*

Write them on the doorframes of your houses and on your gates, so that your days and the days of your children may be many in the land that the Lord swore to give your forefathers, as many as the days that the heavens are above the earth (Deuteronomy 11:18-21).

God promises that, if you know and live according to God's Word, your children will be blessed:

✚ *The righteous man leads a blameless life; blessed are his children after him* (Proverbs 20:7).

We are also told to teach our children about the blessings and miracles that God has done in our lives and in the lives of those who went before us:

✚ *Only be careful, and watch yourselves closely so that you do not forget the things your eyes have seen or let them slip from your heart as long as you live.* **Teach them to your children and to their children after them** (Deuteronomy 4:9).

✚ *In days to come, when your son asks you, "What does this mean?" say to him, "With a mighty hand the Lord brought us out of Egypt, out of the land of slavery. When Pharaoh stubbornly refused to let us go, the Lord killed every firstborn in Egypt, both man and animal. This is why I sacrifice to the Lord the first male offspring of every womb and redeem each of my firstborn sons." And it will be like a sign on your hand and a symbol on your forehead that the Lord brought us out of Egypt with His mighty hand* (Exodus 13:14-16).

ACTION & VISUALIZATION

Teach and train your children in the ways of God.

Discipline Your Children

We are also encouraged to discipline our children so that they will learn God's ways and choose to follow Him.

Do not withhold discipline from a child; if you punish him with the rod, he will not die. Punish him with the rod and save his soul from death (Proverbs 23:13-14).

Disciple your son, for in that there is hope; do not be a willing party to his death (Proverbs 19:18).

Folly is bound up in the heart of a child, but the rod of discipline will drive it far from him (Proverbs 22:15).

He who spares the rod hates his son, but he who loves him is careful to discipline him (Proverbs 13:24).

Discipline your son, and he will give you peace; he will bring delight to your soul (Proverbs 29:17).

To be effective, discipline *must* be applied in *love with peace, patience, kindness, goodness, faithfulness, gentleness, and self control*. Discipline applied in any other way can be damaging to your relationship with your child.

Action & Visualization

Only discipline your children in love.

Honor Your Parents

Finally, God wants us to respect our own parents (even as adults):

✠ *Listen, my son, to your father's instruction and do not forsake your mother's teaching. They will be a garland to grace your head and a chain to adorn your neck* (Proverbs 1:8-9).

✠ *A wise son brings joy to his father, but a foolish man despises his mother* (Proverbs 15:20).

Even if your parents were not good parents because of the sin and self-focus in their lives, you still can (and should) honor them and show God's love to them. The fifth commandment promises long life and blessings for those who honor their father and mother:

✠ *Honor your father and your mother, as the Lord your God has commanded you, so that you may live long and that it may go well with you in the land the Lord your God is giving you* (Deuteronomy 5:16).

To those without parents or who were forsaken by them, God offers this comforting promise:

✛ *...You* [God] *are the helper of the fatherless* (Psalm 10:14).

✛ *Though my father and mother forsake me, the Lord will receive me* (Psalm 27:10).

RELATIONSHIPS ARE PRIORITY

Establishing good relationships in life is your highest priority—your relationship with God being your highest. It's a given that each relationship will take time and effort on your part to properly maintain. This leads us to ask *how* we do this and everything else when 24 hours doesn't seem to be enough time in a day. Consider this story:

A teacher stood before his class one day with some items in a box on his desk. He began by picking out of the box a large glass mayonnaise jar, and he proceeded to fill it with golf balls. He then asked the students if the jar was full. They agreed that it was full.

The teacher then picked out of the box a container of pebbles and poured them into the jar. He shook the jar lightly. The pebbles rolled into the open areas between the golf balls. He then asked the students again if the jar was full. They agreed it was full.

The teacher next picked out of the box a bag of sand and poured it into the jar. Of course, the sand filled up everything else. He asked the students once more if the jar was full. At this point, perplexed, the students agreed.

The teacher reached one more time into the box and pulled out a bottle of wine and proceeded to empty it into the jar, effectively filing the empty spaces between the grains of sand. The students were amazed.

"Now," the teacher said "The jar represents your life and the golf balls all your important relationships with God, your spouse, your children, your family, your friends, and yourself (your physical, mental, and spiritual health). So if everything else in life was lost and these things remained, your life would still be full. The pebbles are the other things important to you, like your ministry, your job, and your favorite passions. The sand represents everything else in life—your possessions and everything else you do. If you put the sand or pebbles in the jar first, then there is no room for the golf balls. The same is true in life. If you spend all your time and energy on your ministry, your job, pastimes, etc, then you will never have time for the developing of the things most important to you—your *relationships*. You need to set your priorities in life from the beginning, filling your life with good relationships by paying attention to and dealing with the small things required to maintain and develop each one of those relationships."

A student then asked, "What does the wine represent?" The teacher responded, "The wine represents having Christ in everything you do so you can have joy in everything you do because you are doing it in the freedom of His Blood."

I wish I had understood this analogy early in my life. For once you fill up your jar with the wrong things, you will find life very unsatisfying—nothing fits. You will also find it more difficult to change the contents of your life once it is already full. Of course, the part of your life that has gone by and the opportunities it represents can never be brought back, so start now to set your priorities straight.

God offers us both freedom and blessings in earthly relationships if we receive, unwrap, and use them the way that God intended. The Gift of Relationship is worth the time, effort, and energy that relationships take to nurture and grow. So unwrap this special gift and invest your life in those whom God has placed into your story.

ACTION & VISUALIZATION

Take full advantage of the relational gifts that God offers you.

✠ *It was just before the Passover Feast. Jesus knew the time had come for Him to leave this world and go to the Father. Having loved His own who were in the world, He now showed them the **full extent** of His love (John 13:1).*

Go out and show the full extent of your love to the people that God gives you, just as Jesus did.

MEDITATION POINT

God offers and encourages us to lean on healthy relationships
in the midst of a struggle.

If you are married or planning to get married, I recommend further reading on this subject. Here are a few books to consider: *Sacred Marriage*, by Gary Thomas; *Making Love Last Forever*, by Gary Smalley; *The Five Love Languages: How to Express Heartfelt Commitment to Your Mate*, by Gary Chapman; *Every Man's Marriage: An Every Man's Guide to Winning the Heart of a Woman*, by Stephen Arterburn, Mike Yorkey, and Fred Stoeker; and *The Act of Marriage*, by Tim and Beverly LaHaye.

Go to Chapter 5 in the Study Guide section on page 325.

ENDNOTES

1. *Consumer Expenditure Survey* (U.S. Department of Labor conducted 1990-92 updated to 2001 dollars using the Consumer Price Index) www.moneycentral.msn.com/articles/ family/kids/tlkidscost.asp.

2. Hara Estroff Marano, "The New Sex Score Card," *Psychology Today*. (July/August 2003).

3. Ibid.

4. Ibid.

5. Jean Beth Eshtain, "Family Matters: The Plight of America's Children," *The Christian Century* (July 1993), 14-21.

6. Judith Wallerstein, Julia Lewis, Sandra Blakesley, *The Unexpected Legacy of Divorce: A 25 Year Landmark Study* (New York, NY: Hyperion, 2000).

Chapter 6

GIFT #11—YOUR DESTINY

HOW DO YOU FIND YOUR DESTINY?

Before you begin to read, pray that the Holy Spirit will give you and all readers of this book understanding and application.

✝ *My frame was not hidden from You* [God] *when I was made in the secret place. When I was woven together in the depths of the earth, Your eyes saw my unformed body. All the days ordained for me were written in Your book before one of them came to be* (Psalm 139:15-16).

✝ *So will it be with the resurrection of the dead. The body that is sown is perishable* [our current bodies], *it is raised imperishable* [our new heavenly bodies]; *it is sown in dishonor, it is raised in glory; it is sown in weakness, it is raised in power; it is sown a natural body, it is raised a spiritual body...* (1 Corinthians 15:42-44).

If you've ever traveled around Christmas season, you know how challenging a trip to the airport can be. There's the drive to the terminal, the hunt for a parking spot, long lines at check-in, luggage to cart around, airport security, crying babies, disgruntled passengers, and lots and lots of waiting. Of course, that's if everything goes smoothly. So why do we put ourselves through such torture year after year? We endure this hardship because there's something on the other side of the chaos, the discomfort, the challenges, and the long lines. We've planned and prepared to reach a goal, a destiny—typically, it's a Christmas reunion with family and loved ones.

Our pursuit of our earthly destiny as followers of Christ is similar. However, many believers are content to sit at home for the holidays— they're content to make a phone call or send an e-mail. But if they don't make that flight, they'll miss the wonder and fulfillment of face-to-face communication! They'll miss the joy that is on the other side of this important journey. This chapter is for those who truly want to take flight.

Webster's New World Dictionary defines destiny as "the seemingly inevitable succession of events or [one's] fate." The question many of us wonder about is, who decides our destiny: God, us, or chance? This is the question we will explore in this chapter.

TWO DESTINIES

God offers us two destinies that we can receive, unwrap, and use. The first verse above speaks to your *earthly* destiny and the second to your *eternal* destiny.

Our eternal spiritual destiny is received and unwrapped when we accept the gift of eternal life. However, the full experience of our eternal spiritual destiny will not be realized until Jesus' return—we'll explore this further in the next chapter. The other destiny that God offers is the one we have in this world of chances, where "in the beginning" man's decision to put his will above God's opened a Pandora's Box. Once opened, this box released sin, which goes against the will of God—resulting in an infected world:

The creation waits in eager expectation for the sons of God [born again believers] *to be revealed. For the creation was subjected to frustration, not by its own choice, but by the will of the one who subjected it* [God]*, in hope that the creation itself will be liberated from its bondage to decay and brought into the glorious freedom of the children of God. We know that the whole creation has been* **groaning** *as in the pains of childbirth right up to the present time. Not only so, but we ourselves, who have the firstfruits of the Spirit, groan inwardly as we wait eagerly for the adoption as sons, the redemption of our bodies* (Romans 8:19-23).

While we await the full manifestation of this eternal destiny, God offers each of us a unique and specific destiny on earth. Jesus had a destiny that He could embrace or reject when He came to earth, and likewise, we each have a unique destiny for which God made us—we too can embrace or reject it.

Listen to Me [Jesus said prophetically through Isaiah]*, you islands; hear this, you distant nations: Before I was born the Lord called Me; from My birth He has made mention of My name. He made My mouth like a sharpened sword, in the shadow of His hand He hid Me; He made Me into a polished arrow and concealed Me in His quiver* (Isaiah 49:1-2).

Jesus knew His destiny on earth and has offered His followers a life with purpose too. Have you ever considered God's destiny for your life? What plans has He laid out for you individually? You too were designed to be a sharp arrow in God's quiver crafted by Him for a specific purpose; however, you can choose to be used or not. Truth is, God has embedded within you what you will need to complete that destiny with Him; you can't achieve your destiny alone. From this day forward, you will be faced with a choice: will you choose to live out your destiny or deny it.

YOUR DESTINY ON EARTH

Receiving, unwrapping, and using the gift of your earthly destiny is a lifelong process. I believe this gift is what all the other gifts work toward. They all work in conjunction with each other to free or enable you to fulfill your God-given destiny. Without receiving, unwrapping, and using the other gifts, you cannot fully unwrap and use your Gift of Destiny.

You can choose to follow God's will, as Jesus did, or you can be distracted by the desires of your flesh or pride. If you chose the latter, you will be on your own in a world of chance. You will be left to your own devices, and you will miss out on God's *perfect power* and *plan*. If you only opened the Gift of Life—salvation—and not the Gift of Destiny, God will still be in you, but you won't know the fullness or abundance of the earthly life that He offers those who die to self and follow His will. It is in this abundant life (the manifestation of your earthly destiny) that you will find *true fulfillment*, regardless of the circumstances you encounter.

The apostle Paul and others in the Bible spoke about this sort of life— when you give yourself over to God's plan, your life becomes inevitable. Hear what the Bible says to this end:

✠ *For we are God's workmanship, created in Christ Jesus to good works, which God prepared in advance for us to do* (Ephesians 2:10).

✠ *...He who began a good work in you will carry it on to completion until the day of Christ Jesus* (Philippians 1:6).

✠ *Many are the plans in a man's heart, but it is the Lord's purpose that prevails* (Proverbs 19:21).

✠ *The Lord will fulfill His purpose for me; your love, O Lord, endures forever—do not abandon the works of Your hands* (Psalm 138:8).

✠ *This is what the Lord says—He who made you, who formed you in the womb, and who will help you: Do not be afraid, O Jacob, my servant, Jeshurun, whom I have chosen* (Isaiah 44:2).

✠ *I know that You* [God] *can do all things; no plan of Yours can be thwarted* (Job 42:2).

✠ *He* [God] *will not let your foot slip—He who watches over you will not slumber* (Psalm 121:3).

✠ *I cry out to God Most High, to God, who fulfills His purpose for me. He sends from heaven and saves me, rebuking those who hotly pursue me; Selah. God sends His love and His faithfulness* (Psalm 57:2-3).

✠ *In his heart a man plans his course, but the Lord determines his steps* (Proverbs 16:9).

✟ *A man's steps are directed by the Lord. How then can anyone understand his own way* (Proverbs 20:24).

For those who decide to answer God's call, Paul raises an important question to which we need to know the correct answer:

✟ *And those He [God] predestined, He also called; those He called, He also justified; those He justified, He also glorified. What, then, shall we say in response to this? If God is for us, who can be against us?* (Romans 8:30-31)

ACTION & VISUALIZATION
Have faith that God can deliver to you the destiny He offers you.

GO WITH THE FLOW

Your earthly life is like a river, and your destiny or destination in life should be to follow that river to its end. At the center of the river, the water flows at a faster pace, and as you move to the sides, the water flows slower and slower. You can try to fight the currents and swim upstream, but this will only tire you out, and you will have little fulfillment to show for much effort. Or you can choose to swim through your life downstream, either in the middle where the current is strong, or by the bank where it's weaker.

If you choose the sides of the river, you may have some semblance of control in your progress and direction, but if you choose to find the center of God's will—your earthly destiny—then He will take you for an unbelievable ride in His power. This ride in the strongest currents won't be easy, and it will be scary at times, especially when you face challenges that bounce you around on the rapids; however, it will be the most exhilarating and fulfilling life possible. God desires for us to choose the strongest current and then, letting go, to give our direction over to Him so that we can experience the excitement of the life He desires for us.

When you do this, you will know deep inside the progress that you are making toward your destiny, even in adversity and trials. Living out your destiny is God's will for your life—at the center of the river of life.

As you find the strong current, you will know more and more that God is working in and through you in a progressive way. Our lives can be powered in supernatural ways by the strongest current—destiny. You must be a consummate seeker, always searching for the center, because it is so easy to slip into idle habits or to succumb to fears, fleshly desires, and the demands of life that take you back to the sides of the river. You must consciously reprogram your thinking and actions. Once your earthly destiny is offered to you, it will take your persistent faith to fully manifest it. So if you always seek God's will for your life and continue to receive, unwrap, and use all of the Gifts of Freedom, then you will find your way to the center of the river.

TRUE FULFILLMENT

Once you set out on God's journey, He will be there to encourage you when you run into troubles. As you know, the apostle Paul had a challenging destiny to fulfill, but He came to understand His purpose and kept the end in sight:

Do you not know that in a race all the runners run, but only one gets the prize? Run in such a way as to get the prize. Everyone who competes in the games goes into strict training, they do it to get a crown that will not last; but we do it to get a crown that will last forever.

Therefore I do not run like a man running aimlessly; I do not fight like a man beating the air. No, I beat my body and make it my slave so that after I have preached to others, I myself will not be disqualified for the prize (1 Corinthians 9:24-27).

✠ *Therefore, since we are surrounded by such a great cloud of witnesses* [on earth and in the spirit realm], *let us throw off everything that hinders and the sin that so easily entangles, and let us run with perseverance the race **marked out for us*** [the destiny God offers us]. *Let us fix our eyes on Jesus, the author and perfecter of our faith, who for the joy set before Him endured the cross, scorning its shame, and sat down at the right hand of the throne of God. Consider Him who endured such opposition from sinful man, so that you will not grow weary and lose heart. In your struggle against sin, you have not yet resisted to the point of shedding your blood* (Hebrews 12:1-4).

Paul goes on to say that we should see the hardships that we encounter in life as a necessary part of moving us from where we are into our destiny. He then directs us to find God's path to avoid danger and to receive healing instead:

✠ *Therefore, strengthen your feeble arms and weak knees. "Make level paths for your feet," so that the lame may not be disabled, but rather healed* (Hebrews 12:12-13).

Look at how he concludes, exhorting us to have confidence in our final, eternal destination:

✠ *You have come to Mount Zion, to the heavenly Jerusalem, the city of the living God. You have come to thousands upon thousands of angels in joyful assembly, to the church of the firstborn* [Jesus], *whose names are written in heaven. You have come to God, the judge of all men, to the spirits of righteous men made perfect, to Jesus the mediator* [between us and God] *of a new covenant, and to the sprinkled blood* [of Jesus] *that speaks a better word than the blood of Abel.... If they did not escape when they refused Him who warned them on earth, how much less will we, if we turn away from Him who warns us from heaven? At that time His voice shook the earth,* [in the day of Moses] *but now He has promised, "Once more I will shake not only the earth but also the heavens." The words "once more" indicate the removing of what can be shaken—that is, created things—so that what cannot be shaken may remain* [our eventual home will only consist of eternal things]. *Therefore, since we are receiving a kingdom that cannot be shaken* [even while on earth, by obeying the Word, we build our house on the unshakable solid rock], *let us be thankful, and so worship God acceptably with reverence and awe, for our "God is a consuming fire"* (Hebrews 12:22-29).

Paul had an intimate relationship with God, so when Paul encountered situations that appeared to be setbacks in his life, his intimate relationship with God was vital and encouraging.

✝ *Last night an angel of the God whose I am and whom I serve stood beside me and said, "Do not be afraid, Paul. You must stand trial before Caesar; and God has graciously given you the lives of all who sail with you"* (Acts 27:23-24).

As I've already mentioned, Paul had many ups and downs in his life; he had bouts with satan and his flesh that he didn't always win. But in his second letter to Timothy, Paul wrote about the satisfaction and fulfillment that he had in living out his story as God had written it:

✠ *For I am already being poured out like a drink offering, and the time has come for my departure* [physical death]. *I have fought the good fight, I have finished the race, I have kept the faith. Now there is in store for me the crown of righteousness, which the Lord, the righteous Judge, will award to me on that day—and not only to me, but also to all who have longed for His appearing* (2 Timothy 4:6-8).

Paul was an ordinary human with all the frailties that you and I experience. Yet he still encourages us through the trials of life to keep our eyes fixed on our Author and Finisher, *not* on our present circumstances. Clearly, we should not count on our own strength or brilliance to win this race:

✠ *...The race is not to the swift or the battle to the strong, nor does food come to the wise or wealth to the brilliant or favor to the learned; but time and chance happen to them all* (Ecclesiastes 9:11).

Action & Visualization

Despite trying circumstances, let God be in control of fulfilling your destiny.

Keep the End in Sight

Our success at living out God's will is dependent on our faith, and specifically, on our ability to exercise it to the maximum while keeping our earthly and eternal destinies in sight. If you wore a blindfold and were told to walk in a long, straight line to a location far away, you'd probably end up walking in circles because you are imperfect. One of your legs is stronger than the other, and that would cause you, over time, to stray from walking that straight line. To get to our destination, we need to keep our destiny locked in sight, always pressing on toward our goal and making adjustments when our weaknesses try to pull us off course.

✠ *...he who guards his way guards his life* (Proverbs 16:17).

So what if we lose our focus? The problems and pleasures of our earthly life will turn us every which way until we are completely lost. Pride will also turn us away from God's destiny.

✠ *We all, like sheep, have gone astray, each of us has turned to his own way...* (Isaiah 53:6).

✠ *The one who received the seed that fell among the thorns is the man who hears the word, but the worries of this life and the deceitfulness of wealth choke it, making it unfruitful* (Matthew 13:22).

✠ *For everything in the world—the cravings of sinful man, the lust of his eyes and the boasting of what he has and does—comes not from the Father but from the world* (1 John 2:16).

✠ *Pride goes before distruction* [of your life and destiny]...(Proverbs 16:18).

When you are experiencing the same thing over and over in life, it's time to consider whether you're moving in circles rather than truly moving toward your destiny. Taking our eyes off God leads us to a self-focused life that lacks purpose and direction. We should not confuse what we believe our destiny should be with what God says it is to be. Of course, knowing the difference isn't always easy. How do we know with certainty that we're hearing Him correctly? How do we find the powerful current that He created at the center of the river—at the center of His will?

ACTION & VISUALIZATION

Keep your destiny in sight so that you don't drift off course or make unnecessary circles.

FINDING THE PATH

God Himself unfolds His will for us, but it is our job to continually seek that developing path.

☩ *This is what the Lord says: "Stand at the crossroads and **look**; **ask** for the ancient paths, **ask where the good way is**, and walk in it...* (Jeremiah 6:16).

Like the psalmist you must ask for and seek out God's assistance to keep your focus.

☩ *Turn my eyes away from worthless things; preserve my life according to your word* (Psalms 119:37).

Your growing relationship with Him is the context in which He begins to unfold your destiny.

✠ *Whether you turn to the right or to the left, your ears will hear a voice behind you saying, "This is the way; walk in it"* (Isaiah 30:21).

✠ *But eagerly desire the **greater gifts**. And now I will show you the most excellent way* (1 Corinthians 12:31).

It's all about God in you and you in Him, as well as receiving, unwrapping, and using all the Gifts of Freedom to find growth in your relationship and communication with Him—allowing you to receive and manifest your God-given destiny directly from Him.

✠ *You [God] have made known to me the path of life...* (Psalms 16:11).

✠ *As for God, His way is perfect...* (2 Samuel 22:31)

For many years, I was stuck on the bank of the river. I was not only spiritually dead, I was headed recklessly for physical death. I had an addiction to alcohol, to many different drugs, to the earthly pleasures of life, and to extreme living. Even in high school, my friends had a running bet that I wouldn't live to see my 21st birthday. So when I turned 21, it only encouraged me to test fate with even harder living—it seemed that I could go beyond the edge.

However, God clearly had other plans. He held my destiny out for me when I was ready to receive, unwrap, and use it. As we have read, God has long-suffering patience, and this was certainly true in how He related to me. He waited for me to get into the river. I did not live for God for the first 36 years of my life. Indeed, I was involved in a widerange of sin, including murder, the murder of my unborn child. Yes, God was patient with me as He watched me choose to waste away day after day. Even as a father and husband, I did not deserve or qualify to enter the river in any way. (None of us qualify, by the way. This is what God's grace is all about.)

How then did I get into the river? One day I simply decided to seek God. I said *yes* to a relationship with Him. That day in church, God became real to me. I did not know how or why God did it that morning—I can only describe my experience as supernatural. My life had radically changed—I was now in the river.

✝ [Jesus said,] *"**On that day you will realize** that I am in My Father, and you are in Me, and I am in you"* (John 14:20).

But even though I was in the river and my heart had changed, I still had *my mind* dwelling on the places that *I* wanted to go. I still had *my* pride and *my* old selfish habits. I thought, "Surely now that I'm a Christian, Jesus will help me accomplish *my* goals and dreams in life." I didn't understand that God does not fill you with His power to help you accomplish *your* goals in life, but to fulfill *His* goals.

So for years after I was saved, I tried swimming upstream! As you can imagine, I eventually grew tired. However, as I tired, I eventually started receiving, unwrapping, and using the additional Gifts of Freedom. These gifts brought me into a closer relationship with God. This close relationship enabled intimacy with God—communication with Him in my daily life that led to a better understanding of His power, His will, and what it looked like to live out my God-given destiny.

I eventually stopped swimming upstream and started letting His current carry me. Initially, I stayed close to the riverbank so that I could keep some control. (It's hard to let go of control when you're used to being "in control.") Little by little, I learned how to swim out into the current for a while. I continued growing closer to God. I started trusting and surrendering to God my work, my family, my finances, my relationships, and my future. Consequently, I moved closer to the center of the river where the rapids were faster and more powerful.

Now it's important to note that as I was getting closer to the center of the river, it became harder for me to accomplish *my* goals because the current often took me in another direction. At the same time, though, God was putting new desires in my heart. I began to realize that I just needed to let go of *my goals* and find His will. I needed to relax and start *going with the flow—His flow.*

When I did, life started falling into place. In some ways, it became easier, but *not* any less scary. In fact, the ride started getting more thrilling and exciting because I had to navigate by faith and *not* by my sight. New unfamiliar obstacles and challenges were coming at me faster and faster all the time. The stakes became higher and higher so now, clearly, I had a lot to talk to God about in the midst of all the excitement and obstacles that came my way.

I learned that, as I got closer to the center of God's will, I could only navigate by letting go. Also the further from the center I was, the harder it was to see my destiny; however, as I found the center of the river, it was easier to see further down the river to my earthly goal. I became better at navigating down the center of the river. It was all about receiving, unwrapping, and using the Gifts of Freedom. As I became more successful at this, I began moving at full force—centered within God's will.

ACTION & VISUALIZATION

Receive, unwrap, and use the Gifts of Freedom while seeking your earthly destiny. Think about how you will use each gift to find your earthly destiny.

Expect the Unexpected

Then out of nowhere came this book series. The idea of writing a book never even crossed my mind. I wasn't a qualified writer. If you talked to people who know me, they'd tell you that I'm not a writer. Could I write an entire series of books? "Highly unlikely," "impossible," they might say. It is not something I dreamed of doing or something I had the knowledge or ability to do. I am actually a very poor writer. In fact, in my business, I prefer to communicate by E-mail whenever I can (and when I do write letters, I have my assistant or administrator draft or at least edit them).

When I began, I didn't have the spiritual insight or knowledge to write. And yet, as I began writing the chapters, I was amazed at what my hand was putting on the page. The more I wrote, the more the books took shape, the more inevitable they became, and the closer I came to God. I was *receiving* His Gift of Destiny in the very work of writing this book.

I became a consistent seeker of God and constant finder of God as I walked and worked out my story. When I first began writing the books, I was far from perfect, but I was a seeker—I had a heart for God. I thought that's why God had given me these books. When I arrived at this chapter, it became clear that my consummate seeking had helped me *find* my destiny—the center of the river.

However, it was also clear that the privilege of writing these books was *not* something that I earned or deserved as a result of my seeking; it was simply my destiny—God's choice, and only He knows the reason. *A gift!* Indeed a *surprise* gift that I found in the center of my river. There will certainly be a *surprise* for you too when you find the center of your river—indeed, God's gift of your destiny will have *many* surprises in it.

The greatest joy that God offers us through His gifts is that they keep on giving. For example, these books hold a battle plan that I can continue to strive toward and conform my life to. Let me be clear: I may have written this book, but I am *not* fully living it in all areas of my life. I can tell you, living out what I have written is a far greater task than writing it. Though when I let go and relax in quiet and stillness before God, He helps me conform. God will help you conform too. Remember, life is a journey—you don't automatically get to your destination just because you decide to go somewhere. It takes a persistent pursuit in faith to be successful.

GETTING ON AND LETTING GO

Getting on the road toward your destiny is not easy because it takes faith. Remember it is by the Spirit that we receive the gifts, and it is by faith that we unwrap and use all of them. The same is true with your gift of earthly destiny—you receive God's will by the Spirit of God and unwrap it with your faith. In order to go on an earthly trip to the Grand Canyon, you would need to use your faith to plan, pack, check the car, etc. Once you are on the road, you will run into challenges that your faith can help you overcome. In the pursuit of your earthly destiny, you'll find that the devil may even challenge you. Only your *intimate relationship* with God will allow you to resist the enemy's attempt to pull you off the path to your destiny:

✟ *With flattery he* [the enemy] *will corrupt those who have violated the covenant, but the people who* **know** *their God will firmly* **resist** *him* (Daniel 11:32).

The world will also try to lead you off your road. Again, your *intimate relationship* with God and your ability to allow the Holy Spirit to lead you down the right path are the keys to finding your destiny:

✟ *Enter through the narrow gate* [you start by doing something that may be difficult in the physical realm—walking in the Spirit]. *For wide is the gate and broad is the road that leads to destruction* [living life in the flesh and mind], *and many enter through it. But small is the gate and narrow the road that leads to life, and only a few find it* (Matthew 7:13-14).

On the right road to your destiny is also where you will find your abundant life:

✠ [Jesus said,] *"For My yoke is easy and My burden is light"* (Matthew 11:30).

✠ *Your* [God's] *paths drip with abundance* (Psalm 65:11 NKJV).

When you're living an abundant life, you will walk out the destiny that God offers you—one in which you will seek His will above all else. Your will must die to make room for His will in your life:

✠ *Foolish one, what you sow is not made alive unless it dies* (1 Corinthians 15:36 NKJV).

Jesus' Example

Just as we all have a very specific, God-offered destiny, Jesus had one as well—to come to earth as a man and die for our sins:

✠ *All that the Father gives Me will come to Me, and whoever comes to Me I will never drive away. For I have come down from heaven not to do My will but to do the will of Him who sent Me. And this is the will of Him who sent Me, that I shall lose none of all that He has given Me, but raise them up at the last day. For My Father's will is that everyone who looks to the Son and believes in Him shall have eternal life, and I will raise him up at the last day* (John 6:37-40).

Receiving your destiny requires a great action of faith. In Jesus' case, this act of faith was unto death. Walking out this brutal death was not easy for Jesus. He asked His Father three times if He could follow a different path to fulfill His destiny:

✠ [Jesus] *went away a second time and prayed, "My Father, if it is not possible for this cup to be taken away unless I drink it, may Your will be done." When He came back, He again found them sleeping, because their eyes were heavy. So He left them and went away once more and prayed the* **third** *time, saying the same thing* (Matthew 26:42-44).

There will be times when you too need to pray for strength to help you move forward to fulfill your destiny, times when you will ask Him if there is another way, another path. God will encourage and strengthen you just as He did His Son:

✠ *An angel from heaven appeared to Him* [Jesus] *and strengthened Him. And being in anguish, He prayed more earnestly, and His sweat was like drops of blood falling to the ground* (Luke 22:43-44).

Clearly Jesus was wrestling to let go of His will and to do God's will so that He could fulfill His destiny. At times you too will have to overcome the difficult task of letting go of your will. This may involve also letting go of multiple issues that are keeping you from freedom to fulfill your destiny.

Let me illustrate this with a story from nature. A certain type of monkey is so enamored with bananas that it will make a decision that puts its life in risk—refusing to let go. This allows its predators to *catch* and *kill* it in a most unique way.

In Africa, poachers will place a cage filled with bananas in the jungle—a cage with bars just wide enough for a monkey to slip its open hand in, but not wide enough for it to pull the banana out with a closed fist. The poachers know the monkey will forfeit its freedom just to clutch the precious bananas. With its fist wrapped around the fruit, the monkey cannot escape, and it becomes easy prey. The acrobatic monkey becomes stationary, a slave to its own desire, and it needlessly gives itself over to be captured or killed. Sounds foolish, doesn't it? Why give up your freedom needlessly? Yet, how often do we get ourselves into this same predicament? Can you see how this applies to our lives? When we hang onto things so tightly that they hold us in bondage, we're easy prey for our predator—*satan*. I've already mentioned some of these things—drugs, smoking, an expensive lifestyle, overworking, pride, stress, overeating, toxic friends or relationships, sexual habits, a stingy attitude…the list goes on and on. If we don't learn to let go of these things, we will be hindered from fulfilling our full destiny. Remember what Paul wrote:

"Everything is permissible for me"—but not everything is beneficial. "Everything is permissible for me"—but I will not be mastered by anything (1 Corinthians 6:12).

This can be very confusing for us at times. Just like bananas are good for monkeys, so too, what we are holding on to seems like a good thing. However, we need to be sensitive to the possibility that the thing we are holding on to, no matter how good it seems, could be creating another problem in our life or keeping us from reaching our destiny.

Refusing to let go of hindrances can cause us to fall short of our earthly destinies, but don't be misled: once we have the incorruptible seed of Jesus in us, our *eternal* destiny is assured.

ACTION & VISUALIZATION

Let go of the things that are hindering you.

AGAINST THE FLOW

You may find that your destiny leads you against the customs of your time (here is another example of a contradiction), but you still must say *yes* to destiny as Mary, the mother of Jesus, did when visited by an angel:

*The angel went to her and said, "Greetings, you who are highly favored! The Lord is with you." Mary was greatly **troubled** at his words and wondered what kind of greeting this might be (Luke 1:28-29).*

Yes it is possible that, when you receive God's call, you will initially be troubled by what you hear, but keep listening. Do not shut God's messenger off, whether it be the Holy Spirit within you, your circumstances, a prophet, an angel, or any other method that God uses.

But the angel said to her, "Do not be afraid, Mary, you have found favor with God. You will be with child and give birth to a son, and you are to give Him the name Jesus. He will be great and will be called the Son of the Most High. The Lord God will give Him the throne of His father David, and He will reign over the house of Jacob forever; His kingdom will never end." "How will this be," Mary asked the angel, "since I am a virgin?" The angel answered, "The Holy Spirit will come upon you, and the power of the Most High will overshadow you. So the Holy One to be born will be called the Son of God. Even Elizabeth your relative is going to have a child in her old age, and she who was said to be barren is in her sixth month. For nothing is impossible with God" (Luke 1:30-37).

What an incredible destiny God offered to Mary. Note that she does not respond by asking "why me?" or by questioning her worthiness.

✠ *"I am the Lord's servant," Mary answered, "May it be to me as you have said." Then the angel left her* (Luke 1:38).

The destiny that God offered Mary defied *physical logic*, and yours may as well. It presented Mary with a real dilemma—it was customary in her time for an unmarried, pregnant woman to be *stoned to death*. And yet, in the face of this grave possibility, Mary's answer to God was "I am the Lord's *servant*. May it be to me as you have said." Unwrapping the Gift of Destiny for Mary meant being a servant to God. Her destiny was to serve Him as the mother of His son. Your prescribed destiny is *no less* important to God—your role in His redemptive plan is equally as essential. I urge you to get this truth into your spirit, to live in confidence of your calling because that confidence will produce great joy and peace.

TAKE THE BALL AND RUN WITH IT

Look at the next line after Mary's response to God's messenger: "Then the angel *left* her." At some point, God will tell or show you a piece of your destiny, and then it is up to you to *take* the ball and *run* with it. The message has been given; now the messenger is *gone*; that is all that you may get for awhile. By *faith* and through your connection with God, you are expected to take the next steps.

Remember the verse that tells us not to worry about what to say or how to say it? Jesus tells us that, at the necessary time, we will know what to say, for it will not be us speaking, but the Spirit of our Father speaking through us. (See Luke 12:11.) Likewise when you are in the center of the river—in His will—then you will not have to speak in your own words or act in your own power. God will provide the words and the power. This *reliance* on God will further enhance your relationship with Him.

A LITTLE AT A TIME

Think for a minute about how little God initially told Mary about the destiny that He was offering her. He didn't tell her where to have the baby, how to deal with the impending persecution, how to raise the baby, what to teach the baby, where she would raise the baby, what her relationship would be with the baby, what the baby would do, and most importantly— what the future would bring for her and the baby.

Sometimes God may give you as little as *one word* and expect you to *run* with it. Remember the verse:

☩ *Your word is a lamp to my feet and a light for my path* (Psalm 119:105).

God is only lighting the immediate path before you, perhaps only the spot where your foot is to land next. It does not say that He uses a beacon or floodlight to light your journey. This "little-by-little" method serves God's purpose because the unwrapping process, which is continually unfolding in your life, keeps your faith vibrant. This creates a foundation for growing your relationship with Him—His reason for creating you.

Listening to the angel's simple message, Mary had no way of knowing how the circumstances would work out. And certainly she could not tell what it would mean to give birth to the Messiah. Her natural mind could not conceive of this. Yet when she received this word from God, she did not look at her circumstances, but kept her focus on God's *words*. Mary had faith that *nothing* was impossible with God, and she stayed focused on His promises.

Your destiny will start to unfold at some point. It may take time, or it may come quickly once you are saved. Every person is different and is on a specific, *unique path*, so avoid comparing yourself to other Christians and how their destinies unfold. And do not be jealous. Celebrate with others what they receive from God and where He sends them. Resenting or envying another's path and relationship with God will only lead you out of His will, as Jesus illustrated in this parable:

✠ *For the Kingdom of heaven is like a landowner [God] who went out early in the morning to hire men to work in his vineyard. He agreed to pay them a denarius for the day and sent them into his vineyard. About the third hour he went out and saw others standing in the marketplace doing nothing. He told them, "You also go and work in my vineyard, and I will pay you whatever is right." So they went. He went out again about the sixth hour and the ninth hour and did the same thing. About the eleventh hour he went out and found still others standing around. He asked them, "Why have you been standing here all day long doing nothing?" "Because no one has hired us," they answered. He said to them, "You also go and work in my vineyard." When evening came the owner of the vineyard said to his foreman, "Call the workers and pay them their wages beginning with the last ones hired, and going on to the first." The workers who were hired about the eleventh hour came and each received a denarius. So when those came who were hired first, they expected to receive more. But each one of them also received a denarius. When they received it, they* began to grumble against the landowner. "These men who were hired last worked only one hour," they said, "And you have made them equal to us who have borne the burden of the work and the heat of the day." But he answered one of them, "Friend, I am not being unfair to you. Didn't you agree to work for a denarius? Take your pay and go. I want to give the man who was hired last the same as you. Don't I have the right to do what I want with my own money? Or are you envious because I am generous?" (Matthew 20:1-15)

ACTION & VISUALIZATION

Take your instructions from God and start the process,
by faith, of unwrapping and living out your destiny.

UNUSUAL WAYS

Our destinies aren't all revealed in the same way. Take the apostle Paul's destiny, for example. It started unfolding quickly, wrapped up with his salvation, and arrived in a very dramatic fashion. In fact there is a term, "Damascus road experience," which refers to the beginning of Paul's conversion and his introduction to God's destiny for his life. At the time Paul was called Saul, and he was a vigilant, well-known persecutor of Christians. Here is the beginning of His spiritual journey, as recorded in Acts:

Meanwhile, Saul was still breathing out murderous threats against the Lord's disciples. He went to the high priest and asked him for letters to the synagogues in Damascus, so that if he found any there who belonged to the Way [the Church], whether men or women, he might take them as prisoners to Jerusalem. As he neared Damascus on his journey, suddenly a light from heaven flashed around him. He fell to the ground and heard a voice say to him, "Saul, Saul, why do you per-secute Me?" [Jesus said this in reference to His Body, the Church] *"Who are you, Lord?" Saul asked. "I am Jesus, whom you are perse-cuting," He replied. "Now get up and go into the city, and you will be told what you must do." The men traveling with Saul stood there speechless; they heard the sound but did not see anyone. Saul got up from the ground, but when he opened his eyes he could see nothing. So they led him by the hand into Damascus. For three days he was blind, and did not eat or drink anything* (Acts 9:1-9).

There are three things I would like to call to your attention in this passage. First, God did not initially give Saul (Paul) a vision of his entire destiny. Second, after Saul's initial contact with God, his sight was removed from him. It is not unusual for God to remove some physical aspect of our lives in order to enable us to see spiritually—making way for His Gift of Destiny.

Third, the men traveling with Saul (Paul) could not see what Saul saw. It was something personal between Saul and God. Saul (Paul) was having an individual experience. You too are a unique individual before God, and He will give you experiences specific to who you are. Let us continue with the account:

In Damascus there was a disciple named Ananias. The Lord called to him in a vision, "Ananias," "Yes, Lord," he answered. The Lord told him, "Go to the house of Judas on Straight Street and ask for a man from Tarsus named Saul, for he is praying. In a vision he has seen a man named Ananias come and place his hands on him to restore his sight." "Lord," Ananias answered, "I have heard many reports about this man and all the harm he has done to Your saints in Jerusalem. And he has come here with authority from the chief priest to arrest all who call on Your name" (Acts 9:10-14).

Ananias and Saul (Paul) each had a destiny that crossed paths with the other. In fact, the verse indicates that Saul (Paul) at this point already had a vision where he saw Ananias would restore his sight. Ananias was scared to follow through with his assigned destiny, and rightfully so. Remember, Saul (Paul) had a reputation as a violent, hostile man—especially toward Christians.

*But the Lord said to Ananias, "Go! This man is My **chosen instrument** to carry My name before the Gentiles and their kings and before the people of Israel. I will show him how much **he must suffer for My name**"* (Acts 9:15-16).

Before Saul (Paul) was saved, God told Ananias that He had a specific destiny in mind for Saul—one we know (through the biblical accounts) that he lived out as Paul. Even though at that exact moment Saul (Paul) was an enemy of the Church, still God said he was *destined* to become a messenger to facilitate growth in the Church. Perhaps you may have been an enemy of the Church, but that does not preclude or hinder you from receiving your destiny from God and doing great things for His Kingdom. Also note that God described for Ananias the unusual sufferings that Saul (Paul) would eventually experience. Likewise, God had spoken to Saul (Paul) about Ananias's prayer to restore his sight even before He spoke to Ananias. As the story continues, we see how Ananias is responsible for catching up with his future—that which Saul (Paul) had already seen in a vision. Here's how the story continues:

Then Ananias went to the house and entered it. Placing his hands on Saul, he said, "Brother Saul, the Lord—Jesus, who appeared to you on the road as you were coming here—has sent me so that you might see again and be filled with the Holy Spirit." Immediately, something like scales fell from Saul's eyes, and he could see again. He got up and was baptized, and after taking some food, he regained his strength (Acts 9:17-19).

You too will have to catch up to your future if God's will is going to be manifested through your life and into others.

Knowing Through Relationship

God did not give Saul (Paul) a detailed account of his destiny or specific instructions for how to unfold his destiny. God simply installed in Saul (Paul) His guidance system, the Holy Spirit. Through that relationship, Saul's (Paul's) destiny began to unfold:

*Saul spent several days with the disciples in Damascus. At once he began to preach in the synagogues that Jesus is the Son of God. All those who heard him were astonished and asked, "Isn't he the man who raised havoc in Jerusalem among those who call on this name? And hasn't he come here to take them as prisoners to the chief priests?" Yet Saul **grew** more and more powerful and baffled the Jews living in Damascus by proving that Jesus is the Christ (Acts 9:20-22).*

God started growing Saul (Paul) into his destiny right away. For several years though Saul (Paul) had to be discipled by others. God converted him from being an enemy of the Church to being one of the leading apostles of the Church—writing approximately *one-third* of the New Testament. Saul, who would soon change his name to Paul, received pieces of his destiny as he went through his journey. He learned where he would go, what he was supposed to do, and what would happen to him in different ways as he unwrapped and used his destiny.

These Scriptures all highlight times when Paul received further understanding of his destiny through his *relationship* with God:

✠ *While they* [the disciples] *were worshiping the Lord and fasting, the Holy Spirit said, "Set apart for me Barnabas and Saul for the work to which I have called them." So after they had fasted and prayed, they placed their hands on them, and sent them off. The two of them, **sent on their way by the Holy Spirit**, went...* (Acts 13:2-4).

✠ *Paul and his companions traveled throughout the region of Phrygia and Galatia, having been kept by the Holy Spirit from preaching the word in the province of Asia. When they came to the border of Mysia, they tried to enter Bithynia, but **the Spirit of Jesus would not allow them to*** (Acts 16:6-7).

✠ *After Paul had seen the vision, we got ready at once to leave for Macedonia, **concluding that God had called us to preach the gospel to them*** (Acts 16:10).

✠ *About midnight Paul and Silas were praying and singing hymns to God* [witnessing to the other prisoners, despite their troubles], *and the other prisoners were listening to them. Suddenly there was such a violent earthquake that the foundations of the prison were shaken. **At once all the prison doors flew open, and everybody's chains came loose*** (Acts 16:25-26).

✠ [While Paul was in Corinth, after a bad experience with an abusive crowd] ***One night the Lord spoke to Paul in a vision****: "Do not be afraid; keep on speaking, do not be silent. For I am with you, and no one is going to attack and harm you, because I have many people in this city." So Paul stayed for a year and a half, teaching them the word of God* (Acts 18:9-11).

✠ *And now, **compelled by the Spirit**, I am going to Jerusalem, not knowing what will happen to me there. I only know that in every city the Holy Spirit warns me that prison and hardships are facing me. However, I consider my life worth nothing to me, if only I may finish the race and complete the **destiny** the Lord has given me—the task of testifying to the gospel of God's grace* (Acts 20:22-24).

It is clear in Scripture that Paul received, unwrapped, and used the Gifts of Freedom. Paul ran his race and learned to be satisfied with receiving his instructions a step at a time from the Holy Spirit. May you also take hold of that kind of faith.

Action & Visualization

Live out your destiny, step-by-step, when God presents it to you that way.

Owning Your Destiny

The Gift of Destiny is the most fulfilling gift that you can receive here on earth. It is a unique gift that God has specially designed just for you, but it is meaningless unless you receive, unwrap, and use it. Remember that when you receive, unwrap, and use a gift from God, you are in turn giving God a gift as well. The Gift of Destiny is also the most fulfilling gift that you can give to God while you are still on earth because it fulfills His purpose for you as well as others. Even with God, your life will never reach perfection here on earth, but you can fulfill your destiny.

No matter who you are or how much faith you have, you will have times when you question your destiny. That is natural because you are human. John the Baptist illustrates this for us. Jesus said of him:

I tell you the truth: Among those born of women there has not risen anyone greater than John the Baptist... (Matthew 11:11).

John the Baptists' destiny was to be the voice announcing the coming Messiah to the world:

This is the one about whom it is written: "I [God] will send My messenger [John the Baptist] ahead of You [Jesus], who will prepare Your way before You" (Matthew 11:10).

This was John the Baptist's destiny from the beginning, and indeed, even from before his birth. Look what happened when Mary, who was pregnant with Jesus, visited John's mother, Elizabeth, while she was pregnant with him:

When Elizabeth heard Mary's greeting, the baby leaped in her womb, and Elizabeth was filled with the Holy Spirit. In a loud voice she exclaimed: "Blessed are you among women, and blessed is the child you will bear! But why am I so favored, that the mother of my Lord should come to me? As soon as the sound of your greeting reached my ears, the baby in my womb [John the Baptist] leaped for joy" (Luke 1:41-44).

So John the Baptist should never have had a question about whether he was fulfilling his destiny, right? Well, keep in mind, he was human just like you and me; when he found himself in a *prison*, he questioned whether he was fulfilling his destiny. Indeed he sent a messenger to Jesus, questioning Him:

When John heard in prison what Christ was doing, he sent his disciples to ask Him, "Are you the one who was to come, or should we expect someone else" (Matthew 11:2-3).

You may have times when it seems you've hit a lowly place and begin to question your destiny; nonetheless, you should never give up or lose faith. Remain persistent in your pursuit. Remember Joseph? God gave Joseph his destiny in a dream, telling him that his brothers would someday bow down to him. But first he was left in a hole, sold as a slave, wrongfully accused, and sent to jail. Through it all, Joseph never gave up, and indeed, all those unlikely, tragic, and painful events were required to put Joseph into a position to actually *receive* his destiny. They were all an integral part of his destiny.

Your circumstances may cause you to question your destiny, but regardless of what you encounter along the way, if you follow God's will, He will illuminate His specific, unique path for you to follow. Your destiny awaits…

MEDITATION POINT

Opening all the other Gifts will allow you to piece together the Destiny
your creator intended for you.

Go to Chapter 6 in the Study Guide section on page 333.

Chapter 7

THE GIFT—GOD OF THE TRINITY

WHAT WILL YOUR RELATIONSHIP ULTIMATELY BE WITH HIM?

Before you begin to read, pray that the Holy Spirit will give you and all readers of this book understanding and application.

✟ *The Lord had said to Abram, "Leave your country, your people and your father's household and go to the land I will show you. I will make you into a great nation and I will bless you; I will make your name great, and you will be a blessing. I will bless those who bless you, and whoever curses you I will curse; and all peoples on earth will be blessed through you* (Genesis 12:1-3).

✟ *Now we who have believed enter that rest...* (Hebrews 4:3).

L et me tell you a classic story about a poor married couple, Jim and Della. As Christmas approached, they began to think of gifts for each other—wonderful gifts that would accurately represent the depth of their love for one another. But they could barely afford rent and food, let alone expensive gifts! Jim wasn't content to show up giftless on Christmas morning, so he sold his most prized possession—a gold watch. Sadly, he had never worn the watch because the band was broken and it was too costly to repair. After selling the watch, he bought Della a most wonderful gift.

Unbeknownst to Jim, Della was also selling her most prized possession—her beautiful hair—in order to buy him a gift. They were both eager to give each other their gifts. On Christmas Eve, Della threw the door open, holding up her gift for Jim: a gold watch band. Jim stood there, stunned, motionless. Without a word, he slid a wooden box across the table to Della so that she could open his gift to her: a most elegant ivory hair comb. They had sold their most prized possessions to give each other seemingly unusable gifts.

Were Jim and Della fools? Some might say so. And some might also call us fools for giving up our lives—our most prized possessions—to follow Jesus Christ. However, what we get in return for our sacrifice is of infinite value—real love. When we surrender our lives, our most valuable possession, to God, He gives it back better. We find a new renewed life that has real *intimacy* with Him, real love, and real freedom—the kind of *life* that is only found when you are willing to give up everything.

The Ultimate Relationship with God Himself

Who is this God for whom we're to give up our lives? You have read about the three persons or personalities of God—the Father, the Son, and the Holy Spirit. We often think of them as three separate persons, yet the Bible repeatedly tells us there is clearly only *one* God.

☩ *So then, about eating food sacrificed to idols: We know that an idol is nothing at all in the world and that there is no God but **one**. For even if there are so-called gods, whether in heaven or on earth (as indeed there are many "gods" and many "lords"), yet for us there is but **one***

God, the Father, from whom all things came and for whom we live; and there is but one Lord, Jesus Christ, through whom all things came and through whom we live (1 Corinthians 8:4-6).

✠ *Make every effort to keep unity of the Spirit through the bond of peace. There is one body and one Spirit—just as you were called to one hope when you were called—one Lord, one faith, one baptism; one God and Father of all, who is over all and through all and in all* (Ephesians 4:3-6).

✠ *Hear, O Israel: The Lord our God, **the Lord is one**. Love the Lord your God with all your heart and with all your soul and with all your strength* (Deuteronomy 6:4-5).

Due to our bodies, which seem to separate us from all else in this physical world, it is difficult for us to fully understand the concept of the Trinity. We learn about them as separate individuals, but they are all part of our *one* God. The last verse may give us some clues on how we can understand God as three in one, specifically when it describes how we're to love Him: with all our heart and with all our soul and with all our strength—heart, soul, and strength. Couldn't Jesus be the heart of God, the Father, the soul or mind of God, the Holy Spirit, the strength (or accomplishing mechanism) of God all working in concert with one another and all yielding in perfect harmony to one another? Indeed, we have similar divisions within ourselves. We are called to love with our heart, mind, and strength, though in our life we have a general tendency to rely on our physical strength rather than spiritual strength. Remember what three things Peter had to offer Jesus to develop His relationship with God: mind, heart and hands.

Clearly, our understanding of the Trinity and their interworking relationship is limited, as well as our understanding of how the Trinity relates to us; however, I believe this process of discovery will make exploring the whole universe of knowledge and eternity exciting. Imagine the limitless,

☩ *One God and Father of all, who is over all and through all and **in** all* (Ephesians 4:6).

The fact that God is everywhere and in all things says that we will be able to experience everything through Him, that is through our intimate relationship with Him. And how do we achieve an intimate relationship with God? For most of us, intimacy with God is a journey. It is a process, a Spirit to spirit connection that happens between us and our Creator that opens up a new world for us. However, to fully experience it we must leave the old one behind.

For example, Abram (also known as Abraham) modeled this for us nearly 6,000 years ago. Abraham's journey with God was just like yours and mine. He had doubts, insecurities, and areas of disbelief, though when God spoke, he obeyed. In fact, God called Abraham to leave his country, family, friends, job and move to a foreign country—a promised land. What was the purpose of this move? Why would God call him to leave what *he loved* behind? Well, Abraham didn't know, he obeyed because of a promise God made him: pursue the Promised Land and you will be greatly blessed. Sound familiar?

Isn't our promised land to dwell in an intimate relationship with God and see His image and likeness in us? Isn't this the source of life's *greatest blessing*? However, just like Abraham, we will face resistance both from our own hang-ups as well as the world we live in. Like Abraham, it will cause you to leave the comfort and familiarity of your homeland—the habits, thoughts, and surroundings familiar to you to relocate somewhere different and unfamiliar. This is the journey of walking by faith toward intimacy with God.

The Gifts of Freedom are all about helping you to reach your Promised Land. Of course, you won't enter the fullness of the Promised Land until you are welcomed into the physical presence of God Himself in the Kingdom of Heaven. It is impossible at this point to fully imagine and comprehend eternity with Him, especially in our current state. In Heaven, God's image and likeness reign supreme—pure love! If we consider just how far we are from perfect love, we begin to realize just how far we are from that closeness and intimacy that God desires.

In Heaven, we will have complete intimacy with our Creator. An *infinite* God can meet and exceed every one of our individual expectations, not just daily or hourly but minute by minute. I truly believe it will blow our minds and surpass even our wildest dreams—no words or feelings we have on earth come close to describing it. In that place, His fullness will be on you and you will enjoy a face-to-face relationship with God, the fullness of the Trinity.

✠ *And I heard a loud voice from the throne saying, "Now the dwelling of God is with men and He will **live with them**. They will be His people, and **God Himself** will be with them and be their God* (Revelation 21:3).

At that time He will complete your transformation into His image and likeness as well as bring you into His perfect rest. But those two wonderful things are *not* just for Heaven. God Himself invites you to begin this incredible journey toward intimacy with *Him* now.

✠ *God, who has called you into fellowship with His Son Jesus Christ our Lord, is faithful* (1 Corinthians 1:9).

Where are you headed in your life? Where is your journey taking you today? As a believer, you are asked to set out for His Kingdom, beginning the journey of moving closer and closer to His image and likeness, toward intimacy with Him. As we *grow* in our spiritual relationship with Him, we can start possessing our Promised Land *now* in His presence—this is the Kingdom of God inside of us. But like Abraham, to answer this call, we too *may* have to leave our countries, families, or jobs. In other words, are you willing to face discomfort to find your Promised Land? Listen to what Jesus said about sacrifice in the Kingdom:

☦ *I have come to bring fire on the earth, and how I wish it were already kindled! But I have a baptism to undergo, and how distressed I am until it is completed! Do you think I came to bring peace on earth? No, I tell you, but division. From now on there will be five in one family divided against each other, three against two and two against three. They will be divided, father against son and son against father, mother against daughter and daughter against mother, mother-in-law against daughter-in-law and daughter-in-law against mother-in-law* (Luke 12:49-53).

☦ *"I tell you the truth," Jesus replied, "no one who has left home or brothers or sisters or mother or father or children or fields for me and the gospel will fail to receive a hundred times as much in this present age... and in the age to come...* (Mark 10:29-30).

So how do we get to our Promised Land? We follow what is sometimes a slow, winding, and difficult journey. Like Abraham, in order to receive this gift, we must start out on the journey, with an action of faith, and then continue to walk in faith despite the adversity that will come upon entering into our Promised Land.

✦ *By faith Abraham, when called to go to a place he would **later** receive as his inheritance, obeyed and went, even though he did not know where he was going* (Hebrew 11:8).

✦ *Though you have not seen Him, you love Him; and even though you do not see Him now, you believe in Him and are filled with an inexpressible and glorious joy* (1 Peter 1:8).

To receive this joy, you need the kind of faith that trusts God to take you to your Promised Land:

✦ *I am with you and will watch over you wherever you go, and I will bring you back to this land. I will not leave you until I have done what I have promised you* (Genesis 28:15).

This applies as well to our transformation into His image and likeness when as believers we partner with Him.

✦ *Because of your **partnership** in the gospel from the first day until now, being confident of this, that He who began a good work in you will carry it on to completion until the day of Jesus Christ* (Philippians 1:5-6).

ACTION & VISUALIZATION

On this long journey of faith, which may take you through unfamiliar and difficult territory, believe that God is with you and that He will complete your journey to your Promise Land.

GOD'S PRESENCE NOW

In the first recorded sermon (commonly referred to as the Sermon on the Mount), Jesus presented clear instructions on how to start this journey toward receiving, unwrapping, and using the Gift of God:

✠ *Blessed are the poor in spirit, for theirs is the kingdom of heaven. Blessed are those who mourn, for they will be comforted. Blessed are the meek, for they will inherit the earth. Blessed are those who hunger and thirst for righteousness, for they will be filled. Blessed are the merciful, for they will be shown mercy. Blessed are the pure in heart, for they will see God. Blessed are the peacemakers, for they will be called sons of God. Blessed are those who are persecuted because of righteousness, for theirs is the kingdom of heaven* (Matthew 5:3-10).

In construction, if you compromise the foundation or the superstructure, you create an unstable building. The same thing is true of your relationship with God. Each step that Jesus outlines in His sermon needs to be properly completed in order to create a stable relationship. God took the first step in building this relationship by offering the greatest gift one could give—the gift of eternal life given in ultimate love.

✠ *For God so loved the world that He gave His one and only Son, that whoever believes in Him shall not perish but have eternal life* (John 3:16).

In this eternal life, which is a gift God offers everyone, we have a promise to receive, an invitation to a relationship with God Himself forever—which is the *ultimate* gift.

Need God Constantly

Let's look at the first requirement that Jesus establishes for receiving this aspect of the gift of life, the Gift of God. (I've included three translations of this verse to help illuminate its meaning.)

✟ *Blessed are the poor in spirit, for theirs is the kingdom of heaven* (Matthew 5:3).

✟ *You're blessed when you're at the end of your rope. With less of you there is more of God and His rule* (Matthew 5:3 TM).

✟ *Blessed (happy, to be envied, and spiritually prosperous—with life-joy and satisfaction in God's favor and salvation, regardless of their outward conditions) are the poor in spirit (the humble who rate themselves insignificant) for theirs is the kingdom of heaven* (Matthew 5:3 AMP).

If you want to go from any point A to point B, you first need to determine where you are: the location of point A. Remember what God asked Adam: "Where are you?" (See Genesis 3:9.) Well, this is a question He asks you *every* single day of your life on earth. It is a question He is asking for *your* benefit. He knows where you are; however, you need to know the answer to that question to properly navigate toward Him. If you don't know where you are (point A), how could you possibly know how to get to Him (point B)? Would you even know you need to move to get there? Look at this parable:

✟ *To some who were confident of their own righteousness and looked down on everybody else, Jesus told this parable: "Two men went up to* *the temple to pray, one a Pharisee and the other a tax collector. The Pharisee stood up and prayed about himself: 'God, I thank you that I am not like other men—robbers, evildoers, adulterers—or even like this tax collector. I fast twice a week and give a tenth of all I get.' But the tax collector stood at a distance. He would not even look up to heaven, but beat his breast and said, 'God, have mercy on me, a sinner.' I tell you that this man, rather than the other, went home **justified before** God..."* (Luke 18:9-14).

The second man, who was humble and contrite, correctly knew where he was in relation to God and in so doing allowed himself to be justified before God. Likewise, you need to begin your journey with God by *conceding* that you are poor in spirit—in need of something more. That more that you need is God, and therefore, you reached out to Him for your salvation. *Here is the important part*: you need to have this realization *every* morning when you wake up, even *after* you have received the gift of salvation. You need to realize that, while you have gained something wonderful, you are *still* spiritually *lacking*. You are incapable of real success without Him, minute to minute, hour to hour, day to day. If you know you need Him every day, every hour, every minute, you will *seek* Him in everything all the time. This is the catalyst for the growth process that leads to an intimate relationship with God.

Mourn Loss of His Presence

Jesus then instructs us in the next verse to appreciate and appropriately respond to where we are versus where we *should be*. Doing this produces a *mournful* spirit:

Blessed are those who mourn, for they will be comforted (Matthew 5:4).

✠ *You're blessed when you feel you've lost what is most dear to you [God's fullest presence in you]. Only then can you be embraced by the One most dear to you* (Matthew 5:4 TM).

If you did something that seriously offended your earthly spouse, you would experience some grief as a result of your actions. Likewise, when we are not walking and operating in the Spirit, we lose the most precious thing—*intimacy* in our relationship with God. If we recognize and wrestle with this, we will experience a spirit of sorrow about missing God and His mark for us, and this will prompt us to change our behavior. Paul said it this way:

✠ **Godly sorrow** *brings repentance that leads to salvation and leaves no regret...* (2 Corinthians 7:10).

When Jesus used the word *mourn*, it was the strongest possible word that He could have used to describe inner pain expressed in an outward way. However, mourning under the conviction of the Holy Spirit over that which we long for will *not* end in discouragement:

✠ *Grieve, mourn and wail. Change your laughter to mourning and your joy to gloom. Humble yourselves before the Lord, and He will **lift you up*** (James 4:9-10).

We are *not* to dwell on our sins and failures—God knows that we are weak and will fall. Indeed we are simply to acknowledge that weakness and to respond by bringing Him into the picture to help us change. *Godly* sorrow produces a *change* in behavior that will *lift us up*; it will *not* bring crippling regret.

The word used in the Bible when John the Baptist told the people they should repent was *metanoeo* (met-an-ah-eh-oh). (See Matthew 3:1-2.) This meant that the people should change their minds and actions—reverse their course. The word *repent* comes from two words: *meta* ("after") and *noeo* ("to think"). Repentance is a decision that results in a change of mind, which in turn leads to a change in our purpose, our actions, and our course.[1]

It's interesting that today the word *repent* breaks down into *pent*, meaning "top" (as in pent-house or top house), and *re*, meaning "get back." So the word *repent* today means "*to get back to the top.*" And that's where God wants our focus when we fail—on getting back to the top. Of course, getting there sometimes means letting go of things that weigh us down so that we can move in the right direction—*up.*

When we see the things that hold us down, we should have the sorrow that's produced by the conviction of the Holy Spirit. Then we let go so that God can lift us up—*back to the top.* You will find that, when you are successful at doing this, your top will ascend higher and higher each time.

You may wonder, *How long must we mourn?* As long as it takes to make a change. Mourning must come from the *heart* in order to bring change—a change of heart. With a change of heart there is a change of direction. There is a strong connection between our heart and mind in our decision-making process. So when our heart changes our minds are guided by its direction.

Your heart is not just a pump; it also acts like a mini brain. Science demonstrates that your heart has its own independent nervous system, a complex system with at least 40,000 neurons, as many as are found in various sub-cortical centers of the brain. In effect, your "heart's brain" acts like a checking station or conscience for all the emotions generated by the flow of chemicals from our thoughts.

Science is discovering that your "heart's brain" is a real "intelligent force" behind the intuitive thoughts and feelings you experience. The "heart's brain" produces an important biochemical substance called ANF or arterial peptide, the balance hormone that regulates many of your brain's functions and motivates behavior.

Your heart is in constant communication with your brain and the rest of your body in three scientifically documented ways: neurologically (through transmissions of nerve impulses), biochemically (through hormones and neurotransmitters), and biophysically (through pressure waves). A growing body of scientific evidence also suggests that your heart communicates with the brain and body in a fourth way: energetically through electromagnetic field interaction.

Through all these biological communication systems, the heart has a significant influence on the function of your brain and all your other body systems. The signals the heart sends to your brain influence not just perception and emotional processing, but higher, cognitive functioning as well. New scientific evidence on the heart's neurological sensitivity points to feedback loops between the brain and the heart that checks the accuracy and integrity of our thought life.[2] We find confirmation for this in the Bible.

✝ *...the Lord searches every **heart** and understands every motive behind the **thoughts**...* (1 Chronicles 28:9).

✝ *Jesus knew what they were thinking and asked, "Why are you **thinking** these things in your **heart**?"* (Luke 5:22)

Your brain alone can have endless thoughts and therefore needs a ruddering or anchoring mechanism that comes from our inner-most soul. The direction of your mind and actions are set by your heart.

✠ *For as he thinks in his heart, so is he…* (Proverbs 23:7 NKJV).

✠ *Keep your heart with all diligence, for out of it spring the issues of life* (Proverbs 4:23 NKJV).

✠ *…doing the will of God from your heart…*(Ephesians 6:6).

✠ *…For out of the overflow of his heart his mouth speaks* (Luke 6:45).

Indeed our very salvation comes from the faith and belief that resides in our hearts.

✠ *That if you confess with your mouth "Jesus is Lord" and believe in your* **heart** *that God raised Him from the dead you will be saved.* **For it is with your heart that you believe** *and are justified…*(Romans 10:9-10).

Be clear on something, mourning is different from regret, which denotes something of the mind. God does not want us to cripple ourselves in regret, but we do need to remember daily that it was you and me who nailed Jesus' hands and feet to that cross. It was our sin that He paid the price and suffered for. Remembering this should produce in our hearts a meaningful attitude of mourning that will change the direction of our hearts. Indeed, it will lead to life, freedom, and greater intimacy with our Creator. This change will get us where we want to go—back to the *top.*

TAKE YOUR PROPER PLACE

Jesus' next instruction is for us to accept our proper place in this new relationship. It is from this place, and only this place, that we can have access to all of the things in the world that God created for us to enjoy. So what is our place? What should our attitude be in the relationship?

✠ *Blessed are the meek, for they will inherit the earth* (Matthew 5:5).

Some translations of the Bible use different words for *meek*, such as *gentle* (NASB), *content* (TM), and *lowly in spirit*. All are meant to convey the idea that we're to be sensitive to the Spirit of God's teaching and leading for our lives. When we do this, a greater world opens up to us—a world where we can obtain our full inheritance from God. This includes a greater awareness of God's presence—greater intimacy with Him.

I want to clarify that the word *meek* does *not* mean weak. Think of *meek* as being bridled like a horse. A Belgian mare is not weak, but when you put a bridle in its mouth, the horse can be guided to places it would not go otherwise. When we allow ourselves to be bridled by the Holy Spirit, we are able to go to places where we can receive more of God in our lives. As the verse says, then we will inherit the earth, then the whole world will open up to us. The contradiction is that we are not fully free in this life until we allow ourselves to be fully bridled, until we surrender our daily lives to God. So choose to find that vital place in relationship with God—the place of humility and contentment.

✠ *"...God opposes the proud but gives grace to the humble." Submit yourselves, then, to God.... Come near to God and He will come near to you... Humble yourselves before the Lord, and He will lift you up* (James 4:6-8,10).

✠ *You're blessed when you're content with just who you are—no more, no less. That's the moment you find yourselves proud owners of everything that can't be bought* (Matthew 5:5 TM).

Hunger and Thirst for Him

The next thing that Jesus teaches us about fulfilling our relationship with God is that we must be hungry and thirsty for righteousness, or right standing with Him.

✠ *Blessed are those who hunger and thirst for righteousness, for they will be filled* [satisfied] (Matthew 5:6).

God loves those who *seek* Him, and those who do so will find Him and, therein, true satisfaction. If we don't seek Him, He will not become intimately real in our lives; however, if we do seek Him, He will draw closer to us.

✠ *Come near to God and He will come near to you...* (James 4:8).

Take note: God does not say that we can achieve our *own* righteousness. God is *not* seeking perfect people. You will fail at that and put yourself back into bondage trying to follow the Law. He is seeking people who are *hungry* and *thirsty*. This attitude is embodied by the writers of these psalms:

✠ *As the deer **pants** for streams of water, so my soul pants for You, O God. My soul **thirsts** for God, for the living God. When can I go and meet with God?* (Psalm 42:1-2)

✠ *My soul **yearns**, even faints, for the courts of the Lord; my heart and flesh **cry out** for the living God* (Psalm 84:2).

It's *not* your current location as it relates to Him that's important to God, it's your desire to move closer that moves Him. It's your desire to continue the journey into Him that God desires. He encourages us to *seek* righteousness (relationship/likeness) now and to not just wait for Him to shower it on us. We should not wait passively for Him to perfect us.

✠ *Sow for yourselves righteousness, reap the fruit of unfailing love and break up your unplowed ground; for **it is time to seek** the Lord, until He comes and showers righteousness on you* (Hosea 10:12).

Remember though, the key to achieving righteousness is not by seeking it, but it is achieved by seeking *Him*—by showing a constant hunger and thirst for *Him*.

One of the keys to maintaining that hunger and thirst is making sure that you don't fill yourself up with the *wrong* foods. Remember the Samaritan lady that Jesus spoke to at the well? She was trying to fill the hunger in her life with men. Jesus offered her *living water*, real sustenance, instead (see John 4:1-26). Jesus also said that we *cannot* live by bread alone (by the things of the world that satisfy our flesh and ego). Instead, He said that real sustenance is found in the Word of God (see Matt. 4:4). Jesus is telling us not to fill ourselves up with worldly pursuits, but to remain hungry for His spiritual nourishment. We must be careful in our pursuits because many things that we pursue in this world can fill up our time, attention, mind, and heart. A continued hunger and thirst for right standing with God Himself above all else will allow us to be truly fulfilled.

Offer Mercy

The next instruction Jesus gives us, in building our relationship with God, is to be merciful:

✠ *Blessed are the merciful, for they will be shown mercy* (Matthew 5:7).

To understand the meaning of mercy we can consult the meaning of the Latin root word from which it is derived, *misericordia*. It is composed of two words: *miserans*, pitying, and *cor*, the heart; or *miseria cordis*, pain of heart. Mercy supposes two things: 1) A distressed object; and 2) A disposition of another's heart, through which it is affected at the sight of such object.[4] In other words, mercy is an aspect of love involving an emotion that one feels when he or she sees the trial or distress of another. Mercy is shown when we enter into the miseries of our neighbor, feel for and mourn with him. It is as if you "get into someone else's skin and are feeling what they feel." Have you ever wished you could take away the pain of a loved one by actually taking on the pain yourself?

Mercy and *hesed* (God's covenant love) are closely related. In the Bible, hesed by definition is viewed in terms of mercy. In this relationship, mercy then comes to be seen as the quality in God that directs Him to forge a relationship with people who absolutely do not deserve to be in relationship with Him.[5] Offering mercy means "refraining from giving people what they deserve."

Truly, seeking to understand where someone is coming from makes it easier to have mercy on that individual. Jesus Himself embodied this. He came and got into our skin, living as we live. He dealt with all of the same temptations that we deal with (see Heb. 2:17-18). Jesus extended mercy to us; therefore, we should do the same for others, especially since they answer to God and *not to us*:

✟ *Who are you to judge someone **else's** servant? To his own master he stands or falls...* (Romans 14:4).

We are no one's master. However, God is everyone's Master, and He has elected to judge no one until after they die and the final chapter of their lives has been written.

✟ *Just as a man is destined to die once, and **after that** to face judgment...* (Hebrews 9:27).

God Himself has given everyone an inalienable right to *not* be judged until their final chapter is closed, a right of redemption. How then can *you* judge someone, and even before that person's time has come? It is because of sin—because we ate from the tree of the knowledge of good and evil—that we are so quick to judge others. That very act of judging has caused us to *lose* our innocence. This is because, when we judge others, we're also judged by the *same* measure. What you plant or sow you will reap:

✟ *Do not judge, or you too will be judged. For in the same way you judge others, you will be judged, and with the measure you use, it will be measured to you* (Matthew 7:1-2).

✟ *You, therefore, have no excuse, you who pass judgment on someone else, for at whatever point you judge the other, you are condemning yourself, because you who pass judgment do the same things* (Romans 2:1).

✝ *...Why do you judge your brother? Or why do you look down on your brother? For we will all stand before God's judgment seat* (Romans 14:10).

On the other hand, showing mercy will likewise bring you mercy—bring God lovingly into your circumstances, sharing your pain. Your own expression of mercy allows you to avoid judgment. So our own lack of mercy validates our disobedient acts as sins that require punishment. Without our mercy interceding for us, we then rely solely on His mercy which can only be obtained through our acknowledgement of our need for it. This is confirmed in an exchange that Jesus had with a Pharisee:

✝ *Jesus said, "For judgment I have come into this world, so that the blind* [who cannot judge good and evil] *will see* [life] *and those who see* [and judge things as good and evil] *will become blind* [to life]." *Some Pharisees who were with Him heard Him say this and asked, "What? Are we blind too?" Jesus said, "If you were blind, you would* **not** *be guilty of sin; but now that you claim you can see, your guilt remains"* (John 9:39-41).

I believe this is why innocent children who die before receiving Christ will be able to enter the Kingdom of God. It is their very innocence (or lack of judging) that keeps them blind from judgment, and therefore, judgment will be blind to their sins.

In our dealings with other people, we must remember that God has personal relationships with many of them and that He seeks oneness with others. God wants the best for them, just as He wanted the best for us even before we knew Him and were cleansed by Him.

Perhaps when you see someone acting outside of God's will, you will be tempted to judge them. Well, guess what: you're not qualified for that job.

First, you are not sinless. Remember, Jesus said, "Let the one without sin throw the first stone" (see John 8:7). Second, you can't see the future like God can. Only He knows where that person is going. Third, you don't know how much God loves that person. This is why He does *not* want you to see yourself as their judge, but rather as their *friend*. This is also why the second greatest commandment (after loving God) is about loving others:

✝ *The second is this: "Love your neighbor as yourself." There is no commandment greater than these* (Mark 12:31).

Simply put, we enhance our relationship with God by enhancing our relationship with others. Jesus Himself offers this account of the final judgment to show us how our relationship with God is intricately tied to our relationships with others:

✝ *Then the King will say to those on His right, "Come, you who are
blessed by My Father; take your inheritance, the kingdom prepared for
you since the creation of the world. For I was hungry and you gave Me
something to eat. I was thirsty and you gave Me something to drink, I
was a stranger and you invited Me in, I needed clothes and you clothed
Me, I was sick and you looked after Me, I was in prison and you came
to visit Me." Then the righteous will answer Him, "Lord, when did we
see You hungry and feed You, or thirsty and give You a drink? When
did we see You sick or in prison and go to visit You?" The King will
reply, "I tell you the truth, whatever you did for one of the least of these
brothers of Mine, you did for **Me**." Then He will say to those on His left,
"Depart from Me, you who are cursed, into the eternal fire prepared for
the devil and his angels. For I was hungry and you gave Me nothing to
eat, I was thirsty and you gave Me nothing to drink, I was a stranger
and you did not invite Me in, I needed clothes and you did not clothe
Me, I was sick and in prison and you did not look after Me!" They also*

will answer, "Lord when did we see You hungry or thirsty or a stranger or needing clothes or sick or in prison, and did not help You?" He will reply, "I tell you the truth, whatever you did not do for one of the least of these, you did not do for Me." Then they will go away to eternal punishment, but the righteous to eternal life (Matthew 25:34-46).

Show mercy to others where you are able and you will receive mercy where needed.

SEE BETTER WITH PURITY

The next thing that Jesus says we need to do to fully receive God is to put our hearts and minds in the right place. Without righteous hearts and minds, our spiritual vision will be too distorted to see God.

Blessed are the pure in heart, for they will see God (Matthew 5:8).

If our temple is not clean, we won't see God in the way that we should. An impure heart distorts our insight, blocking clear vision of God:

For God did not call us to be impure, but to live a holy life (1 Thessalonians 4:7).

For it is written, "Be holy, because I am holy" (1 Peter 1:16).

*Make every effort to live in peace with all men and to be holy; without holiness **no one will see the Lord*** (Hebrews 12:14).

✠ *You're blessed when you get your inside world—your mind and heart—put right. Then you can see God in the outside world* (Matthew 5:8 TM).

Unfortunately what we don't see, we don't know is missing or distorted. This is why we are exhorted over and over to keep a pure heart. It has a fundamental effect on our relationship with God, which affects every other aspect of our lives. You see, our hearts represent the innermost part of ourselves, which as you read earlier in the chapter gives direction to the mind and body. Indeed a good book to read on this subject is *Who Switched Off My Brain* by Dr. Caroline Leaf. In the book she goes through the scientific data which shows the need for us to have "positive faith-based emotions" (love, joy, peace, happiness, kindness, gentleness, self-control, forgiveness and patience) versus "negative fear-based emotions" (hate, worry, anxiety, anger, hostility, rage, ill-will, resentment, frustration, impatience, and irritation). These "negative fear-based emotions" produce toxic attitudes, which produce toxic chemical responses in the body, causing sickness and disease. Through the book she shows you how to use "positive faith-based emotions" to detox your mind and heart, which allows you to detox your body and be healed.[3]

So when our hearts are pure and in *tune* with God (the key), our whole life benefits— physically and spiritually—allowing us to see and experience the life God desires for us.

✠ *A cheerful heart is good medicine…*(Proverbs 17:22).

✠ *Above all else, guard your heart, for it is the wellspring of life* (Proverbs 4:23).

Dear friends, if our hearts do not condemn us, we have confidence before God and receive from Him anything we ask, because we obey His commands and do what pleases Him (1 John 3:21-22).

God looks at your heart and *knows* your heart. He wants to uphold the innermost part of your being, which makes guarding the purity of your heart vital. We can't do this by our efforts alone—we need Jesus' help.

*His divine power has given us everything we need for life and **godliness through our knowledge of Him** who called us by His own glory and goodness. Through these He has given us His very great and precious promises, so that through them you may participate in the divine nature and escape the corruption in the world caused by evil desires* (2 Peter 1:3-4).

You see, in this passage, that to escape the corruption of the world we must embrace His divine nature and purity within us. Our godliness or purity will only come through our knowledge of Him or intimacy with Him. We cannot achieve purity alone. It comes through our willingness to align ourselves with Him.

Also being holy is *not* simply a matter of doing good. For example, you can give someone money to leverage them or for selfish recognition. Purity is all about the motives of your heart, as you can do seemingly "good things," even "Christian things," with worldly intentions.

All a man's ways seem innocent to him, but motives are weighed by the Lord (Proverbs 16:2).

✝ ...[God] *will expose the motives of men's hearts* (1 Corinthians 4:5).

When our heart is holy, sin does not distort our vision, and when our vision is clear we can see God in our world and everyday circumstances. This allows us to do His will and to fulfill our purpose in sometimes confusing situations. He will lead and guide you into righteousness if you allow Him.

✝ *He* [God] *guides me in the paths of righteousness for His name sake* (Psalms 23:3).

PRACTICE PEACE

The next step that Jesus gives us, toward our efforts to unwrap our relationship with God, is to be at peace with God and those around us.

✝ *Blessed are the peacemakers, for they will be called sons of God* (Matthew 5:9).

We are called to foster peace, first with our Father God and then with those He created.

✝ *Peacemakers who sow in peace raise a harvest of righteousness* (James 3:18).

You will not have peace with God until you have peace with other people because you cannot separate your relationship with people from your relationship with God—they are intertwined. They are intertwined because He is inseparably in other people, just as they are in Him.

✠ *...Father, just as You are in Me and I am in You, may **they** also be in Us...* (John 17:21).

When you were a child, I'm sure your earthly parents were upset when you and your siblings would fight. If a fracture happens in a family, that fracture interrupts the will of God for that family. Lack of unity denies relationships their full potential. Remember, Heaven on earth can't exist unless *all* relationships reach their full potential.

Love and *humility* are a critical part of becoming a true peacemaker. A peacemaker doesn't just avoid arguing with others, but also refrains from speaking negatively about those same people behind their backs. *All* of your actions should seek unity among your brothers and sisters.

✠ *You're blessed when you can show people how to cooperate instead of compete or fight. That's when you discover who you really are, and your place in God's family* (Matthew 5:9 TM).

Endure Persecution

The last thing that Jesus teaches in this portion of His sermon is that we will face persecution in this world because of the relationship that we have with God—and that we're to hang in there and endure it. Let's look at two translations of this verse:

✠ *Blessed are those who are persecuted because of righteousness, for theirs is the kingdom of heaven* (Matthew 5:10).

You're blessed when your commitment to God provokes persecution. The persecution drives you even deeper into God's kingdom (Matthew 5:10 TM).

Let me be clear that, if you are on track with the other seven ingredients for a deeper and more intimate relationship with God, you *will* encounter persecution. This is because you'll be living in contradiction to the way that the world is living. Indeed if you are *not* encountering persecution, you may want to review whether you're pursuing the other seven ingredients as readily as you ought. As I have said before, if you and satan are going in the same direction, you won't encounter any problems with him. However, if you're going in the opposite direction, he will attempt to oppose you. Listen to what Jesus said about persecution:

*Remember the words I spoke to you: "No servant is greater than his master." If they persecuted Me, then they will persecute you **also**..."* [assuming you have made Him the Master of your life] (John 15:20).

This is why Jesus goes on to encourage us in His Sermon on the Mount to rejoice in persecution:

Blessed are you when people insult you, persecute you and falsely say all kinds of evil against you because of Me. Rejoice and be glad, because great is your reward in heaven, for in the same way they persecuted the prophets who were before you (Matthew 5:11-12).

The apostle Peter said it this way:

✠ *Dear friends, do not be surprised at the painful trial you are suffering, as though something strange were happening to you. But rejoice that you **participate** in the sufferings of Christ, so that you may be overjoyed when His glory is revealed. If you are insulted because of the name of Christ, you are blessed, for the Spirit of glory and of God rests on you. If you suffer, it should not be as a murderer or thief or any other kind of criminal, or even as a meddler. However, if you suffer as a Christian, do not be ashamed, but praise God that you bear that name. For it is time for judgment to begin with the family of God; and if it begins with us, what will the outcome be for those who do not obey the gospel of God* (1 Peter 4:12-17).

ACTION & VISUALIZATION

Build your relationship with God carefully, using all of the steps that Jesus teaches in His Sermon on the Mount.

SERVICE AND OBEDIENCE = LOVE

The gift of relationship with God should be our primary focus and concern in life:

✠ *One of the teachers of the law came and heard them debating. Noticing that Jesus had given them a good answer, he asked Him, "Of all the commandments, which is the most important?" "The most important one," answered Jesus, "is this: 'Hear, O Israel, the Lord our God, the Lord is one. Love the Lord your God with all your heart and with all your soul and with all your mind and with all your strength'"* (Mark 12:28-30).

So how do we express loving God with all of our heart, soul, mind, and strength? In its simplest definition, the expression of our love for God can be summed up in two words: *serve* and *obey.*

✞ *And now, O Israel, what does the Lord your God ask of you but to fear the Lord your God, to walk in all His ways, to love Him, to* **serve** *the Lord your God with all your heart and with all your soul, and to* **observe** *the Lord's commands and decrees that I am giving you today for your own good?* (Deuteronomy 10:12-13)

Remember that, the greater degree you serve and obey, the greater God's presence will be in your current life. Of course, the reference here to obeying does not mean enslaving ourselves ritualistically to the Law for obedience sake alone, but it means to obey in love. True obedience comes from the heart; it is lead by the Spirit and thirsts for that which leads to a deeper commitment to God.

When we reach Heaven, God will completely purify our temples, at which time we will walk perfectly with Him; however, until then we obey Him to please Him:

✞ *What agreement is there between the temple of God and idols? For we are the temple of the living God. As God has said: "I will live with them and walk among them, and I will be their God, and they will be My people"* (2 Corinthians 6:16).

Until then, we look to Jesus as our example for how to relate to God:

✞ [Jesus] *replied, "Blessed rather are those who hear the word of God and* **obey** *it"* (Luke 11:28).

✠ *As the Father has loved Me, so have I loved you. Now remain in My love. If you **obey** My commands, you will remain in My love, just as I have **obeyed** My Father's commands and remain in His love. I have told you this so that My joy may be in you and that your **joy may be complete*** (John 15:9-11).

Note that, *when* you obey God to please and enter a deeper relationship with Him, not only will you be expressing your love to God, but also you personally will experience joy—as you will be living out that which you were created for. God ties things together in amazing ways—all of which are for our benefit.

ACTION & VISUALIZATION

Look for ways that you can serve and obey God.

DEPENDENCE BRINGS YOU CLOSE

When we serve and obey God's will (even when we don't fully understand God's plan) we are acknowledging our dependence on God. Dependency is a virtue that enhances our relationship with God because it allows more of Him in us. Paul offered these conclusions:

✠ *But He said to me, "My grace is sufficient for you, for My power is made perfect in weakness." Therefore I will boast all the more gladly about my weaknesses, so that Christ's power may rest on me. That is why, for Christ's sake, I delight in weaknesses, in insults, in hardships, in persecutions, in difficulties. For when I am weak, then I am strong* (2 Corinthians 12:9-10).

Paul knew that his weaknesses caused him to be dependent on God in those areas, which then became his strengths. It was the same for all of the Bible heroes:

✠ *...Gideon, Barak, Samson, Jephthah, David, Samuel and the prophets, who through faith conquered kingdoms, administered justice, and gained what was promised; who shut the mouths of lions, quenched the fury of the flames, and escaped the edge of the sword; whose **weakness** was **turned to strength**; and who became powerful in battle and routed foreign armies* (Hebrews 11:32-34).

Paul also wrote that Jesus is our model for how we become weak in order to gain God's strength:

✠ *For to be sure, [Jesus] was crucified in **weakness**, yet He lives by God's power. Likewise, we are **weak** in Him, yet by God's power we will live with Him to serve you* (2 Corinthians 13:4).

God finds His place in your weakness to form a partnership with you. This happens when you realize that you cannot find victory on your own. God wants this type of relationship with you—oneness. The more room you give God to inhabit your efforts, the more of God (and the less of you) will dwell in them.

As you have learned, a very important part of growing with God is preparation. I am referring to the inner you; the part of you that God is most concerned with is not your strength or exterior beauty. Rather, He is concerned with your heart:

✠ *But the Lord said to Samuel, "Do not consider his appearance or his height for I have rejected him. The Lord does not look at the things man looks at. Man looks at the outward appearance, but the Lord looks at the heart"* (1 Samuel 16:7).

✛ *The lamp of the Lord searches the spirit of a man; it searches out his innermost being* (Proverbs 20:27).

✛ *Woe to you, teachers of the law and Pharisees, you hypocrites! You are like whitewashed tombs, which look beautiful on the outside but on the inside, are full of dead men's bones and everything unclean* (Matthew 23:27).

✛ *Stop judging by mere appearances, and make a right judgment* (John 7:24).

God is most concerned about what's on the inside of you because He expects His children to live from the inside out—reflecting what is inside of them (Him) outward for the world to see. Remember even Jesus' appearance was described as being ordinary (see Isaiah 53:2). Sometimes we get so caught up in preparing our outward appearances that we place little focus on preparing our hearts. The outward appearance is temporal. Confidence in exterior things will *eventually* disappoint, for in time our outward self grows old and wears out. Instead, we need to be focused on improving our inner selves because, in contrast, our inner selves can become better and better, brighter and brighter every year that we live.

Your effort will not go unnoticed by people. As you operate, fully connected to your primary purpose, projecting His image and likeness, others will notice. On the other hand, Paul said that such people, who seem outwardly powerful, are of no account to God or His message to the world:

✝ *As for those who seemed to be important—whatever they were makes* **no** *difference to me; God does not judge by external appearance—those men added nothing to my message* (Galatians 2:6).

So what **is coming out** of us is *more* important than the *outside* of us. Remember the light bulb analogy from Book One? What is inside of us determines what comes out. This is why we need to hang tight, fully depending on Him who is in us so that He can perform His great works through us.

✝ *I can do everything through Him who gives me strength* (Philippians 4:13).

✝ *...Do not grieve, for the joy of the Lord is your strength* (Nehemiah 8:10).

✝ *Be strong in the Lord and in His mighty power* (Ephesians 6:10).

✝ *In all these things we are more than conquerors through Him who loved us* (Romans 8:37).

Obeying God and preparing yourself for Him will not only make your relationship with God stronger, but it will also give you much more *freedom* in your life.

✝ *To the Jews who had believed Him, Jesus said, "If you hold to My teaching, you are really My disciples. Then you will know the truth, and the truth will set you free"* (John 8:31-32).

ACTION & VISUALIZATION

Work at obediently preparing yourself so that you can project the right image and likeness.

INTIMATE UNION

Our relationship with God begins as a spiritual one that will eventually manifest itself as a holy union. The Bible likens this union to that of a husband and wife; Jesus, the husband, marries His Bride, the collective Church.

✝ *For the husband is the head of the wife as Christ is the head of the church, His body, of which He is the Savior* (Ephesians 5:23).

This infers that we will become one with God, just as God says that husbands and wives are one. Indeed, just like a husband and wife prepare for their union, so we are betrothed to Christ and are commanded to prepare for and respect our union.

✝ *Let us rejoice and be glad and give Him glory! For the wedding of the Lamb has come, and His bride has made herself ready* (Revelation 19:7).

✠ *At that* [end] *time the kingdom of heaven will be like ten virgins* [the Church] *who took their lamps and went out to meet the bridegroom* [Jesus] (Matthew 25:1).

✠ *At midnight* [the endtimes] *the cry rang out: "Here's the bridegroom* [Jesus]*! Come out to meet him"* (Matthew 25:6).

This is why the Bible exhorts us to keep ourselves clean and pure:

✠ *"Food for the stomach and the stomach for food"—but God will destroy them both* [when we get our heavenly bodies]. *The body is not meant for sexual immorality, but for the Lord, and the Lord for the body. By His power God raised the Lord from the dead, and He will raise us also. Do you not know that your bodies are members of Christ Himself? Shall I then take the members of Christ and unite them with a prostitute? Never! Do you not know that he who unites himself with a prostitute is one with her in body? For it is said, "The two will become one flesh." But he who unites himself with the Lord is one with Him in spirit* (1 Corinthians 6:13-17).

✠ *I saw the Holy City, the new Jerusalem, coming down out of heaven from God, prepared as a bride beautifully dressed for her husband* (Revelation 21:2).

✠ *I am jealous for you with a godly jealousy. I promised you to one husband, to Christ, so that I might present you as a pure virgin to Him* (2 Corinthians 11:2).

Relationship with Jesus is an invitation to the water of life. This living water, which Jesus spoke of with the Samaritan woman, is actually Jesus Himself.

*The Spirit and the bride say, "Come!" And let him who hears say, "Come!" Whoever is thirsty, let him come; and whoever wishes, let him take the **free gift** of the water of life* (Revelation 22:17).

ACTION & VISUALIZATION

Begin preparing yourself now for your holy union with Jesus.

YOUR ETERNAL DESTINY

There remains one unanswered question. Was our salvation predetermined from the beginning? Consider these verses:

*Therefore He has mercy on whom He wills, and whom He wills He hardens. You will say to me then, "Why does He still find fault? For who has resisted His will?" But indeed, O man, who are you to reply against God? Will the thing formed say to him who formed it, "Why have you made me like this?" Does not the potter have power over the clay, from the same lump to make one vessel for honor and another for dishonor? **What** if God, wanting to show His wrath and to make His power known, endured with much longsuffering the vessels of wrath prepared for destruction, and that He might make known the riches of His glory on the vessels of mercy, which He had prepared beforehand for glory...* (Romans 9:18-23 NKJV).

✠ *For [God] chose us in Him before the creation of the world to be holy and blameless in His sight. In love He predestined us to be adopted as His sons through Jesus Christ, in accordance with His pleasure and will—to the praise of His glorious grace, which He has freely given us in the One He loves* (Ephesians 1:4-6).

Was the current so strong, the way so clear for those of us who have received Jesus? Was saying "yes" to God inevitable for you and me? Whatever the case, those who received the gift of salvation have an eternal destiny, an eternal future with God, the head of the Trinity.

✠ *They will make war against the lamb, but the lamb will overcome them because He is Lord of lords, and King of kings—and* **with** *Him will be His called, chosen and faithful followers* (Revelation 17:14).

At that time, we will receive the fullness of our Promised Land (transformation into the image and likeness of God) and live eternally in His very presence. All that has been infected by sin on the earth will be destroyed, burnt up, and God will replace it with a new Heaven and earth; however, all of His promises to us will remain:

✠ *Heaven and earth will pass away, but My words will never pass away* (Matthew 24:35).

✠ *Behold, I will create new heavens and a new earth. The former things will not be remembered, nor will they come to mind* (Isaiah 65:17).

✠ *By calling this covenant "new," He has made the first one obsolete; and what is obsolete and aging will soon disappear* (Hebrews 8:13).

✠ *All the stars of the heavens will be dissolved and the sky rolled up like a scroll; all the starry host will fall like withered leaves from the vine, like shriveled figs from the fig tree* (Isaiah 34:4).

✠ *Lift up your eyes to the heavens, look at the earth beneath; the heavens will vanish like smoke, the earth will wear out like a garment and its inhabitants die like flies. But My salvation will last forever, My righteousness will never fail* (Isaiah 51:6).

✠ *"As the new heaven and the new earth that I will make endure before Me," declares the Lord, "so will your name and descendants endure"* (Isaiah 66:22).

✠ *I tell you the truth, until heaven and earth disappear, not the smallest letter, not the least stroke of a pen, will by any means disappear from the Law until everything is accomplished* (Matthew 5:18).

✠ *But the day of the Lord will come like a thief. The heavens will disappear with a roar; the elements will be destroyed by fire, and the earth and everything in it will be laid bare. Since everything will be destroyed in this way, what kind of people ought you to be? You ought to live holy and godly lives as you look forward to the day of God and* speed its coming. *That day will bring about the destruction of the heavens by fire, and the elements will melt in the heat. But in keeping with His promise we are looking forward to a new heaven and a new earth, the home of righteousness* (2 Peter 3:10-13).

All evil will be consumed from earth, which leaves only His unshakable promises standing. Only His Kingdom will remain, where we can be the people He wants us to be—fully consumed in our relationship with Him.

✞ *Therefore, since we are receiving a kingdom that cannot be shaken, let us be thankful, and so worship God acceptably with reverence and awe, for our "God is a consuming fire"* (Hebrews 12:28-29).

IMAGE AND LIKENESS

Not only will the current world we live in be purified, but also our very own bodies. Consider these verses about our eternal bodies:

✞ *But our citizenship is in heaven. And we eagerly await a savior from there, the Lord Jesus Christ, who, by the power that enables Him to bring everything under His control, will transform our lowly bodies so that they will be like His glorious body* (Philippians 3:20-21).

✞ *And after my skin has been destroyed, yet in my [**new**] flesh I will see God* (Job 19:26).

✞ *According to the Lord's own word, we tell you that we who are still alive, who are left till the coming of the Lord, will certainly not pre-cede those who have fallen asleep* [died]. *For the Lord Himself will come down from heaven, with a loud command, with the voice of the archangel and with the trumpet call of God, and* **the dead in Christ will rise first**. *After that, we who are still alive and are left will be caught up together with them in the clouds to meet the Lord in the air. And so we will be with the Lord forever* (1 Thessalonians 4:15-17).

✠ *Now we know that if the earthly tent we live in* [our body] *is destroyed, we have a building from God, an eternal house* [body for our mind and spirit] *in heaven, not built by human hands. Meanwhile we groan, longing to be clothed with our heavenly dwelling, because when we are clothed,* **we will not be found naked**. *For while we are in this tent, we groan and are burdened, because we do not wish to be unclothed but to be clothed with our heavenly dwelling* [God's glory], *so that what is mortal may be swallowed up by life. Now it is God who has made us for this very purpose and has given us the Spirit* [which we received when we were saved] *as a deposit, guaranteeing what is to come* [complete fulfillment of our intimate relationship and transformation into His image and like-ness] (2 Corinthians 5:1-5).

✠ *I consider that our present sufferings are not worth comparing with the glory that will be revealed in us. The creation waits in eager expectation for the sons* [and daughters] *of God to be revealed. For the creation was subjected to frustration, not by its own choice, but by the will of the one who subjected it, in hope that the creation itself will be liberated from its bondage to decay and brought into the glorious freedom of the children of God. We know that the whole creation has been groaning as in the pains of childbirth right up to this present time. Not only so, but we ourselves, who have the firstfruits of the Spirit, groan inwardly as we wait eagerly for our adoption as sons* [and daughters], *the redemption of our bodies* (Romans 8:18-23).

✠ *But someone may ask, "How are the dead raised? With what kind of body will they come?" How foolish! What you sow does not come to life unless it dies. When you sow, you do not plant the body that will be, but just a seed, perhaps of wheat or of something else. But God gives it a body as He has determined, and to each kind of seed He gives its own body. All flesh is not the same: Men have one kind of flesh, animals have another, birds another and fish another. There are also heavenly bodies and there are earthly bodies; but the splendor of the heavenly bodies is one kind, and the splendor of the earthly bodies is another. The sun has one kind of splendor, the moon another and the stars another; and star differs from star in splendor. So will it be with the resurrection of the dead. The body that is sown is perishable,* **it is raised imperishable**; *it is sown in dishonor,* **it is raised in glory**; *it is sown in weakness,* **it is raised in power**; *it is sown a natural body,* **it is raised a spiritual body**. *If there is a natural body, there is also a spiritual body. So it is written: "The first man Adam became a living being"; the last Adam* [Jesus], *a life-giving spirit. The spiritual did not come* **first**, *but* **the natural**, *and* **after that the spiritual**. *The first man was of the dust of the earth, the second man* [Jesus] *from heaven. As was the earthly man, so are those who are of the earth; and as the man from heaven* [Jesus], *so also are those who are of heaven. And just as we have borne the likeness of the earthly man,* **so shall we bear the likeness of the man from heaven** [Jesus]. *I declare to you, brothers that flesh and blood cannot inherit the kingdom of God, nor does the perishable inherit the imperishable. Listen, I tell you a mystery: We will not all sleep* [remain dead], *but* **we will all be changed in a flash, in the twinkling of an eye, at the last***

*trumpet. For the trumpet will sound, the dead will be raised imper-
ishable, and we will be changed. For the perishable must clothe itself
with the imperishable, and the mortal with immortality. When the
perishable has been clothed with the imperishable, and the mortal
with immortality, then the saying that is written will come true:
"Death has been swallowed up in victory. Where, O death, is your
victory? Where, O death, is your sting?" The sting of death is sin, and
the power of sin is the law. But thanks be to God! He gives us the victory through our Lord Jesus Christ* (1 Corinthians 15:35-57).

*Dear friends, now we are children of God, and what we will be has
not yet been made known. But we know that when He appears, we
shall be like Him, for **we shall see Him** as He is. Everyone who has
this hope in him purifies himself, just as He is pure* (1 John 3:2-3).

YOUR PROMISED LAND

So what will this new Heaven be like? Well the Bible gives us some
exciting clues; however, when reading these descriptions, remember that
the authors could only use words and concepts that they and we can relate
to and understand. The reality is, Heaven will actually be so different from
anything we have ever experienced that the words we now know cannot
fully or properly describe it in either a respectful or accurate way. Here is
what the Bible says about Heaven:

*Then I saw a new heaven and a new earth, for the first heaven and
the first earth had passed away, and there was no longer any sea. I
saw the Holy City, the new Jerusalem, coming down out of heaven
from God, prepared as a bride beautifully dressed for her husband.*

*And I heard a loud voice from the throne saying, "Now the dwelling of God is with men, and **He will live with them**. They will be His people, and **God Himself** will be with them and be their God. He will wipe every tear from their eyes. There will be no more death or mourning or crying or pain, for the old order of things has passed away." He who was seated on the throne said, "I am making everything new"*... (Revelation 21:1-5).

✠ *The ransomed of the Lord* [Christians] *will return. They will enter Zion* [God's presence] *with singing; everlasting joy will crown their heads. Gladness and joy will overtake them, and sorrow and sighing will flee away* (Isaiah 51:11).

✠ *Never again will they hunger; never again will they thirst. The sun will not beat upon them, nor any scorching heat* (Revelation 7:16).

✠ *The Lord their God will save them on that day as the flock of His people. They will sparkle in His land like jewels in a crown. How attractive and beautiful they will be! Grain will make the young men thrive, and new wine the young women* (Zechariah 9:16-17).

✠ *Then the angel showed me the river of the water of life, as clear as crystal, flowing from the throne of God and of the Lamb* [Jesus] *down the middle of the great street of the city. On each side of the river stood the tree of life, bearing twelve crops of fruit, yielding its fruit every month. And the leaves of the tree are for the healing of the nations. No longer will there be any curse* [brought on by man]. *The throne* *of God and of the Lamb will be in the city, and His servants will serve Him. They will **see His face**, and His name will be on their foreheads. There will be no more night. They will not need the light of a lamp or the light of the sun, for the Lord God will give them light. And they will reign for ever and ever* (Revelation 22:1-5).

✝ *I did not see a temple* [place of worship to meet God] *in the city, because the Lord God Almighty and the Lamb are its temple. The city does not need the sun or the moon to shine on it, for the **glory of God gives it light**, and the Lamb is its lamp* (Revelation 21:22-23).

The Bible is clearly telling us here that our final destination will be in direct relationship with *God Himself.* Put the book down for a few minutes to just let your imagination flow and dwell on what it means to see the face of God. How can we truly comprehend that, given our current limitations and understanding of time and space? Remember, God does not have a physical presence. He is, for lack of a better term, an action—love, life, goodness, mercy, etc. So what does the face of God Himself look like? For us, of course, it would be the experience of pure love as well as the full knowledge of His thoughts and knowledge. Think of the infinite mind of God that imagined then created every physical *detail* you see in nature right down to the smallest molecule and the furthest galaxy. This is something we really can't fathom. Consider the unique design of every butterfly, snowflake, or even feelings. Because of His infinite capacity, God is always with each of us now; however, in our heavenly experience we will have a face to face intimate relationship that allows us to personally explore the depths of His love, knowledge and power.

The verse also says He will be our temple or, you could say, the place in which we experience Him (see Rev. 21:22). The verse continues with:

*The nations will walk by its light, and the kings of the earth will bring their splendor into it. On no day will its gates ever be shut, for there will be no night there. The glory and honor of the nations will be brought into it. **Nothing impure** will ever enter it, nor will anyone who does what is shameful or deceitful, but only those whose names are written in the Lamb's book of life* (Revelation 21:24-27).

How is this heavenly experience, where everything goes well and no one feels disappointment, possible? What does a "perfect world" look like? Well, perfection can only happen when everything and *everyone* is acting in complete obedience to the will of God, when all people are only experiencing love from God and giving God's love to *one another*. We all will help create the heavenly experience, as revealed in the Bible, for each other because God will conform us back into His image and likeness. We will be heavenly beings.

We gain entry into Heaven when we accept the Gift of Salvation, when we accept Jesus as our Savior and have our names written in the Lamb's book of life. This starts that process of our transformation that is required to get to Heaven. We volunteer, allowing Him to conform us into His image and likeness, into heavenly beings. We become heirs of our Father's Kingdom. And when we reach this Promised Land, after we are transformed into His image and likeness, we will no longer know evil. We will all be in *perfect harmony* with God and each other.

IMPROVE YOUR ETERNITY

While salvation gets us into Heaven, we do *not* all have the same experience in Heaven. The Gift of God Himself can begin to be unwrapped on earth enabling us to walk in greater obedience, submission, and love. Remember, when we receive, unwrap, and use a gift that God offers, we are in turn giving Him a gift. Gift-giving is the manifestation of intimacy, as in a marriage, the *most* intimate earthly relationship. God's goal is to have an ultimate intimacy with you for eternity. The Bible suggests that, while on earth, we can influence our future relationship with God by how well we unwrap our relationship with Him now:

✠ *Behold, I am coming soon! My reward is with Me, and I will give to everyone according to what he has done* (Revelation 22:12).

✠ *But store up for yourselves treasures in **heaven** [by planting good seeds on earth], where moth and rust do not destroy, and where thieves do not break in and steal* (Matthew 6:20).

✠ *Then I heard a voice from heaven say, "Write: Blessed are the dead who die in the Lord from now on." "Yes," says the Spirit, "they will rest from their labor, **for their deeds will follow them**"* (Revelation 14:13).

✠ *Blessed are you when people insult you, persecute you and falsely say all kinds of evil against you because of Me. Rejoice and be glad, because great is your reward **in heaven**, for in the same way they persecuted the prophets who were before you* (Matthew 5:11-12).

✠ *The Lord has made proclamation to the ends of the earth: "Say to the Daughters of Zion, 'See your Savior comes! See, His reward is with Him and His recompense accompanies Him'"* (Isaiah 62:11).

☩ *Do not work for food that spoils, but for food that endures to **eternal life**, which the Son of Man will give you...* (John 6:27).

☩ *Sell your possessions and give to the poor. Provide purses for yourselves that will not wear out, a treasure in heaven that will not be exhausted, where no thief comes near and no moth destroys* (Luke 12:33).

☩ *"I tell you the truth," Jesus replied, "No one who has left home or brothers or sisters or mothers or fathers or children or friends for Me and the gospel will fail to receive a hundred times as much in this present age...**and the age to come**..."* (Mark 10:29-30).

☩ *For the Son of Man is going to come in His Father's glory with His angels* [at His Second Coming], *and then He will reward each person **according to what he has done*** (Matthew 16:27).

Another theme that runs through the Bible is that our actions of faith earn us *crowns* that we will wear in Heaven. Some we gain simply by placing our faith in Jesus as our Savior, and some come by other *actions* of faith.

☩ *Everyone who competes in the games goes into strict training. They do it to get a **crown** that will not last; but we do it to get a **crown that will last forever*** (1 Corinthians 9:25).

✝ *Now there is in store for me the **crown** of righteousness, which the Lord, the righteous Judge, will award to me on that day—and not only to me, but also to all who have longed for His appearing (2 Timothy 4:8).*

✝ *Blessed is the man who perseveres under trial, because when he has stood the test, he will receive the **crown** of life that God has promised to those who love Him (James 1:12).*

✝ *And when the Chief Shepherd appears, you will receive the **crown** of glory that will never fade away (1 Peter 5:4).*

✝ *I am coming soon. Hold on to what you have, so that no one will take your **crown** (Revelation 3:11).*

An interesting passage in the Book of Revelation says that the 24 elders lay down their crowns before Jesus' throne as an act of submission and worship:

✝ *The twenty-four elders fall down before Him who sits on the throne, and worship Him who lives for ever and ever. They lay their **crowns** before the throne... (Revelation 4:10).*

The question I would ask you now is, how many *crowns* would you like to lay at the feet of Jesus on that day?

God is going to complete His promise to you.

✟ *Being confident of this, that He who began a good work in you will carry it on to completion until the day of Christ Jesus* (Philippians 1:6).

What will you do for Him? Now is the time to consider what *gifts* you can receive to lay at His feet.

MEDITATION POINT

In heaven, your relationship with God will become one in presence and spirit.

Go to Chapter 7 in the Study Guide section on page 341.

ENDNOTES

1.   Jack Hayford, ed., *Spirit-Filled Life Bible for Students* (Nashville, TN: Thomas Nelson Publishers, 1995), 1188.

2.   Dr. Caroline Leaf, *Who Switched Off My Brain* (Dallas, TX: Switch on Your Brain USA Inc., 2008), 123-124.

3.   Ibid, 19-120.

4.   Adam Clarke, "Commentary on Matthew 5," *The Adam Clarke Commentary*, http://www.studylight.org/com/acc/view.cgi?book=mt& chapter=005. 1832.

5.   Ibid.

Study Guide

INTRODUCTION

Please don't think of this study guide as a homework assignment. It *isn't* about giving the "right answer"—it's about giving an honest answer. It *isn't* about "getting it done"—it's about letting the questions stir your heart. It *isn't* about "filling in the blanks"—but instead letting the Holy Spirit speak to your soul. Think of this as a spiritual experience or potential encounter between you and God rather than an exercise to check off your "to do" list.

We are conditioned to believe that our answers to questions in a textbook will be graded; however, that mindset stifles the purpose of this study guide. This is an opportunity to write honestly about your faith, to grow and go deeper in God's Word, to pray earnestly about His will for your life, and most of all to cultivate an intimate relationship between you and your Creator.

If possible, devote time for quiet reflection as you read the material, think about your life, and write accordingly. Answer the questions as you truly feel, even if it seems wrong or troubling. Remember that "the truth will set you free" and growth can only happen when the soil is soft. You get what you give. You could burn through this entire study guide in half an hour if you like, but it would offer little to no lasting benefit.

I pray that you will put in the time and effort to maximize this material and actualize the full impact of His Gifts of Freedom into your life.

The Gifts of Freedom Study Guide

Book Three

Increase, Gifts of the Spirit, Relationships, Destiny, and God Himself

How to Use the Study Guide

You can use this study guide in a variety of ways, including individually, as part of a small group Bible study, or in a Sunday school setting. If you are working through this book on your own, use this study guide to record your personal growth journey. Take the time after each chapter to answer the questions. Some are designed to help you remember the main concepts in the chapter, while others are designed to help you personalize the content and apply it to your own life. Seriously pray in closing that God will fill you with His gifts—and that you will recognize and accept them. You can also visit our Website (www.giftsoffreedom.com) and see how others have applied this information to their lives.

If you're reading this book in a small group, use the study questions to prompt lively discussion. Discuss the action steps with at least one other group member to build accountability in your plans for action, then close your time together with prayer. For more information on how to lead a group or Sunday school class and get additional resources, visit our Website at www.giftsoffreedom.com.

If you are not currently in a group study of the book, you might want to consider starting one after you finish, so you can spread to others the new freedoms you have discovered. As you help others, you will deepen your understanding and relationship with God—gaining even more freedoms.

Go to www.giftsoffreedom.com for additional resource materials and instructions.

Chapter 1

GIFT #8—INCREASE (PART 1)

WHERE, HOW, AND WHY IS THERE INCREASE?

STUDY QUESTIONS

1. What is the primary purpose of an investment? How do earthly investments differ from investments in God's Kingdom? What does this suggest about a successful investment strategy?

   _____

   _____

   _____

   _____

2. Does an investment in knowing God cause increase in other areas of our lives? Are we prone to ignore this? Why?

   _____

   _____

   _____

   _____

The measure of your faith is found through the actions of your faith.

3. What does your measure of faith look like today?

_____

_____

_____

_____

Knowing and believing that God gives you all your increase will enhance your relationship with Him each day.

4. How does pride get in the way of increase? What changes when you trust God to be the sole provider of increase?

_____

_____

_____

_____

_____

Regardless of what the world and your ambition may tell you, it is God who you need to trust and see as your provider.

5. Who is your ultimate provider? Why is understanding this important to you? How is it vital to what you will actually receive?

_____

_____

_____

_____

_____

6. If you reap what you sow, what are some seeds that you would like to uproot? What are some seeds you would like to see growing in your life that you need to begin planting? (Also consider non-physical things such as love, mercy, truth, etc.)

_____

_____

_____

_____

_____

_____

Allow time to be the opportunity to grow your faith as you wait for your seeds to bear fruit.

7. Reflect on this verse: *"And let us not grow weary while doing good, for in due season we shall reap if we do not lose heart"* (see Gal. 6:9 NKJV). Why did Paul write, "if we do not lose heart"? What is he talking about? What are some seeds that you have planted in faith that you may have to not lose heart over before you see growth? Following the analogy, what are some ways that you can water, nourish, and facilitate growth?

_____

_____

_____

_____

_____

_____

_____

_____

_____

_____

It is up to us what we sow and what we consume as bread. One will give us an additional return. So choose wisely what you will consume and what you will replant for long-term reward.

8. What is the best way to determine which portion of our increase we consume and which portion we use for seed?

_____

_____

_____

_____

Just like the seed must die to be made alive as a plant, you as well must die to yourself so you can have spiritual growth that brings you alive.

9. What does it mean to "die to yourself"? Why is this important for bearing fruit? Conversely, how does living for self stifle growth?

_____

_____

_____

10. Why is the spiritual growth timeline from seed to harvest becoming shorter? What does this mean for you, practically speaking?

_____

_____

_____

_____

_____

_____

God sowed His Son into physical death so that He could receive a spiritual harvest of eternal sons and daughters.

11. Why was it important for God to sow His most precious possession? What can we learn in our lives about sowing and reaping from this most precious gift?

_____

_____

_____

_____

_____

_____

12. Most of us believe that God is the source of increase, but our lives often suggest that we are the ultimate source of increase, not Him. What areas can you change to reflect this new, abundant way of thinking and living?

_____

_____

_____

_____

_____

_____

ACTION STEPS

Summarize the nine spiritual truths of sowing and reaping contained in this chapter. What have you learned about sowing and reaping that can help you in your day-to-day walk of faith? How will these truths help you grow closer to God? Consider practical ways that you will put this new knowledge into practice every day.

_____

_____

_____

_____

_____

_____

Closing Prayer

(Pray this prayer or come up with your own to close this study time.)

Lord, thank You for the Gift of Increase. Teach me how to use these steps in my own life and to wait patiently on Your increase.

Chapter 2

GIFT #8—INCREASE (PART 2)

HOW DO YOU GET THE GOOD KIND?

STUDY QUESTIONS

1. After reading the story that opens the Chapter, what do you think the sports car could represent in your life? What do you think caused the son to miss his father's gift? Is your ultimate desire for the "bigger gift" first and foremost, blinding you to the gift that God is offering you?

_____

_____

_____

_____

_____

_____

_____

_____

_____

After the Fall, increase was found in hard work; yet our true increase is found when we accept, unwrap, and use God's help-increase.

2. How do you go about exercising your faith? What are some principles with physical exercise that relate to our spiritual growth? Can you see some possible areas in your life where this may apply?

_____

_____

_____

The only challenge God makes to you in the Bible is to bring your tithe into His house. He promises that He will open the windows of Heaven and pour out such a blessing that there will not be enough room to receive it.

3. Why do you think God challenges us to "test" Him when it comes to tithing? How do you do this? What kind of blessings could come from God's response to your obedience?

_____

_____

_____

A dire financial situation may not really be a need for money, as much as a need for more of God's presence in your life.

4. What are some examples of *dire situations* that you've experienced that have compelled you toward God? Do difficult times always send people toward God? Why or why not?

_____

_____

_____

A generous heart will help build up your eternal account and impede the devour.

5. What does a *generous heart* look like in your story? How have others been generous toward you? How are you generous toward others? What are the spiritual benefits of generosity?

_____

_____

_____

When the enemy is stealing your possessions you can count it joy because your retribution can be double.

6. Think of times when you've been troubled by satan. What would a doubled repayment look like in these times? How has God blessed you or others after times of trial and testing? Why do God's blessings typically follow a winter season, a period of trial and testing?

_____

_____

_____

_____

_____

_____

_____

_____

_____

_____

_____

_____

Listen to God and His advice during the good times so you won't have to experience things He didn't intend for you.

7. "If God wants to say something to me, I'm right here." Is this attitude different from actively seeking and listening? How do you go about listening to God? Are there other ways that you could seek His input? Why is this important in relation to increase?

_____

_____

_____

A gift opens the way for the giver to in turn generously receive.

8. What are the gifts that you can give to God? What spiritual doors are *opened* by giving gifts to God?

_____

_____

_____

The actions of our heart put spiritual things in motion that create the things in life that we later run into.

9. What are some ways that you need to guard your heart in current relationships? How might this play into future circumstances?

_____

_____

_____

_____

_____

_____

_____

_____

_____

_____

_____

_____

_____

_____

Your planted seed God can use to give you and others rest and shade in ever increasing amount.

10. What are some kingdom-building seeds that you have planted? Imagine how and in what way these could grow.

_____

_____

_____

_____

_____

_____

_____

_____

_____

11. Jesus said that we should seek first God's Kingdom (see Matt. 6:33), yet most of us, in all honesty, seek God's Kingdom only when there's time or when it's not too stressful. What if a farmer had this attitude with his crops? How could this apply to you?

_____

_____

_____

_____

_____

_____

12. In the author's story, God used money to bring increase after intense and repeated testing. What is He using in your life? What good seeds are you planting right now in faith that will bring increase?

_____

_____

_____

_____

_____

_____

_____

ACTION STEPS

Take a look at the way you currently give to God. Are you tithing? Are you generous with your increase (look at your check stubs for the answer)? Even if you don't have much money, you can give from what you do have to God. Consider adjusting your giving habits if you need to. Then trust God to deliver on His promise to bless you. Consider all of the other areas in which you can give.

_____

_____

_____

_____

_____

_____

_____

_____

_____

_____

_____

_____

_____

_____

_____

_____

_____

CLOSING PRAYER

(Pray this prayer or come up with your own to close this study time.)

Lord, thank You for Your blessings. Help me to become a generous giver and to trust Your hand as I learn to obey and anticipate Your increase in my life.

Chapter 3

GIFT #9—GIFTS OF THE SPIRIT (PART 1)

HOW DO YOUR GIFTS BRING LIFE TO YOUR LIFE?

STUDY QUESTIONS

1. What are some ways in which becoming a parent alters your perspective on life and, therefore, the way you live it? What similar changes take place when you become a follower of Christ? Can you do it on your own? Who can help?

_____

_____

_____

_____

_____

_____

_____

_____

Let the world see God through your actions and REACTIONS.

2. What does it look like to let the world see God through your actions and reactions? In tense or stressful situations, what do your actions and reactions say about your faith? Give an example of this from your own life.

_____

_____

_____

_____

_____

3. True or False: God gives Christians gifts when they deserve them and can properly use them. Why or why not? What happens if you don't exercise your gifts?

_____

_____

_____

_____

_____

Jesus as the head of the Church Body orchestrates it through the Holy Spirit to fulfill God's plan for the world. You are God's hands to reach a dying world.

4. How do the different gifts work together to make something beautiful? How does unity in the Body of Christ impact the reach of God's hands into our world? How well have you done at submitting your head, heart, and hands to God as Peter did? What could you do to improve?

_____

_____

_____

_____

_____

_____

_____

_____

_____

_____

_____

_____

_____

_____

Our words and Gifts will be received based on how well they are wrapped with God's Spirit.

5. Of what value are the gifts when love is not a part of the process? Why? How do you infuse love with the gifts?

_____

_____

_____

_____

_____

6. How does love fulfill the Law? Are we called to love or to live by the Law? How does love develop our relationship with God?

_____

_____

_____

_____

_____

_____

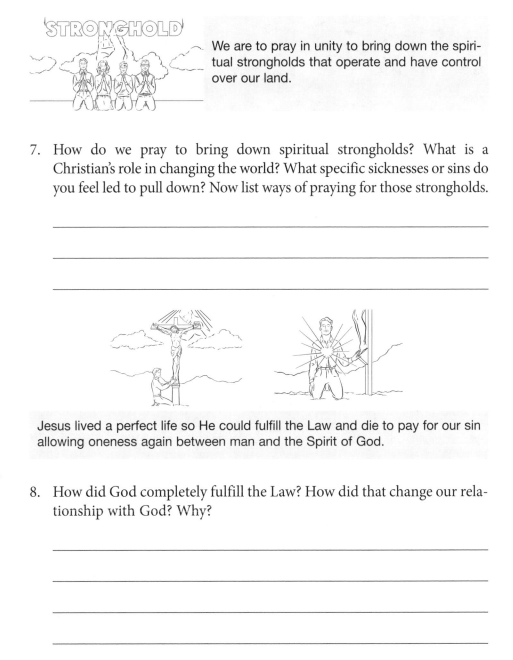

We are to pray in unity to bring down the spiritual strongholds that operate and have control over our land.

7. How do we pray to bring down spiritual strongholds? What is a Christian's role in changing the world? What specific sicknesses or sins do you feel led to pull down? Now list ways of praying for those strongholds.

_____

_____

_____

Jesus lived a perfect life so He could fulfill the Law and die to pay for our sin allowing oneness again between man and the Spirit of God.

8. How did God completely fulfill the Law? How did that change our relationship with God? Why?

_____

_____

_____

_____

When you can see what is happening in the spirit realm in your everyday life, using your gifts will be much easier.

9. What does it mean to contradict the world? When we do this and want people to follow us, what condition should we live in? Make a plan for when, where, and how you are going to be in fruit-bearing condition.

_____

_____

_____

_____

Wrapping your gifts in God's love will allow them to be accepted and therefore used.

10. Think of some of God's gifts and how you would wrap them in pure love. What's likely to happen when you do? And when you don't?

_____

_____

_____

_____

11. List ways that you could be tempted to use your gifts for applause, personal gain, power, or other self-focused means. How do you guard yourself against these temptations?

_____

_____

_____

_____

_____

_____

12. Love is God's essence, and our charge is, "[To make known] *the manifold wisdom of God to the rulers and authorities in the heavenly realms, according to His eternal purpose which He accomplished in Christ Jesus our Lord*" (see Ephesians 3:10-11). If Jesus returned today and asked you how you're fulfilling this mandate, what would you say? Where are you lacking, and how could you become more active?

_____

_____

_____

_____

_____

_____

_____

Action Steps

Think about how well you're using your gifts in love. Are there some things that you need to change (attitudes or actions) to better live them out with God's love? Make those needed changes and watch to see how God will use you in surprising and powerful new ways.

_____

_____

_____

_____

_____

_____

_____

_____

_____

_____

Closing Prayer

(Pray this prayer or come up with your own to close this study time.)

Lord, You have given me unique and important Gifts of the Spirit. Help me to exercise them only in love so that they will impact the world in powerful ways.

Chapter 4

GIFT #9—GIFTS OF THE SPIRIT (PART 2)
HOW DO YOU FIND YOUR GIFTS?

STUDY QUESTIONS

1. Have you ever been to the symphony? What are some areas in which you may be unpracticed, out of sync, or out of tune with the Conductor?

_____

_____

_____

_____

_____

_____

_____

_____

_____

_____

Gifts offered in anything other than God's love will be rejected or even backfire.

2.   What are some examples of what happens to our gifts when our motivation becomes pride or self-interest? How does this damage our relationship with God? With others?

_____

_____

_____

_____

_____

3.   What if you have a gift such as teaching but never use it? If you have a gift, does that automatically make you a good teacher, prophet, leader, etc. from the start? Or does it take time to fully develop your gifts? How do we sharpen and refine our gifting?

_____

_____

_____

_____

_____

4. As you read about the different gifts, which one(s) did you identify with most clearly? How can you experiment with all of the different gifts to see which ones you may possess?

_____

_____

_____

_____

_____

Use discernment to identify the root cause of someone's heart and actions.

5. Do you have or know someone who has the gift of discernment? How can this gift help your own life story?

_____

_____

_____

_____

_____

The gift of knowledge can allow you to know the core issues in someone's life.

6. If you had the gift of knowledge, how would you use it to glorify God? What is the value of seeking this gift out?

_____

_____

_____

_____

_____

_____

7. How do you see the gift of leadership exercised by the leaders in your church? God's idea of a leader can be much different from the way that many corporate leaders lead. How so? How did Jesus show leadership?

_____

_____

_____

_____

_____

_____

Acts of mercy will be noticed by others who will question their source.

8. Mercy is something that we're all supposed to have in some measure. What can someone who has this gift offer that the rest of us can't?

_____

_____

_____

Prophecy will encourage others and build their faith in the face of struggle and pain.

9. Do you have or know of someone who has the gift of prophecy? How can finding those who have this gift help you?

_____

_____

_____

_____

Using wisdom will allow your decisions in life to be on a rock solid foundation.

10. What are some areas in your life where you could benefit from the gift of wisdom? Why is this particular gift important to you? To the Body of Christ?

_____

_____

_____

_____

_____

_____

11. The saying "receive, unwrap, and use the gifts" is written throughout the book. How does this apply to spiritual gifts? What steps are you taking toward finding, trying out, and developing your specific gifting?

_____

_____

_____

_____

_____

12. Have you exposed yourself to those who possess these powerful gifts so that you can mature and become perfected in Christ? List the people who have blessed you with their use of specific gifts. Which ones are missing? How will you expose yourself to these missing, yet vital gifts?

_____

_____

_____

_____

_____

ACTION STEPS

Do you know what your gift(s) are? Take time to review the descriptions in this chapter and on the Website: www.buildingchurch.net. They have a questionnaire which can help you determine which gifts you possess in greater quantities. You may have gifts that you didn't know you had, or they may be right in line with what you expected. Learn all you can about your gifts and how they may benefit the Body of Christ, and talk with church leaders about how you can better make use of your gifts.

_____

_____

_____

_____

_____

_____

CLOSING PRAYER

(Pray this prayer or come up with your own to close this study time.)

Father, thank You for the gifts that You've given me. Help me to identify them and use them fully according to Your purpose.

Chapter 5

GIFT #10—RELATIONSHIP

HOW DO RELATIONSHIPS COMPLETE YOU AND YOUR DESTINY?

STUDY QUESTIONS

1. Why do we talk about *investing* in relationships? How does that investment look in your life with those closest to you? What do you potentially gain and lose? Are you really too busy to make the investment, or do you just think it is too much work? If so, how could you change?

_____

_____

_____

_____

_____

_____

_____

_____

2. How do the gifts that you've already learned about impact the way you relate to friends, family, co-workers, and strangers? How do you make friends and improve the friendships that you already have?

_____

_____

_____

_____

_____

Relationships can remove limits and thereby give us more freedom—physically and spiritually.

3. How do relationships help improve us? What are some of the ways relationships can give us more freedom?

_____

_____

_____

_____

_____

_____

Focusing on other's needs and lack rather than your own will make the journey more enjoyable. It will ultimately open up a gift of freedom for you to walk to further places in life.

4. What are some practical ways that you can focus on others' needs? How does this impact your relationship with them? With God?

_____

_____

_____

_____

5. What does it look like to love your neighbor as yourself? Is this always easy? Why or why not? Looking at the parable of the Good Samaritan, how can you "go and do likewise," as Jesus said? (See Luke 10:25-37.)

_____

_____

_____

_____

_____

_____

Only relationships can birth real life here on earth.

6. How can God's love, exuding through you, bring life to others?

_____

_____

_____

7. God spiritually binds a man and a wife together as one; however, physically speaking, each of them must take actions that keep the bond together as one. List some ways that you could see this happening in a marriage.

Man's design and function is more straight-forward and to the point while woman's function is more complex and robust.

_____

_____

_____

_____

8. Think of some examples that support the truth about the specific differences between the way men and women are wired. How does knowing this help you in your relationships? In what ways do you think you can benefit and enjoy these differences?

_____

_____

_____

_____

The Fall distorted our view of the world and made it difficult to see beyond ourselves. However, in marriage seeing beyond ourselves is essential.

9. Describe some of the ways that a marriage on earth is similar to our relationship with God. What are some of the truths about our relationship with God that we can discover through marriage? How can marriage help build your character? If you are married, what are some things that you can change to build a better marriage?

_____

_____

_____

_____

10. Why is basing a marriage on romance a poor foundation? What is one way to add romance to your marriage? Whose responsibility is it?

_____

_____

_____

_____

_____

_____

When you could not take care of yourself, God gave you the wonderful gift of relationship—respect and treasure this God-given gift.

11. How can you respect your parents even when you disagree with them or when you've been hurt by them?

_____

_____

_____

_____

_____

_____

12. What are some of the blessings and freedoms that you can gain when you receive, unwrap, and use the Gift of Relationship?

_____

_____

_____

_____

_____

_____

ACTION STEPS

Take a close look at the relationships that you are involved in today. If you're married or dating, consider how well you're living out the sort of relationship that God would desire for you as a couple. What are some ways that you can work on improving all of your earthly relationships? What steps do you need to take to avoid unnecessary conflict? To grow a deeper friendship? Make plans to enact these steps in the days to come.

_____

_____

_____

_____

_____

_____

Closing Prayer

(Pray this prayer or come up with your own to close this study time.)

Dear God, thank You for the Gift of Relationship. Give me wisdom in relating to family, friends, co-workers, and strangers. And show me Yourself through these relationships so that I might learn more about You and grow closer to You.

Chapter 6

GIFT #11—YOUR DESTINY

HOW DO YOU FIND YOUR DESTINY?

STUDY QUESTIONS

1. What are some ways that you've sought your own earthly destiny? Are you seeking to live out the destiny God offers you or are you trying to create your own? What happens when you reject the one God offers you? What do you have to do to find the one God offers?

_____

_____

_____

_____

_____

_____

_____

_____

_____

2. What are some of the desires of the flesh that can distract you from discovering or fulfilling your destiny?

_____

_____

_____

_____

Keep your end in sight so you can keep on your course.

3. How can you keep your eyes on your destination? What weaknesses (in faith, trust, prayer, worship, dying to self, etc.) do you think might have you going in circles—repeating the same mistakes over and over and causing you to cover the same ground repeatedly?

_____

_____

_____

_____

_____

Attaining goals outside of God's will be a struggle without fulfillment. Instead, find your destiny in the river of life, it will be far more exhilarating and fulfilling.

4. What are some of the ways that you've tried to swim upstream? What was the end result for your effort? What was the motivation for your direction during these times? What are some things that you might need to do in order to move into the current where God wants you?

_____

_____

_____

_____

The closer to the center of the river you are, the easier it will be to see your destiny.

5. Why is it more difficult to see your destiny when you are farther from the center of God's will? What are some things you need to do in order to see better?

_____

_____

_____

You will find surprise gifts enroute to your destiny.

6. What are some different ways that God surprises us as we seek our destiny? How have you been surprised so far? How can you live your life so that you're prepared for and welcoming of God's surprises along the way? Why is it hard for our flesh to recognize His surprises?

_____

_____

_____

_____

_____

_____

7. What was Jesus' destiny on earth? What can we learn from how He lived out His destiny? How can it help us with our own?

_____

_____

_____

_____

_____

_____

This is not what God wants for you, but the result of not "letting go" of what he didn't intend for you.

8. What are some things that you might need to let go of in order to reach your God-intended destiny?

_____

_____

_____

_____

_____

9. Could your appointed destiny defy physics and logic, contradict customs, lead you into new areas, be unbelievably challenging, and be a tall order all at the same time? How would God ask you to respond to these potentially uncomfortable circumstances? Do you see parts of your destiny starting to unfold yet? What challenges might come with it?

_____

_____

_____

_____

_____

10. Respond to this quote, regarding your destiny: "Do not worry about what to say or how to say it. At that time you will be given what to say, for it will not be you speaking..." (see Matt. 10:19-20). How does this encourage you as you pursue your destiny? In what ways does it lead you to grow in faith?

_____

_____

_____

_____

_____

_____

11. Review Paul's destiny as described in this chapter. How do you see God working through Paul's life in surprising or creative ways? Are you looking for and expecting God to reveal your path in surprising ways? How are you doing this?

_____

_____

_____

_____

_____

_____

Your Gift of destiny, if received and used, is the most fulfilling gift that you can receive from God and is the most fulfilling gift that you can give God in return.

12. In what ways is the Gift of Destiny the most fulfilling gift that you can receive, open, and use? How can you best deal with those times when you question whether your destiny even exists? What is the Holy Spirit's vital role in this? How about all the other Gifts of Freedom— what part do they play?

_____

_____

_____

_____

_____

_____

_____

_____

_____

_____

_____

_____

_____

Action Steps

Spend some time thinking about the life you've lived so far. Then write down ways that you think God might have used your circumstances to bring you to where you are today. What might He be preparing you for? In what areas could you become a witness to others? In what areas could you show compassion? Talk with a friend about what you discover, and then spend time together in prayer, inviting the Holy Spirit to reveal to you what is next in your pursuit of your unique, God-given destiny. Keep checking back with God so that you can stay focused on this destiny and so that you can be aware of His hand in your life and the creative, evolving ways that He continues to shape your future.

_____

_____

_____

_____

_____

_____

_____

_____

Closing Prayer

(Pray this prayer or come up with your own to close this study time.)

Dear God, thank You for my unique destiny. Help me to discover Your will for me in everything that I do. Give me purpose and clarity as I seek Your will and uncover the plans that You have for my life—my earthly destiny.

Chapter 7

THE GIFT—GOD OF THE TRINITY

WHAT WILL YOUR RELATIONSHIP ULTIMATELY BE WITH HIM?

STUDY QUESTIONS

1. What is the primary purpose of the Gifts of Freedom?

   _____

   _____

   _____

2. What are some of the steps that you need to follow to create a stable foundation for your relationship with God? How will living this out help you discover the Promised Land that God has in mind for you?

   _____

   _____

   _____

   _____

Before you can figure out how to get to point "B" you need to know where you currently are —point "A".

3. What is your current "point A" in life? Where is that in relation to Him—to your Promised Land? What do you need to do to properly reposition yourself?

_____

_____

_____

_____

Godly sorrow brings you to a change in the way you do things that will lift you up, and unlike regret that will bring you down.

4. Where have you known or felt godly sorrow in your life? How has that changed you in good ways? If you haven't known godly sorrow yet, how do you think you can find it? How can you use it to bring about spiritual growth and not despair?

_____

_____

_____

5. What does Jesus mean when He says "Blessed are the meek"? What is the difference between meek and weak? What will you find when you're meek?

_____

_____

_____

_____

_____

_____

_____

Your heart sets the issues of life in motion, issues you will encounter in the future.

6. How does an "unclean temple" keep us from seeing God clearly? What do you need to do to clean your heart? To cleanse your mind?

_____

_____

_____

_____

_____

When you are ablaze with the light of Jesus, the devil will attempt to dim or snuff you out.

7. What are some ways that satan tries to persecute or distract those who are seeking an intimate relationship with God? How are we to respond to these attacks? How does God help us respond to them?

_____

_____

_____

_____

_____

_____

8. How do we express our love to God? How are you serving Him? If you are not, what is stopping you? How are you obeying Him? What are the signs of someone who is obedient to Him?

_____

_____

_____

_____

_____

_____

At the resurrection God will restore you with a new body free from sin and shame.

9. What are you most looking forward to when you receive new life after the resurrection? How can this future Promised Land help encourage you today toward obedience, love, and holiness?

_____

_____

_____

_____

_____

10. What does the Bible tell us about what this new Heaven will be like? (List your favorite verses describing this.) What are some reasons you could think of that would make Heaven indescribable?

_____

_____

_____

_____

_____

11. How can the Gifts of Freedom affect your Heaven experience? How does the unwrapping of your relationship with Him now impact your life now? How about in the future?

_____

_____

_____

_____

_____

_____

How many gifts will you have to give when you get to heaven?

12. How many crowns would you like to lay at the feet of Jesus? Are you living to praise Jesus in the end? What can you do to gain more crowns for Him?

_____

_____

_____

_____

_____

_____

ACTION STEPS

Review the Gifts of Freedom in this and the other two books. Then make a plan to read these books again in several months to review what you've learned and to remind yourself of your goals as you seek to discover God's plan for your life. How well are you doing so far in all that you've committed to? What are some things that you can work on in your pursuit of God? Make a plan to keep working on these in the coming months and years. It will be a process that never ends in this life, as long as you remain a seeker.

_____

_____

_____

_____

_____

_____

_____

_____

_____

_____

_____

_____

_____

_____

CLOSING PRAYER

(Pray this prayer or come up with your own to close this study time.)

Father, thank You so much for the Gift of You and all of the Gifts of Freedom. Give me both the desire and the wisdom necessary to receive, unwrap, and use all of these gifts so that I can enter my Promised Land and live out the unique destiny that You have planned for me.

ABOUT THE AUTHOR

Greg Rice began his real estate business in 1971; however, God has taken him on a most unusual journey since then. In 1988, he gave his heart to Jesus Christ—the gift of salvation began to grow, heal, and restore his life. Greg's continual seeking to know God and develop a most intimate relationship with Him has led to many discoveries.

As God was healing him, Greg began to share his new life and success with others through several ministries. Greg has now focused much of his ministry efforts through Solid Rock Media (see www.solidrockmedia.com), and its vision is to illuminate the life and light of Jesus to a dying world through various media outlets.

The Gifts of Freedom book series grew out of this pursuit and in November 2005, the Holy Spirit began to give the words. God's message was clear: "Offer Christians a clear path toward living in wholehearted freedom."

God has an answer for those who find themselves bound in life by things not of God. God's desire is for everyone bound and held captive in life to be set free so they can achieve their purpose and fulfill their destiny. The Gifts of Freedom was written to illuminate the gifts God offers so we can achieve our God-given purpose and calling. Yes, the heart of the book is to shine this light of freedom into churches, marriages, and families. And indeed, this light can even penetrate the steel and cement of prison walls and jail bars.

Men and women held in prison also have a God-given purpose and destiny. With this in mind, Greg's mission is to distribute the Gifts of Freedom free of charge to prisons and jails around the world to facilitate salvation, discipleship, healing, and growth. To this end, Greg has already donated 120,000 copies to prisons across the United States.

It is Greg's prayer that the Spirit of God would bring change within, working from the inside out—as only He can bring true rehabilitation and freedom. Partner with Greg by giving a donation to distribute additional copies of the books—bringing spiritual nourishment to spiritually hungry men and women in prisons worldwide. In the U.S. alone there are over 7,000 incarceration facilities now holding almost 2.5 million prisoners. If this were a city it would be the fourth largest city in the United States after Chicago and before Houston. Certainly, these men and women have the time to consider this life-changing message. What better way is there to positively influence the crime statistics as well as the negative human results of those crimes?

WRITE A CHECK TO "GIFTS OF FREEDOM" AND MAIL TO:
GIFTS OF FREEDOM
P.O. BOX 62459
COLORADO SPRINGS, CO 80962
VISIT WWW.GIFTSOFFREEDOM.ORG.

☩ *I, the Lord, have called you in righteousness; I will take hold of your hand. I will keep you and will make you to be a covenant for the people and a light for the Gentiles, to open eyes that are blind, to free captives from prison and to release from the dungeon those who sit in darkness* (Isaiah 42:6-8).

MINISTRY INFORMATION

U nity is what brings us together, creating oneness within the Body of Christ. Together we can unite under one goal, unite under His will, and unite in prayer to pull down strongholds to allow His will to be manifested in His creation. Through the "Gifts of Freedom" newsletter we can pray in one accord, with countless other believers in other cities and countries to restore His will on earth. Our newsletter will also be received by men and women in prison, allowing them, even in their physical captivity, to be unified with the Body of Christ in prayer and fellowship to do the mighty work of setting captives free while still in physical captivity.

Please sign up today, to receive either an electronic or paper form of the newsletter and unite with others in the oneness of Jesus, to see His power change our world.

GIFTS OF FREEDOM
PO BOX 62459
COLORADO SPRINGS, CO 80962
VISIT OUR WEBSITE AT WWW.GIFTSOFFREEDOM.ORG.

Additional copies of this book and other
book titles from DESTINY IMAGE are
available at your local bookstore.

Call toll-free: 1-800-722-6774.

Send a request for a catalog to:

Destiny Image® Publishers, Inc.

P.O. Box 310
Shippensburg, PA 17257-0310

*"Speaking to the Purposes of God for This
Generation and for the Generations to Come."*

**For a complete list of our titles,
visit us at www.destinyimage.com.**